CAMBRIDGE TEXTS IN THE HISTORY OF PHILOSOPHY

MEDIEVAL ISLAMIC
Philosophical Writings

CAMBRIDGE TEXTS IN THE HISTORY OF PHILOSOPHY

Series editors

KARL AMERIKS

Professor of Philosophy at the University of Notre Dame

DESMOND M. CLARKE

Professor of Philosophy at University College Cork

The main objective of Cambridge Texts in the History of Philosophy is to expand the range, variety, and quality of texts in the history of philosophy which are available in English. The series includes texts by familiar names (such as Descartes and Kant) and also by less well-known authors. Wherever possible, texts are published in complete and unabridged form, and translations are specially commissioned for the series. Each volume contains a critical introduction together with a guide to further reading and any necessary glossaries and textual apparatus. The volumes are designed for student use at undergraduate and postgraduate level and will be of interest not only to students of philosophy, but also to a wider audience of readers in the history of science, the history of theology and the history of ideas.

For a list of titles published in the series, please see end of book.

MEDIEVAL ISLAMIC

Philosophical Writings

EDITED BY

MUHAMMAD ALI KHALIDI

American University of Beirut

CAMBRIDGE
UNIVERSITY PRESS

PUBLISHED BY THE PRESS SYNDICATE OF THE UNIVERSITY OF CAMBRIDGE
The Pitt Building, Trumpington Street, Cambridge, United Kingdom

CAMBRIDGE UNIVERSITY PRESS
The Edinburgh Building, Cambridge, CB2 2RU, UK
40 West 20th Street, New York, NY 10011–4211, USA
477 Williamstown Road, Port Melbourne, VIC 3207, Australia
Ruiz de Alarcón 13, 28014 Madrid, Spain
Dock House, The Waterfront, Cape Town 8001, South Africa

http://www.cambridge.org

First published 2005

Printed in the United Kingdom at the University Press, Cambridge

Typeface Ehrhardt 11/13 pt. *System* LaTeX 2ε [TB]

A catalogue record for this book is available from the British Library

Library of Congress Cataloguing in Publication data
Medieval Islamic philosophy / edited by Muhammad Ali Khalidi.
p. cm. (Cambridge texts in the history of philosophy)
Includes bibliographical references and index.
ISBN 0 521 82243 2 – ISBN 0 521 52963 8 (paperback)
1. Philosophy, Islamic. 2. Philosophy, Medieval. I. Khalidi, Muhammad Ali, Professor. II. Series.
B741.M44 2004
181′.07 – dc22 2004048196

ISBN 0 521 82243 2 hardback
ISBN 0 521 52963 8 paperback

For Amal and Zayd,
who never knew each other

Contents

Acknowledgments

I have incurred numerous debts in the course of preparing this volume. Among the scholars who have given me encouragement in pursuing the study of Islamic philosophy are Charles Butterworth, Albert Hourani, Basim Musallam, Parviz Morewedge, George Saliba, Josef Stern, and Paul Walker. My greatest debt is to my father Tarif Khalidi, who provided wise advice at every step, read the translation with great care, and saved me from numerous errors. The book was also expertly read in manuscript by one of the coeditors of this series, Desmond Clarke, whose philosophical and stylistic guidance were very valuable and helped to sustain me in carrying out the project. Hilary Gaskin, philosophy editor at Cambridge University Press, also gave much needed support and recommendations, and shepherded the book through the various stages of production.

A grant from the University Research Board of my home institution, the American University of Beirut, helped me to get started on this project during the summer of 2002. That summer, I was fortunate enough to be hosted by the Center for Middle Eastern Studies at the University of Arizona, where I was provided with much needed office space and library facilities. I am very grateful to the Center's Director, Anne Betteridge, and Assistant Director, Anne Bennett, for their kindness and hospitality. A semester as a visiting professor at the University of Virginia freed me of administrative duties and allowed me to devote more time to this project than I could have in Beirut. I am grateful to colleagues there for stimulating discussion, particularly Jorge Secada, Daniel Devereux, James Cargile, and Mohammed Sawaie.

My debt to my wife Diane Riskedahl is of a different order. While this book was in gestation, she wrote her Ph.D. dissertation, in addition to carrying and giving birth to our son Zayd. That she also managed to read and comment on various parts of this book in manuscript is a testimony to bodily endurance and her generosity of spirit.

Introduction

Developing in the late ninth century AD and evolving without interruption for the next four centuries, medieval Islamic philosophy was instrumental in the revival of philosophizing in Europe in the Middle Ages. Philosophers in the Islamic world were strongly influenced by Greek works and adapted some of the Platonic, Aristotelian, and other ideas to their brand of monotheism. But they also developed an original philosophical culture of their own, which had a considerable, but hitherto largely unexplored, impact on the subsequent course of western philosophy. Their problems and concerns are echoed in medieval European philosophy, and resonate to some extent in early modern philosophy.

Notwithstanding the substantial influence that it has had on western philosophy, medieval Islamic philosophy is not generally regarded as part of the philosophical canon in the English-speaking world, and such figures as Ibn Sīnā (Avicenna) and Ibn Rushd (Averroes) remain obscure by comparison with Augustine and Aquinas. More often than not, they are either considered curiosities deriving from an entirely different philosophical tradition, or preservers of and commentators on the Greek philosophical heritage without a sufficiently original contribution of their own. The reasons for these omissions and for the disparagement of Islamic philosophy are steeped in the often conflicted history of Islam and Christendom. This is not the place to go into an account of the reception of these texts in the west and of their declining fortunes in the canon, since the purpose here is to reintroduce a small portion of these works to readers more familiar with the standard western philosophical corpus. This anthology attempts to provide a representative sample of the Arabic-Islamic philosophical tradition in a manner that is accessible to beginning students of philosophy, as well as to more seasoned philosophers with little or no exposure to this tradition.

The main challenge associated with preparing an anthology of this kind has to do with the selection of texts. The aim has been to choose a small number of approachable texts from some of the most representative practitioners of Islamic philosophy, and to translate them into comprehensible language with a minimum of footnotes and annotations. This volume contains extracts from longer philosophical works rather than entire texts or a large number of brief passages from a variety of texts. The selections assembled here are taken from five texts by five authors: al-Fārābī, Ibn Sīnā (Avicenna), al-Ghazālī, Ibn Ṭufayl, and Ibn Rushd (Averroes). This list includes what many scholars would consider to be the paradigmatic exemplars of the tradition, though some may question the chronological endpoint on the grounds that it perpetuates the mistaken impression that Islamic philosophy died out with Ibn Rushd (1126–98 AD), whereas it actually endured far beyond that point. But despite the survival of philosophical activity of some kind in the Islamic world, I would argue that a "style of reasoning"[1] did indeed decline after Ibn Rushd, one that is seamlessly connected to natural science, a logic-based, Greek-influenced, and rationalist enterprise.

This anthology tries to achieve some thematic unity by focusing broadly on metaphysics and epistemology rather than on ethics and political philosophy. Though the distinction is somewhat artificial in the context of medieval Islamic philosophy, since few texts discuss ethics without bringing in some metaphysics and vice versa, one can often extract portions of texts where the emphasis is decidedly on "theoretical" questions rather than "practical" ones. It might be added that epistemology (unlike metaphysics) was not recognized as a distinct branch of philosophy by these writers, and that this category is therefore something of an imposition. Bearing these two points in mind, it is quite possible to select texts with these complementary foci, broadly construed. The issues discussed in these selections (language, meaning, mind, knowledge, substance, essence, accident, causation, and so on) might be said to reflect our current philosophical predilections rather than to represent Islamic philosophy "as it saw itself." But if the aim is partly to "mainstream" Islamic philosophy,

[1] The phrase is used by Ian Hacking to apply to the history of science, following A. C. Crombie. See I. Hacking, "Five Parables," in *Philosophy in History*, ed. R. Rorty, J. B. Schneewind, and Q. Skinner (Cambridge: Cambridge University Press, 1984).

then the approach should be to select texts that will be of particular interest to a contemporary audience.

Another challenge associated with preparing such a volume consists in choosing texts that will be of interest not just to a philosophical audience, but also to students of Islamic civilization. Orientalist scholars have often regarded philosophy as being marginal to Islamic history and culture, but more nuanced interpreters of the tradition have underscored the latent philosophical content in Islamic civilization, ranging from ubiquitous Arabic terms originally coined for philosophical purposes, to substantive theses concerning the best form of government, to more general attitudes towards the relation between faith and reason. As Albert Hourani has written: "There was a submerged philosophical element in all later Islamic thought."[2] Moreover, many prevailing Islamic attitudes were formulated, at least in part, in reaction to the views of the Islamic philosophers, and such establishment figures as Ibn Ḥazm, al-Shahrastānī, Ibn Taymīyyah, Ibn Khaldūn, and others frequently occupied themselves in responding to them. For obvious reasons, a collection of texts in moral and political philosophy might be thought to have more direct relevance to those interested in Islamic culture, history, and religion, than one that focuses mainly on epistemology and metaphysics. But theoretical philosophy, no less than practical philosophy, had an important impact on foundational debates concerning the conception of God, the place of humanity in the universe, the limits of reason, and the nature of the afterlife, among many others.

In what follows, I will try to provide short introductions to each of the texts excerpted in this volume, trying to strike a balance between textual exegesis and critical commentary. These brief introductions to the individual texts contain minimal historical background on the authors of these texts, since that can readily be gleaned from other sources. I will introduce the texts from the perspective of the "history of philosophy" rather than "intellectual history," to use a distinction that has been drawn in recent years.[3] In other words, in addition to communicating aspects of

[2] Albert Hourani, *Arabic Thought in the Liberal Age, 1789–1939* (Cambridge: Cambridge University Press, 1983), p. 18.

[3] See, for example, Rorty, Schneewind and Skinner, "Introduction," in *Philosophy in History*. In their opinion, an "ideal intellectual history would have to bracket questions of reference and truth," whereas an ideal history of philosophy would not (p. 2). Though I do not agree fully with the way they make the distinction between the two disciplines, I think that there is an important, though elusive, distinction to be drawn.

their content and highlighting their most distinctive positions, I will try to engage critically with some of their arguments and venture occasional assessments of them. This is meant to be a departure from the prevailing tendency to approach these texts as historical oddities with little to say to contemporary thinkers.

Al-Fārābī, *The Book of Letters*

Abū Naṣr al-Fārābī (*c.* 878–*c.* 950 AD) was born in Turkestan on the northeastern border of the lands under Islamic rule, in the town of Fārāb (in present-day Turkmenistan on the border with Uzbekistan). He is said to have moved to Baghdād at an early age when his father, who was a military officer, was one of the Turkish mercenaries recruited by the ᶜAbbāsid court. Some accounts state that he was taught philosophy by Yūḥannā bin Haylān, a Nestorian Christian whose intellectual lineage connected him to the Greek philosophical school of Alexandria. Fārābī lived and taught for almost all his life in Baghdād, but in 942, when he was reportedly in his seventies, he accepted an invitation from the Ḥamdānid ruler Sayf al-Dawlah to move to Aleppo. He died there or in Damascus (accounts differ) eight years later, in 950. His philosophical output was prolific and diverse: over a hundred different texts are attributed to him, including works on logic, physics, metaphysics, ethics, politics, and a well-known treatise on music.

This selection from Fārābī comprises the middle section of *The Book of Letters* (*Kitāb al-Ḥurūf*), which represents a thematic break from the first and last sections of a text that is devoted largely to metaphysical terms and the meanings of Arabic words used in philosophical discourse. By contrast, this portion of the work is a genetic account of the origin of language, as well as the origins of various disciplines, culminating in philosophy and religion. Throughout, Fārābī assumes a tripartite classification of types of discourse or modes of reasoning, which was to become central to a great deal of Islamic philosophy in subsequent centuries. In ascending order of rigor, the types of reasoning are: rhetorical, dialectical, and demonstrative. Rhetorical and dialectical reasoning are associated with the multitude of human beings and are the modes of reasoning adopted in popular disciplines, whereas demonstrative reasoning is the province of an elite class of philosophers, who use it to achieve certainty. The main difference between these three types of discourse consists in the types of premises from which they begin, and hence the extent to which they provide an ultimate justification for their conclusions. Rhetorical disciplines, as Fārābī makes clear elsewhere, base their conclusions on persuasive opinions, while dialectical ones begin from commonly accepted opinions. By contrast, demonstrative disciplines are those that start from first principles or self-evident premises and proceed to prove everything else from them, either directly or indirectly.

In this text, Fārābī makes clear that this ascending hierarchy also corresponds to a genetic progression, rhetoric being the first mode of discourse to appear in human affairs, followed by dialectic, and then demonstration. In addition to these three main types of discourse, sophistical discourse appears alongside dialectic, employing false or dubious premises rather than true (but uncertain) ones. Some disciplines also employ images or similes instead of literal language, further removing discourse from literal truth and certainty. In particular, Fārābī regards religion as couching philosophical truths in the form of similes for popular consumption. Moreover, the two principal religious sciences, theology and jurisprudence, are based on religion and are dialectical or rhetorical in nature, sometimes taking the similes of religion for literal truth. This means that philosophy precedes religion, which in turn precedes the derivative disciplines of theology and jurisprudence.

Before giving an account of the development of the three main modes of discourse, Fārābī proposes a theory of the origin of language. Language arises in a particular nation (*ummah*) when people start to use visible signals to indicate their intention to others, later replacing these visible signs with audible ones. The first signs are those for particular perceptibles, followed by signs for universals that can be derived from perceptibles. The process of assigning words to particulars and universals happens first haphazardly among small groups of people, who effectively develop a convention to use certain words to pick out certain things. They do so not by stipulation, but rather by falling in with a certain practice. Eventually, these scattered efforts are managed by someone, who also invents sounds for things that have yet to be assigned sounds, plugging the gaps in their language by introducing new terms. Then, after expressions settle on meanings, linguistic rules start to be broken, issuing in figurative meanings. A word that has already been attached to a certain meaning comes to be associated with a different meaning, based on some near or distant resemblance between the two meanings.

Fārābī's distinction between literal and figurative language allows him to develop a distinctive view of the relation between reason and revelation, and his distinction between the three modes of reasoning (rhetorical, dialectical, demonstrative) enables him to explain the relationship of philosophy to theology and jurisprudence. The introduction of figurative or metaphorical meanings paves the way for three syllogistic arts to come into being: rhetoric, poetry, and linguistics. As figures of speech and other devices are introduced, rhetoric begins to develop as a skill or "art" (*ṣināʿah*, cf. Greek *technē*), which is the first of the syllogistic arts. It is syllogistic in that it employs logical argumentation, but the premises and intelligibles (or universal concepts) that it deploys are all popular or rhetorical ones. This implies that the art that studies rhetoric, like rhetorical speeches themselves, is not based on first principles but on premises that are persuasive to the multitude. After the appearance of the rhetorical arts, Fārābī needs to explain how dialectical and demonstrative arts originate. The crucial development is that people become interested in ascertaining the causes of things in the natural world and in mathematics. At first, their inquiries are rhetorical and are rife with disputes and differences of opinion, since rhetorical discourse is based merely on persuasive opinions. But as they endeavor to justify their mathematical and scientific claims to one another in argument and debate, their methods begin to achieve more thorough justification and they discover the dialectical methods, distinguishing them from the sophistical methods (which they use "in times of crisis" [141]). Eventually, the method of demonstration or certainty emerges, which is applied to theoretical matters as well as to political affairs and other practical matters, which pertain to human volition. Earlier, political matters had been broached using dialectical methods. But the theoretical and practical sciences are only perfected using demonstrative methods. Once these sciences are discovered using demonstration, the need arises in a society to convey these theoretical and practical matters to the multitude, resulting in a need for lawgiving. Religion then steps in to legislate in such a way as to convey these matters to a wider public through images and similes. Fārābī concludes that the religious lawgiver conveys some of the contents of philosophy to the multitude in the form of images and nonliteral discourse. Finally, the religious sciences of theology and jurisprudence arise in order to infer things that were not openly declared by the founder of the religion, basing themselves not on first principles but on those things that were openly declared in that religion, which makes them dialectical disciplines.

Thus, religion succeeds philosophy and serves mainly to convey its deeper truths in a form that is accessible to the multitude. However, Fārābī is aware that this neat progression can be broken in some cases, notably when religion is imported from one nation to another. In such cases, religion might precede philosophy rather than succeed it, as in the paradigm case that he discusses. In addition, religion might be corrupt, if it is based on a nondemonstrative philosophy, which is still being developed using rhetorical, dialectical, or sophistical methods. This is "philosophy" in name alone, since true philosophy for Fārābī is undoubtedly demonstrative. Such a corrupt religion will inevitably come into conflict with true philosophy, since it is based on a false or dubious philosophy. That is not the only way that religion and philosophy might come into conflict, as Fārābī explains in what might be a veiled reference to the relationship of religion and philosophy in Islam. Sometimes a religion based on a true philosophy is brought to some nation before the philosophy upon which it is based. When that philosophy eventually reaches the nation, the adherents of the religion, who assume that their religion contains the truth rather than similes of the truth, will oppose the philosophy. The philosophers will also be opposed to religion at first, until they realize that it contains figurative representations of philosophical truths. At that point, they will become reconciled to it, but the adherents of religion will remain implacably hostile, forcing the philosophers to defend themselves. However, if a religion is based on a corrupt philosophy, then whichever of the two, religion or philosophy, predominates in a nation "will eliminate the other from it" [150].

At the end of the selection, Fārābī discusses the way in which religion and philosophy are transferred from one nation or culture to another. He holds that when the philosophers of one nation encounter a new philosophical concept that has been imported from another nation, for which they have no expression, they can do one of two things. They can invent a new word, which can either be a neologism or a transliteration of the term in the other language. Alternatively, they can "transfer" a term used for some nonphilosophical or popular concept. In so doing, they can either use the corresponding popular term that has been used by the other nation, or else they can use a different popular term, while preserving the associations that that term had in the first nation. Fārābī thus implies that philosophical concepts are sometimes denoted by terms borrowed from other contexts because of the broader connotations associated with those terms. Indeed, he explains that "one group" is of the opinion that philosophical terms should not be borrowed from other more popular contexts on account of a certain resemblance, but that one should always invent new terms for novel philosophical concepts to avoid confusing the philosophical concept with the popular one. His rejoinder to this opinion is that this resemblance to popular meanings has a certain pedagogical utility when teaching a novice in philosophy, since it enables the student to grasp the philosophical concept more quickly. However, he does admit that one must always guard against confusion in these contexts, as one guards generally against homonymous words.

Ibn Sīnā, *On the Soul*

Abū ᶜAlī Ibn Sīnā (980–1037 AD) may be regarded as the great system-builder among Islamic philosophers, composing compendious works in philosophy, medicine, science, and religion, as well as on literary and linguistic matters. Ibn Sīnā was born of Persian parentage around half a century after Fārābī died, near the town of Bukhārā (in modern Uzbekistan), then capital of the Samānid dynasty, a semi-independent regime generally loyal to the Baghdād-based ᶜAbbāsid caliphate. His father was sympathetic to the Ismāᶜīlīs, a breakaway sect from Shīᶜī Islam, who were influenced by neo-Platonist ideas. He was exposed to these ideas from an early age and had a basic religious education as well as lessons in logic, mathematics, natural science, philosophy, and medicine, all of which he is said to have mastered by the age of 18. He relates that he reread Aristotle's *Metaphysics* forty times without understanding it, until he came upon one of Fārābī's works, which explained it to him. He was appointed a physician at the Samānid court, but their rule disintegrated under Turkish attack in 999 and Ibn Sīnā left to roam the cities of Persia, moving from city to city, serving in various senior posts. He died in 1037, assisting the ruler of Iṣfahān on a campaign against Hamadān, though he had refused an official position. Even more productive than Fārābī, Ibn Sīnā's corpus includes a number of works of a mystical nature written in what is known as the "illuminationist" (*ishrāqī*) style of philosophizing. His celebrated work in medicine, *Kitāb al-Qānūn fil-Ṭibb* (*The Book of the Canon of Medicine*, *The Canon* for short), remained in use in Latin translation in Renaissance

Europe, and is cited as *the* authoritative medical textbook in Chaucer's *Canterbury Tales*.

Ibn Sīnā's magnum opus *The Book of Healing* (*Kitāb al-Shifā'*) is a multivolume overview of the philosophical sciences, including logic, natural science, and divine metaphysics. The text excerpted here, *The Book of Salvation* (*Kitāb al-Najāt*), is a condensed version of that longer work organized into the three divisions mentioned, the second of which includes a section on the soul. Though Ibn Sīnā wrote numerous works in which he discussed the nature of the soul, this section contains perhaps his most succinct yet thorough treatment of the main topics relating to the human soul: the intellect, the acquisition of knowledge, abstraction, the immateriality of the intellect, the origination of the soul, the immortality of the soul, the refutation of reincarnation, the unity of the soul, and the Active Intellect. The selections translated here omit the first three chapters concerning the vegetative soul, the animal soul, and the internal senses of the soul, and begin with a chapter on the (human) rational soul.

When it comes to the topic of the human soul, the basic challenge for Ibn Sīnā and other Islamic philosophers was to reconcile Aristotle's account, which is not unequivocally dualist in nature, with an account which not only conceives of the soul as being a separate self-standing substance, but also subscribes to the immateriality, incorruptibility, and immortality of individual souls. One central aspect of Ibn Sīnā's dualist theory of the soul has to do with the different grades that can be attained by the human soul, depending on the degree to which its potential has been actualized. Initially, the human soul, or more precisely, the theoretical part of it, namely the intellect (*ʿaql*), is pure potential and is known as the "material intellect" (in analogy with prime matter before it receives any forms – not because it is literally material). Once it has acquired the basic building blocks of thinking, namely the first intelligibles or the purely rational principles that are unproven premises underlying the entirety of human knowledge (e.g. things equal to the same thing are equal to one another), it is known as the "habitual intellect." Then, after the soul acquires the rest of the intelligibles, it becomes the "actual intellect"; and at this point it is capable of reasoning and proving (or demonstrating) the totality of knowledge. Finally, whenever it actually grasps the intelligibles or thinks, it turns into the "acquired intellect."

Throughout this process, an agent is needed to effect the transformation of the intellect from potentiality into actuality. That agent is known as the Active Intellect (*al-ʿaql al-faʿʿāl*). The doctrine of the Active Intellect, which was developed by other Islamic philosophers prior to Ibn Sīnā and based ultimately on certain hints in Aristotle, is very distinctive to Islamic philosophy in general and to Ibn Sīnā in particular. Like other Islamic philosophers, Ibn Sīnā identifies the Active Intellect with the last of the celestial intelligences, that is, the intellects that are supposed to govern the motions of each of the ten celestial spheres (the outermost sphere of the heavens, sphere of the fixed stars, and so on).[4] The first celestial intelligence emanates directly from God, the second intelligence emanates from the first, the third from the second, and so on, until eventually the Active Intellect (the tenth intelligence, which governs the sphere of the moon) emanates to serve as a link between the celestial realm and the terrestrial realm. In addition to endowing natural things with their forms (hence, it is sometimes also termed the "bestower of forms"), it is responsible for activating the human intellect at the main stages of its intellectual development. Moreover, in certain exceptional individuals, it is instrumental in speeding up the process whereby the actual intellect becomes an acquired intellect. Such people are prophets and they are said to be endowed with a "holy intellect" or "intuition." At the end of the actualization process (i.e. at the stage of the acquired intellect or the holy intellect), the soul becomes something like a mirror image of the Active Intellect, containing the very same knowledge.

Embedded in this account of the stages through which the intellect progresses is an explanation of the significance of prophecy. Like other Islamic philosophers, Ibn Sīnā was intent on locating prophetic revelation within his overall metaphysical and epistemological system, and he does so in his own distinctive way. Rather than regarding prophecy as mainly a matter of the capacity to convey demonstrative philosophical truths in symbolic idiom, as Fārābī does, he views it as a superior intellectual ability to reach demonstrative conclusions more quickly than the ordinary rational person. Therefore, prophets equipped with holy intellects are capable of acquiring the same demonstrative knowledge as philosophers, but they do so in a shorter time. Ibn Sīnā makes a point of mentioning

[4] In addition to these two spheres, there are seven others, associated with the five known planets (Saturn, Jupiter, Mars, Venus, and Mercury), the sun, and the moon. The celestial intelligences were thought to be represented in religious discourse by the angels.

that they travel the same route as the philosophers, namely by pursuing a chain of deductive reasoning. As he puts it, they do so "not by conforming to convention but rather in an orderly manner that includes the middle terms" of syllogisms [206]. He insists on this, pointing out that beliefs acquired merely conventionally are not certain and rational.

In order to understand Ibn Sīnā's account of knowledge acquisition in more detail, it is necessary to introduce the external and internal senses. The external senses are, of course, the familiar five senses, which are instrumental in the acquisition of knowledge. In addition to these, Ibn Sīnā also posits five internal senses, which constitute the link in the chain between the external senses and the intellect. These are described directly before the excerpt translated in this volume and consist of five psychological faculties, as follows: (1) *phantasy* (Arabic *fanṭāsīyā*, a transliteration of Greek *phantasia*) or the *common sense*: brings together sensory information from the five senses; (2) *representation*: preserves the sensory information; (3) *imagination*: operates on the sensory information by manipulating the images thus preserved; (4) *estimation*: attaches rudimentary evaluative estimations to these images; and (5) *recollection*: preserves these evaluative estimations. The faculties of external sense, internal sense, and intellect eventuate in ever greater degrees of abstraction from the natural world. Like Aristotle, Ibn Sīnā understands sense perception as a process of acquiring the form of a substance, thereby abstracting it from matter. This measure of abstraction (which he also refers to as "extraction") from matter is minimal, as he explains, since the sensory image is only retained as long as the natural substance remains in place, and it disappears when it is removed or annihilated. A somewhat greater degree of abstraction is achieved by the faculty of representation, which abstracts forms from matter but not from the dependents of matter. In other words, though representations remain when the objects of representation are not present, they are not fully general or universal since they retain the accidents that accompany forms in the material world. Thus, for example, a representation of a human being in the soul will not be universal but will instead resemble some human or another, whether real or imaginary. To a first approximation, a representation of a human being may be thought of as some kind of mental image in memory, which must always have a determinate stature, color, shape, and so on. Yet further abstraction is achieved by the faculty of estimation, which attaches value to sensory particulars, such as approval and disapproval. This process of abstraction culminates in the intellect, since intelligible forms are wholly divorced from matter. For example, when it comes to the form *human*, the intellect separates it from matter to such an extent that it is applicable to all exemplars of humanity. How does this method of concept formation square with the process whereby the Active Intellect implants knowledge in the soul? Presumably, we can acquire these concepts only because the Active Intellect simultaneously activates them. Otherwise, we would not recognize them once we have attained them, which is the problem famously posed by Plato in formulating Meno's paradox.

Ibn Sīnā's brand of dualism rests on establishing that the human soul, more properly the intellect, is fundamentally immaterial. His main proof is a *reductio ad absurdum*, which relies on the premise that matter is infinitely divisible. He begins by assuming the opposite, namely that the soul is material, and considers what would follow if the soul were a divisible material entity. If this divisible entity is actually divided and the intelligible or concept contained in the soul is thereby also divided in two parts, various absurdities would ensue. A concept can only be divided into its constituent parts, namely genus and differentia (e.g. the concept *human* would be divided into the parts, *animal* and *rational*). But since a material body is potentially infinitely divisible, the genus and differentia would themselves have to be infinitely divisible. However, they are not, since such conceptual decomposition comes to an end. Moreover, he states that not all concepts are decomposable into genus and differentia, since some are the simplest building blocks of all other concepts. From this, he concludes that the soul must be an immaterial entity.

One thorny philosophical problem that confronted Ibn Sīnā has to do with reconciling the philosophical position that all souls are identical in essence, particularly virtuous souls that have attained the same level of knowledge and have the same intelligible content, with the view that souls remain distinct and separate in the afterlife. In at least one work, his predecessor Fārābī implies that virtuous souls do not maintain their distinctness in the afterlife.[5] Once they are freed of material attachments, there is nothing to distinguish human souls from one another, since they are all essentially reflections of the Active Intellect; hence, they unite with one another and with the Active Intellect. This is tantamount to a denial

[5] This view is expressed in *Kitāb al-Siyāsah al-Madanīyyah*; translated in Alfarabi, "The Political Regime," in *Medieval Political Philosophy*, ed. R. Lerner and M. Mahdi (Ithaca: Cornell University Press, 1963), p. 38.

of the doctrine of personal salvation. Ibn Sīnā's attempt to avoid such an unorthodox conclusion begins with his account of the origination of the soul. An individual soul comes into existence at the point at which a body originates that is suitable for being governed by that soul. Thus, the origination of the body is an accidental cause of the origination of the soul, whose essential cause is the "separate principles" (*al-mabādi' al-mufāriqah*), which are the celestial intelligences. He argues that the soul comes into being at the very instant as the body and does not exist before the body. At the moment of origination, a soul is endowed with "a particular disposition to be attracted to governing a particular body," which is "an essential concern that is specific to it" [220]. Then, in the course of a human life and as a result of its association with a particular body, that soul acquires further specificity and becomes distinguished from other souls. Accordingly, after separating from the body, each soul will have become a separate essence. This enables Ibn Sīnā to assert that individual souls maintain their distinctness in the afterlife, despite the fact that they may have acquired exactly the same degree of knowledge and are therefore identical in intellectual content. However, questions might be raised about Ibn Sīnā's account of the individuality of human souls, which posits souls that are essentially identical and yet also possess "an essential concern" towards governing particular bodies. If this means that they are essentially different in terms of their dispositions to govern particular bodies, then it is not clear how he can reconcile this with his claim that souls are identical in essence.

At the end of this selection, Ibn Sīnā proposes an analogy that illustrates the relation of the human soul to the Active Intellect. In doing so, he makes crucial use of an extended comparison between the influence of the Active Intellect on the soul and the influence of the light of the sun on the terrestrial realm. The use of light as a metaphor for the divine emanation (transmitted via the celestial intelligences) is prevalent in Ibn Sīnā's writing on this subject and is also used by other Islamic philosophers to illustrate the connection between the celestial and the terrestrial realm. Ibn Sīnā begins by explaining the difference between the vegetative, animal, and human souls in terms of the manner in which they have been influenced by the Active Intellect. He compares it to the difference in the way that three material bodies might be influenced by the light of the sun. Some bodies are such that they are merely heated by the sun, others are illuminated by it (better: reflect its light), and yet others are so susceptible to it that they might actually be ignited. Every body that is ignited is also illuminated and heated, and every body that is illuminated is also heated. This metaphor brings out the fact that the animal soul possesses the vegetative faculties, and that the human soul possesses both the animal and vegetative faculties. The metaphor has further respects of similarity, since once a fire has been ignited in a material body, that body goes on to heat and illuminate on its own, just as a human soul activated by the Active Intellect can go on to reason on its own, thereby acquiring some of the attributes of the Active Intellect itself. Finally, just as the sun is both a source of illumination as well as a perceptible, so also the Active Intellect actualizes thinking in the soul and can itself become an object of thought. Once the human soul achieves its highest state of thinking, it manages to conceive of the Active Intellect and to reflect its content.

Al-Ghazālī, *The Rescuer from Error*

Often considered an intellectual autobiography, this text is at best a rational reconstruction of the intellectual life of Abū Ḥāmid al-Ghazālī (1058–1111 AD), specifically his lifelong quest for knowledge or certainty. Indeed, it is often a considerable challenge to determine how his biographical details map on to his intellectual development. To tackle this question, one needs to plot the bare details of Ghazālī's life. He was born in Tus (near Meshhed in what is now northeastern Iran) and grew up there, leaving it in 1077 at the age of 19. For the next fourteen years he was at Nishapur, teaching at the Niẓāmīyyah college until 1085, then serving as court adviser to the famed Seljuk vizier Niẓām al-Mulk until 1091. In 1091, at the age of 33, he moved to Baghdād to take up a teaching post at the Niẓāmīyyah college there. Four years later, he experienced an intellectual crisis that caused him to stop teaching, which lasted six months and led to his traveling to Damascus, Jerusalem, Hebron, Mecca, and Medina. These travels lasted a little over a year, ending some time in 1097, at which point he returned to Baghdād. He spent the next nine years or so in Baghdād in a state of solitude of some kind, during which he refrained from teaching and concentrated on his mystical experiences. By the end of this period, in 1106, Ghazālī was 48 and was summoned back to Nishapur. He returned to teaching in Nishapur, after an eleven-year hiatus, spending the rest of his days there and dying at the age of 53 in 1111.

As for his intellectual quest, it proceeds as follows. He tells us that as a youth he had some dissatisfaction with conformist beliefs (*taqlīdīyyāt*), or beliefs acquired on the basis of tradition and authority. This led him to question many of his beliefs from an early age and to adopt a broadly skeptical outlook. Much later, at the age of 37, he experienced sharp pangs of doubt that caused him to be unsure of all his beliefs, even those based on the senses and on reason, leaving him without any beliefs at all. This intellectual crisis lasted two months and ended only when God enlightened him, casting a light into his breast. Ghazālī is quite explicit that this light from God restored his trust in the necessary truths, that is, those beliefs based on reason alone. We can presume that it also restored his sensory beliefs, since he would surely have needed them to get further in his intellectual quest, which consists in a systematic investigation of what he takes to be the four classes of truth-seekers: theologians, philosophers, Instructionists (an Islamic sect who believe that authoritative teaching is dispensed by an infallible religious leader), and mystics (*Ṣūfīs*). What is certain from the text is that this bout of skepticism coincides with the intellectual crisis described above. However, what is not certain is when he went on to investigate the first three classes of truth-seekers. In the text, he implies that he did so directly after this crisis and before he proceeded to investigate mysticism (the fourth class of truth-seekers), but this is unlikely, since he tells us that philosophy alone took two years of his time. It is more likely, given the fact that he had been the equivalent of a seminary professor, teaching mainly theology and jurisprudence for around eighteen years prior to his skeptical crisis, that he had already undertaken an investigation of these three classes before his bout with skepticism. Thus, after his necessary beliefs (and perhaps sensory beliefs) had been restored, he proceeded to investigate the theory and practice of mysticism, which we can presume occupied him for the next eleven years or so. But before embarking on his investigation of mysticism, he informs us that some of his basic religious beliefs were also restored to him (belief in God, prophecy, and the Day of Judgment). Since these are neither sensory nor necessary beliefs, they must not have been acquired as a result of the light cast by God. Ghazālī is somewhat evasive as to how these beliefs were acquired, telling us simply that they became entrenched in his soul "not as a result of a specific and explicit proof, but rather due to reasons, indications, and experiences, the details of which do not lend themselves to a brief summary" [133–4]. This suggests that these sciences were pursued after his rescue from skepticism and before he embarked on the in-depth study of mysticism. However, we have already seen that the investigation of philosophy alone took two years. Thus, the chronological sequence cannot have been as he implies. One alternative is that the belief in these things had eventuated from a reflection on his earlier studies of theology and philosophy, which took place in the interval between his being rescued from skepticism and his delving into mysticism (an interval that must have been fairly short based on what he tells us about his autobiography). What this shows is that Ghazālī's account of the four main stages of his intellectual development (skeptical crisis, fideist resolution, investigation of the three classes of truth-seekers, and immersion in mysticism) must be a rational reconstruction to some extent. The four stages cannot have been as compartmentalized as he makes out; in particular, the third stage must not have been neatly confined to a single phase in his life.

The parallels with Descartes' intellectual crisis and bout of skepticism, as recounted in the *Discourse on Method* and the *Meditations on First Philosophy*, have often been noted. However, the similarity between the two accounts stops more or less at the point at which the two philosophers find themselves in a state of radical doubt. After that, Ghazālī's solution may be regarded as fideist, while Descartes' is plainly rationalist. Unlike Descartes, Ghazālī makes no attempt to prove the existence of God, stating simply that, "Whoever supposes that enlightenment depends upon explicit proofs has narrowed the expanse of God's mercy" [86–7]. Indeed, he advances a reason as to why there *can be* no rational escape route from a situation of extreme skepticism, pointing out that a proof can only be given by employing certain first principles, but if these are not accepted by the skeptic, then no proof is forthcoming. That is why the fideist solution is the only one open to him, and why he relies on a light from God to restore some of his basic beliefs.

It is evident from this text that Ghazālī did not consider himself a philosopher, but he nevertheless mastered the techniques, vocabulary, and doctrines of the philosophers so thoroughly that he made original philosophical contributions of his own, particularly in his celebrated attack on philosophy, *The Incoherence of the Philosophers* (*Tahāfut al-Falāsifah*). His conflicted relationship with philosophy thus makes him a philosopher despite himself. In this less systematic text, his critique of philosophy is very abbreviated and appears in the context of a foray into both philosophy and theology to determine whether either of them is able to supply him with certainty. Armed with the bare foundations of knowledge, Ghazālī investigates the theologians and the philosophers. Interestingly, he regards the theologians as useless for this purpose on the grounds that they take too much for granted and can therefore be "of little use for someone who only accepts necessary [truths]" [92]. The reason is that their enterprise is primarily a defensive one: they defend religion against the unorthodox by beginning from the beliefs they share with them and proceeding to show them the errors of their ways. Since they do not start from first principles, they fail to serve Ghazālī's purpose. This shows that even though Ghazālī is professionally committed to theology and counts himself among the theologians, he nevertheless shares the philosophers' conception of theology as a dialectical discipline that bases its conclusions on commonly accepted opinions rather than on first principles.

As for the philosophers, Ghazālī dismisses them too, though he does so less summarily than the theologians. In this text, he conveys only a few of his many grievances with the philosophers, whom he splits up into three main groups: materialists, naturalists, and theists. Since the first are atheists and the second deny the afterlife, he gives greatest consideration to the third group, including Plato, Aristotle, Fārābī, and Ibn Sīnā. He finds their main errors to be in metaphysics, over such matters as the denial of bodily resurrection in the afterlife. However, he states that he has exposed their errors elsewhere (primarily in the *Incoherence of the Philosophers*), and proceeds to expose the dangers that arise from such philosophical sciences as mathematics and ethics. In doing so, he defends esotericism, an attitude he shares with most of the Islamic philosophers he opposes. He argues that it is necessary to restrict access to the books of the philosophers and to bar their teachings to the multitude in order to avoid two dangers: blind acceptance by impressionable neophytes and blanket dismissal by intolerant religious fanatics.

Having been disappointed by the theologians and philosophers,[6] Ghazālī goes on to find what he is looking for in mysticism, which he tells us cannot be learned merely from books but must actually be practiced. It turns out not to be a simple matter to articulate precisely what Ghazālī learned from mysticism, though by the end of his mystical experience he appears to have restored all his former beliefs. However, what is certain is

[6] Ghazālī also dismisses a third group of knowledge-seekers, the Instructionists (*al-Taʿlīmīyyūn*), an Islamic sect associated with the Ismāʿīlīs who claim that truth is to be found in the teachings of an infallible religious leader. That portion of the text has not been included in this translation.

that Ghazālī thinks that mystical insight is of a different order from rational thought. There is a fairly consistent distinction throughout this text between knowledge (*ʿilm*) and cognizance (*maʿrifah*, sometimes also linked to *idrāk*, or apprehension), according to which the former is propositional in character, based on reason, and capable of demonstration, while the latter is nonpropositional, based on mystical insight, and capable only of direct acquaintance (literally, "tasting," *dhawq*). Though Ghazālī sometimes uses these terms loosely, they generally mark a distinction between a strictly rational body of thought that is obtained using the demonstrative method that the philosophers advocate, and a type of insight that transcends reason or the intellect and must be obtained through other means, such as mystical experience. This distinction between knowledge and cognizance is underwritten by Ghazālī's proof of prophecy, by which he means, in part, a realm beyond reason or intellect (*ʿaql*) and a source of cognizance that outstrips rational knowledge. Unlike Fārābī, who regards prophecy as a talent for conveying rational truths in symbolic form, and Ibn Sīnā, who regards it as a faculty for reaching rational conclusions speedily and promptly, Ghazālī views it as a capacity to glean insights that lie beyond reason – though that is only one aspect of prophecy, he hastens to add.

One of Ghazālī's main tasks in this text is to show that prophecy, in the sense of a mode of apprehension that surpasses reason, is a genuine phenomenon, and he claims to do so in three distinct ways. First, he offers what he takes to be a rational *demonstration* that nonrational apprehension is possible. He argues that truths of a nonrational nature have been acquired by humanity (in medicine and astrology, among other domains), and goes on to say that they must have come by them thanks to a nonrational source of insight. Secondly, Ghazālī states that prophecy can be affirmed by means of a direct *awareness* of the mystical state, which is "the beginning of prophecy," though it is by no means the whole story. This is what he calls "tasting" (*dhawq*) and it involves a mystical experience, which is, however, not accessible to all people. Indeed, he holds that the things that were revealed to him while he was in the mystical state (*ḥāl*) cannot even be expressed in language, and that any such attempt is liable to distort or falsify. Finally, prophecy is established through trust in testimony and second-hand corroboration, which is what he calls *faith* (*īmān*). This is not faith in the ordinary understanding of the term, since it is a phenomenon not restricted to religious matters, and crops up in many other instances (e.g. his example of the man who is sure that his father is not malevolent to him). His account of faith relies partly on the concept of "recurrent corroboration" (*tawātur*), which indicates a process whereby testimony is supported by numerous different sources, especially in authenticating a saying or report attributed to the prophet Muḥammad (*Ḥadīth*).

One way of understanding Ghazālī's intellectual journey is that it effectively serves to rehabilitate his conformist beliefs (*taqlīd* has been translated here as conformism, but it also connotes: imitation, tradition, convention, and authority). These include such things as the belief that one must pray five times a day at fixed times and that certain religious rituals must be performed during the pilgrimage, among many others. Having questioned these beliefs at an early age, then having set them aside during his skeptical crisis and fideist resolution, he proceeds on his intellectual journey without them. They are rehabilitated not by a simple reversion to the beliefs he had before, since he informs us early on that once "the glass of conformity is fractured . . . the damage is irreparable" [90]. Rather, he arrives at them by a different route and they receive justification on altogether different grounds. The conformist beliefs, which he once accepted merely because they were handed down to him, are later embraced apparently on the basis of his belief in prophecy. Since he vindicates prophecy itself in three different ways (as mentioned above), this renders his erstwhile conformist beliefs no longer conformist. They have become every bit as secure as the sensory or rational beliefs. Moreover, this epistemological transformation is accompanied by an attitudinal change, for Ghazālī insists at the end of his journey that, while he once disseminated the knowledge that brings fame, he now spreads "the knowledge that brings about the rejection of fame, and by means of which one becomes cognizant of its insignificance" [160].

Ibn Ṭufayl, *Ḥayy bin Yaqzān*

Ibn Ṭufayl (*c.* 1109–86 AD) was born around the same time as Ghazālī died, at the opposite end of the Islamic world, near the town of Granada in Spain. Little is known about his early life, though it is clear that he studied medicine and philosophy, and practiced as a physician in Granada, eventually becoming secretary to the governor of the province. He occupied progressively senior positions, eventually serving as court physician to the

Almohad sultan of Spain and parts of North Africa, Abū Ya^{c}qūb Yūsuf, upon whom he exercised considerable influence. The text excerpted here is the only one of his philosophical works to survive, but he also wrote treatises on medicine and astronomy, and is said to have held certain anti-Ptolemaic views in astronomy. After Abū Ya^{c}qūb died in 1184, Ibn Ṭufayl went on to perform the same role for his son and successor Abū Yūsuf Ya^{c}qūb, who was, however, less interested in philosophy than his father, and he died in his service in Marrakesh in 1186.

This work, entitled *Ḥayy bin Yaqẓān* (literally, Alive Son of Awake) after its eponymous hero, recounts the tale of an autodidact who lives by himself on a desert island. The selection translated in this volume constitutes over three-quarters of the work, omitting an extensive introductory section and a concluding epilogue. In this middle section of the text, the emphasis is on showing that a single human being in isolation from others, equipped simply with a superior intellect and a disposition for virtue, can discover for himself the main truths of philosophy (including natural science). Ibn Ṭufayl is also concerned to show that such an individual can surpass the rational realm, crossing over to a mystical state that furnishes him with a vision of the supernatural. In addition, the work functions as a kind of philosophical primer that can serve to introduce neophytes to basic philosophical concepts through the story of their spontaneous discovery by a single individual.

As if to convey the point that there can be both a purely naturalistic or scientific explanation as well as a nonscientific explanation for the same phenomenon, we are provided with two accounts of how Ḥayy came to be on his uninhabited island. The first involves spontaneous generation from clay, while the second consists of a fanciful story of forbidden love, illicit marriage, and the dispatch of a newborn infant in a wooden chest over the waves, a tale that might almost have been drawn from the *Thousand and One Nights*. But the two accounts quickly converge and Ibn Ṭufayl proceeds to recount the stages of Ḥayy's development, which are conveniently divided into seven seven-year periods (taking him up to the age of 50). After being reared in his early years by a doe, Ḥayy embarks on his intellectual journey by undertaking an empirical investigation of the world around him. This leads him to uncover important metaphysical truths, and his journey ends with a discovery of mysticism and the euphoric visions that one obtains from it.

The first four phases of Ḥayy's life are largely taken up with an investigation into the terrestrial realm, though this eventually includes knowledge of matters that originate in the celestial sphere, such as the forms of objects and the rational soul. He gains knowledge not just of the natural sciences, for example by undertaking anatomical dissections of various different species of animals, but also of metaphysics, for example by contemplating the difference between body and soul. In recounting Ḥayy's intellectual progress, Ibn Ṭufayl introduces his readers in an intuitive way to some of the main philosophical and scientific doctrines that he shared with his fellow Islamic philosophers, including the distinction between form and matter, the nature of the four elements (earth, water, air, and fire), the difference between essence and accident, and the role of the Active Intellect. For example, Ḥayy establishes the existence of the Active Intellect after investigating the process whereby the four elements are transformed into one another. As water is heated, it is transformed into steam, a process that he understands in terms of eliminating one form and replacing it with another. He reasons that this necessitates an agent that bestows forms on natural objects, which is none other than the Active Intellect. After completing this inquiry into the natural world, the fifth phase of Ḥayy's life takes him from the terrestrial to the celestial realm, engaging him in discussions of the nature of the universe, which lead him to conclude that it is finite and has been created by an immaterial creator. Thus, this phase of Ḥayy's life (at the end of which he reaches the age of 35) concludes with a proof of the existence of God.

The sixth phase of his life moves Ḥayy from the realm of theory into the realm of practice. Given the absence of other human beings on his island, these practical endeavors involve his conduct towards other living creatures, his conduct towards himself, and his conduct towards God, in the form of spiritual exercises that aim ultimately at constant contemplation of God. Indeed, this phase also brings forth a tension between mystical contemplation and practical attention to the needs of other creatures (which is later heightened in the epilogue to the text). On the grounds that he shares something with animals, celestial beings, and God Himself, Ḥayy sets himself three different tasks or "emulations." The first emulation pertains to the animals and aims to secure Ḥayy's livelihood and ensure his continued survival in such a way that he is not distracted from the vision of God. It therefore involves an ascetic existence that causes the least amount of disruption to the work of the Creator. The second emulation involves imitating three attributes of the celestial bodies (including the sun): caring for his fellow creatures in the realm of generation and corruption, practicing purity and circular motion, and enjoying a vision of God. Finally, the third emulation is continuous with the third part of the second emulation since it also involves reflecting on God. Emulation of God's positive attributes involves knowing Him without associating Him in any way with materiality. Meanwhile, emulation of His negative attributes (mainly, freedom from matter) entails ridding himself of material attachments and preoccupations. At this point, Ibn Ṭufayl informs us that a tension arises between the second and third emulations, since part of the objective of the second is the care of other creatures, whereas the third calls for utter withdrawal from the world. Ḥayy never resolves the tension; instead, he becomes increasingly detached from the material world and seeks ever greater proximity to God. Eventually, he succeeds in achieving an uninterrupted mystical vision for longer periods of time, with minimal pauses to replenish himself and keep body and soul together. Thus, the seventh phase of his life ends with Ḥayy achieving this mystical vision and being imbued with some form of mystical insight.

When it comes to the status of mystical insight and the possibility of a nonrational mode of apprehension, Ibn Ṭufayl's position seems to be situated somewhere between Ibn Sīnā's and Ghazālī's. He does not go so far as the latter in holding that mysticism provides a source of insight that cannot be apprehended through reason. However, he would not appear to concur with Ibn Sīnā's conception of the prophetic faculty simply as an enhanced ability to frame deductive arguments. This emerges most clearly in the prologue to this text (which has not been included in this translation), where he likens the acquisition of mystical insight to the acquisition of the sense of sight by a congenitally blind man. He explains that this does not confer any new information on the man who acquires the new sensory modality, since he knew the shapes and appearances of things by touch as well as by hearsay. It merely presents the same information more vividly.[7] Ibn Ṭufayl agrees with Ghazālī that reason breaks down

[7] This analogy might be interpreted differently, namely, as implying that one does indeed learn something new from mysticism, since some information is available to sight that is not available to touch and the other sensory modalities. This depends on one's view about the ability to transfer information gained from one sensory modality to another. The question has an illustrious history in modern philosophy, beginning perhaps with Locke's discussion of Molyneux's problem. It has

when faced with mystical experience, illustrating this point by showing that it leads Ḥayy into specious argumentation. After awakening from the mystical state, Ḥayy reflects on the fact that his essence is really only a reflection of the essence of God, and since the reflection of the sun in a material body is in reality nothing but the light of the sun itself, he concludes thet he is nothing but the reality of God. Moreover, Ḥayy reasons that God's essence is no different from His knowledge of His essence, and since he has acquired knowledge of God's essence, he has also acquired His essence. Once he acquires this knowledge, it becomes Ḥayy's essence, so he concludes that he is identical with God's essence, and therefore the same as God. However, this is a specious argument, which Ḥayy soon dismisses once he recognizes (by God's grace) the source of his error.

Despite the fact that Ibn Ṭufayl maintains that Ḥayy's vision cannot be fully expressed in words, insisting that his discourse is of a kind that transcends reason, and that a request to understand it in propositional terms is comparable to a request to taste colors, he acquiesces reluctantly in the attempt to convey the gist of what Ḥayy observed in his mystical state. The last part of the text consists in an apocalyptic vision of the essences of the celestial beings and of other human beings, as well as allusive evocations of the Day of Judgment. Ibn Ṭufayl expresses in a vivid form the emanationist cosmology and cosmogony that is broadly shared by many Islamic philosophers, according to which a series of ten celestial intelligences emanate from God, each of which governs one of the celestial spheres. As we have already seen, the last of these ten intelligences is the Active Intellect, which governs the sphere of the moon and gives rise to the vast multiplicity of the sublunar world – though Ibn Ṭufayl also insists that it is a mistake to attribute multiplicity to the Active Intellect. To convey this scheme, he uses an analogy similar to Ibn Sīnā's, whereby the light of the sun (emanation from God) is reflected in a mirror (celestial intelligence), which is reflected in another mirror, and so on until the tenth reflecting surface is shimmering water, presumably an indication of the fact that it scatters the light of the sun in many directions. The essence of this last celestial sphere is multifaceted, each facet glorifying the essence of God. Ḥayy observes that his own essence is in some sense

also recently witnessed a great deal of discussion in the debate surrounding the "Knowledge Argument" concerning qualitative phenomenal states (or qualia), especially those involved in perceiving colors.

part of this essence, though it came into existence with the origination of his body and is specific to his body (recall here Ibn Sīnā's account of the origination of the soul and its relationship to the Active Intellect). Throughout, Ibn Ṭufayl emphasizes that this verbal description of Ḥayy's vision is inadequate to convey it faithfully. Ironically, Ḥayy himself is bereft of language, which renders his entire intellectual journey somewhat questionable, since many philosophers would argue that the concepts he frames and the complex arguments he engages in would not be possible without some kind of linguistic medium. However, given the nature of mysticism in Ibn Ṭufayl's account, that might actually facilitate the crowning achievement of his endeavors: his mystical experience.

Ibn Rushd, *The Incoherence of the Incoherence*

A protégé and contemporary of Ibn Ṭufayl, Abū al-Walīd Ibn Rushd (1126–98 AD) spent most of his career in Islamic Spain. Though he excelled as a jurist and physician, philosophy was his main intellectual preoccupation. Ibn Rushd came from a prominent family of jurists and received a thorough legal training in Islamic jurisprudence. He must also have received a good education in theology, in the philosophical sciences, and in medicine. Ibn Ṭufayl was responsible for introducing him to the philosophically minded ruler of Islamic Spain and parts of North Africa, Abū Ya^{c}qūb Yūsuf, who promptly commissioned him to write a number of commentaries on Aristotle. He also wrote works on medicine, jurisprudence, and other books on philosophy, notably *The Incoherence of the Incoherence* (*Tahāfut al-Tahāfut*), which is excerpted here. In addition to these activities, he served as chief judge of Cordoba and court physician. In 1194, Ibn Rushd fell out of favor at court after Abū Ya^{c}qūb's son came to power and came under the influence of religious extremists. Along with other philosophers, he was sent into exile and a prohibition was issued against the study of philosophy. But shortly afterwards, he was restored to favor and resumed work on philosophy until he died in Marrakesh in 1198. Ibn Rushd (Averroes) is sometimes said to have had a more profound influence on the Latin West than on the Islamic world, even though there was a backlash against Averroism in late thirteenth-century Europe, when the study of his works was pronounced heretical. But what went by the name of "Averroism" was often different from the philosopher's actual doctrines.

Ibn Rushd's *Incoherence of the Incoherence* is very distinctive in form. Conceived as an extensive reply to Ghazālī's assault on philosophy, *The Incoherence of the Philosophers*, Ibn Rushd's work quotes the vast majority of Ghazālī's text, so that his readers can read his opponent's words side by side with his own. To consider *The Incoherence of the Incoherence* a philosophical dialogue may seem somewhat unfair to Ghazālī, since Ibn Rushd always has the last word. However, it does retain much of the character of a debate thanks partly to the fact that Ghazālī has the foresight to anticipate many of the objections to his views, as well as to the fact that Ibn Rushd gives him a fair hearing. This particular exchange concerns the nature of causation, and it constitutes the seventeenth of twenty issues that Ghazālī tackles in criticizing the philosophers (the last four of which are about the "natural sciences").

This debate between Ghazālī and Ibn Rushd is both rich and involved. Not only does it contain their respective positions on the issues of causation and miracles, it also contains what Ghazālī takes to be the position of the philosophers (primarily Ibn Sīnā, though he goes largely unmentioned), what Ibn Rushd takes to be the position of the philosophers (which is not always identical with Ghazālī's interpretation, nor is it always the same as his own position), positions Ghazālī takes for the sake of argument to refute the position of the philosophers, objections raised by Ghazālī to what he takes to be the position of the philosophers, Ibn Rushd's responses to these objections, objections raised by Ibn Rushd to Ghazālī's position, and so on. Needless to say, the dialectical state of play can become difficult to follow at times (e.g. is Ghazālī stating another objection or is he articulating an alternative philosophical position?). However, with some rearranging, two main threads emerge in the dialogue.

In the debate on causation, Ghazālī is advocating an occasionalist view according to which existing things do not have any real causal powers. Rather, every time fire burns cotton, the fire itself does not produce any of the burning effects; they are, instead, caused directly by God. Naturally occurring events do not manifest the causal powers of the objects involved in those events; they are mere occasions for God to insert the appropriate effects in their habitual order. Ghazālī adheres to this view partly because it leaves room for God to refrain from inserting those effects in certain instances, or makes it possible for God to insert effects other than the habitual ones. These instances are none other than miracles. By contrast,

Ghazālī holds that the rival, philosophical conception of causality, according to which things in nature have causal powers that are proper to them and necessitate their effects, does not allow for the possibility of miracles. He also thinks that it represents a limitation on God's omnipotence by ruling out his ability to intervene directly and interrupt the causal order or sever the causal nexus. Thus, a second reason for adhering to occasionalism is that it places fewer limits on God's capabilities.

After enumerating three types of miracle that Ghazālī says the philosophers allow, he states that this falls short of a full endorsement of miracles and fails to allow for other more spectacular types of miracle, for example Moses' conversion of a stick into a serpent, which is mentioned in the Qur'ān (see 7:107, 20:20). The first line of argument that Ghazālī pursues against the necessitarian view of causation consists of denying a necessary connection between cause and effect (or for that matter, between effect and cause). He points out that the "only proof" the philosophers adduce for a necessary connection between fire and burning is the simple fact of the occurrence of the burning upon contact with the fire. However, he responds that observation proves that the occurrence took place *upon* contact with fire, not that the occurrence took place *by virtue of* contact with fire. To underscore this point, he observes that the philosophers themselves acknowledge that at least one such habitual occurrence is not an indication of causation, namely the ensoulment of the embryo in the womb. He tells us that the nonmaterialist philosophers agree that the soul attaches itself to the body at conception not as a result of the operation of natural causes and the effects of the four elements, but as a result of direct causal intervention from the celestial realm (either by God himself, or by the mediation of the celestial intelligences).

Ibn Rushd's response to this proceeds by pointing out that a denial of natural causation is tantamount to a denial that things have fixed natures, definitions, and names. If fire no longer has the causal power of burning, then there is nothing to distinguish it from water, air, and earth. Consequently, natural elements and the substances formed from them can no longer be differentiated from one another in any real sense. This would, according to Ibn Rushd, strip all the various existents of their distinctive natures and make them one; indeed, not even one, since that implies that the resulting undifferentiated natural substance has some causal power or another, and since it does not, one should properly say that it does not exist at all. In addition, in the absence of fixed causal powers, things do not have settled natures, which means that we could have no real knowledge of the natural world. Thus, the removal of cause and effect removes the possibility of human knowledge.

A second argumentative thread pursued by Ghazālī in this debate concerns the philosophers' view that "external principles" (i.e. the celestial intelligences) are somehow involved in endowing natural existents with the natures that they have in the first place. As we have already seen, on a widespread Islamic philosophical view, natural existents in the terrestrial or sublunar realm are subject to the influence of the celestial realm through constant emanation. This divine emanation is mediated by the celestial intelligences, the last of which is the Active Intellect associated with the innermost sphere of the heavens, which was introduced above in connection with Ibn Sīnā's account of the development of the human soul. Moreover, in addition to this psychological role, the Active Intellect (or the "bestower of forms") also endows existents with their forms and essential natures, as Ḥayy bin Yaqẓān discovers in Ibn Ṭufayl's work. Once these natures have been bestowed on existing things, they proceed to act upon one another with necessity through their own causal powers.

Ghazālī raises three points in response to this aspect of the necessitarian account. First, he questions why the philosophers accept that God endows existents with their essential natures in this way, whether directly or through the mediation of the Active Intellect, and do not accept that God intervenes to revoke or suspend these essential natures at the time of a miracle. Second, he states that even if we grant that causal powers, once bestowed on existents, are fixed, there is nothing to prevent God from intervening to limit these causal powers in certain ways, for example restricting the heating effects of fire to a certain circumscribed area and not allowing it to come into contact with the cotton. Third, he wonders why the forms that are bestowed on some material things at certain times could not be bestowed on other material things that are not ordinarily receptive to them. In fact, he finds that the philosophers have no coherent account of why some material entities are disposed to receive certain forms and not others, for example why the sperm of a human being could not receive the form of a horse, or for that matter, why a stick could not receive the form of a serpent.

Ibn Rushd addresses all three of these points, with varying degrees of success. He replies to the first point, concerning the bestowing of forms upon existents, by admitting that external principles are involved in causation, but stating that one must distinguish between perceived, known causes and unperceived, unknown causes. He maintains simply that one should not confuse the former, which operate by endowing existents with the natures that they have, with the latter, which operate when those existents act upon one another. As to the second point, Ibn Rushd replies enigmatically that the natures of material existents are well defined and specific, according to certain quantities and qualities. That is, it is not merely in the nature of fire to burn, but to burn to a certain degree, within a certain range, and so on. This suggests that a limitation or restriction on the causal powers of a material existent amounts to a revocation of those powers. Hence, Ghazālī's contention that the philosophers can have their causal powers without denying miracles, simply by allowing God to intervene in natural processes in a limited fashion, cannot really be acceptable to the philosophers. Finally, when it comes to the third point, Ibn Rushd seems to admit that the philosophers do not have an ultimate explanation for why only certain instances of matter are disposed to receive certain forms, and declares this to lead to a stand-off between the philosophers and the theologians, each deeming their view to be self-evident. He implies that shapes are essential to substances and that substances would not have had the forms and properties that they do if they did not have the shapes that they have. However, he does not advance a real explanation as to why that is so, and the example he gives about the human hand is somewhat obscure. Moreover, he holds that if it were really possible for any form to be received by any matter in this manner, then God would not have seen to it that animals were created through a lengthy process such as the one that occurs in nature. Instead, he would have created animals directly from clay. Thus, when it comes to the second line of argument, concerning the external principles and the manner in which existents are endowed with their causal powers, Ghazālī manages to embarrass the philosophical account sufficiently for Ibn Rushd to declare a stalemate. However, Ibn Rushd also manages to contribute a threatening argument against Ghazālī's position.

In addition to these two main argumentative strands in the text, one can also discern a few supplementary arguments deployed by Ibn Rushd against Ghazālī, at least three of which are worth mentioning. At one point, Ibn Rushd suggests that the theologians themselves employ the notion of causation, though they do not always clearly signal it as such, for example in stating something like the argument from design. In response, Ghazālī might rephrase this in terms of God's habit. However, this response may not succeed if he is trying to prove God's existence based on the alleged reason exhibited in his creation. Secondly, Ibn Rushd raises legitimate doubts concerning what it means to say that the connection between cause and effect is not necessary but habitual. He points out that it cannot be a habit of God (since God's course has no alteration, according to the Qur'ān), nor a habit of natural objects (they are inanimate, and to the extent that they can be said metaphorically to have habits, those are their natures), nor a habit of ours (that would make the sequence of natural events conventional or relative to us). Related to this objection is Ibn Rushd's implicit criticism of Ghazālī's conception of God. He hints that the view of causation put forward by Ghazālī would lead ultimately to an unsatisfactory conception of God, who would be seen to rule over the universe like a despotic tyrant (as opposed, perhaps, to a law-abiding authoritarian). A third objection that Ibn Rushd raises against Ghazālī occurs at the very end of the exchange. Indeed, Ghazālī anticipates this objection, which amounts to the following question: If God can do everything possible, what are the limits of possibility? Can he, for example, square the circle, or make something be the case and not be the case at once? Ghazālī's response rests on a distinction between logical possibility and metaphysical or physical possibility; effectively, he asserts that God cannot contravene the former but can the latter. This response is satisfactory up to a point, but if part of Ghazālī's concern is to preserve God's omnipotence, the inability to contravene logic may also be construed as a restriction on God's capability. That is why Ibn Rushd alleges that it would have been more consistent on Ghazālī's part to allow that God can indeed breach logic, citing at least one theologian who takes this view (although he suggests that the mainstream Ashᶜarites[8] have shied away from it). According to such a position, logic is merely a contingent feature of our intellects – a conclusion that Ibn Rushd finds delusory.

A fundamental issue that looms over this text concerns Ibn Rushd's considered view about miracles. Given his necessitarian view of causation, it would seem to follow that he does not believe in miracles in the sense of disruptions of the causal nexus or interruptions in the causal chain. This is lent credence by the fact that he is decidedly evasive on the issue

[8] Ashᶜarite theology is the dominant school of Islamic theology, founded by Abū al-Ḥasan al-Ashᶜarī (c. 874–936 AD).

and states on at least two occasions in this text that such matters should not be discussed openly – a clear indication of his staunch esotericism on this as well as other thorny philosophical questions. Further evidence that Ibn Rushd does not believe in miracles (in the strong sense) comes from the fact that the only actual example of a "miracle" that he cites is the Qur'ān, which is surely not miraculous in the sense of an interruption in causality, but presumably only in the sense that it has an extraordinary or superlative character.[9]

These brief introductions to the five texts collected in this volume are necessarily selective with respect to the issues they highlight. They are meant to reveal some of the concerns and continuities that characterize these texts, as well as some of the stylistic and substantive differences among them. In introducing these texts, I have tried to suggest interpretations of them and raise questions about them that might serve to encourage a broader discussion, while trying to avoid the twin perils of treating them as contemporaries and of regarding them as incommensurable aliens. In other words, I have tried to consider them simply as one would the canonical texts of the western philosophical tradition, from which they have hitherto been largely excluded.

[9] The Qur'ān is sometimes said to have the power to render imitation of it impossible. This power is denoted by the term *iʿjāz*, which is significantly derived from the same root as the term for miracle, *muʿjizah*.

Chronology

c. 570	Birth of Muḥammad
622	Emigration (*hijrah*) of Muḥammad from Mecca to Medina
632	Death of Muḥammad
632–61	Reign of first four (Rāshidūn) caliphs of Islam
637–44	Muslim conquests of Syria, Iraq, and Egypt
661	Establishment of Umayyad dynasty
710	Muslim forces cross into Spain
750	Establishment of ^{c}Abbāsid dynasty; end of Umayyad dynasty
754–75	Reign of caliph al-Manṣūr, patron of early translations of scientific texts from Greek
c. 800	Teaching hospital established in Baghdād
813–48	Flourishing of Mu^{c}tazilite philosophical theology
832	Establishment of Bayt al-Ḥikmah library in Baghdād by caliph al-Ma'mūn
c. 873	Death of al-Kindī, often considered the first philosopher of Islam
c. 878	**Birth of al-Fārābī in Turkestan**
c. 936	Death of al-Ash^{c}arī, founder of dominant school of Islamic theology
c. 950	**Death of al-Fārābī in Syria**
973	Founding of al-Azhar mosque and university in Cairo
980	**Birth of Ibn Sīnā in Persia**
1037	**Death of Ibn Sīnā in Persia**
1058	**Birth of al-Ghazālī in Persia**
1095	Pope Urban calls for Crusade
c. 1109	**Birth of Ibn Ṭufayl in Spain**

1111	**Death of al-Ghazālī in Persia**
1126	**Birth of Ibn Rushd in Spain**
1186	**Death of Ibn Ṭufayl in North Africa**
1187	Crusaders defeated by Ṣalāḥ al-Dīn
1191	Death of Suhrawardī, illuminationist philosopher influenced by Ibn Sīnā
1198	**Death of Ibn Rushd in North Africa**
1204	Death of Maimonides, Jewish philosopher and physician influenced by Ibn Rushd
1236	Christians capture Cordoba in Spain
1258	End of ᶜAbbāsid dynasty in Baghdād
1261	Mamlūk dynasty established in Egypt
1303	Mongols defeated by Mamlūks in Egypt
1406	Death of Ibn Khaldūn, philosopher of history and society

Further reading

Translations

All but one of the five texts collected in this volume have been previously translated into English, but most of these translations are now somewhat dated. Ibn Sīnā has been translated in F. Rahman, *Avicenna's Psychology* (Oxford: Oxford University Press, 1952), Ghazālī in W. M. Watt, *The Faith and Practice of al-Ghazali* (London: Allen & Unwin, 1952) and in R. McCarthy, *Freedom and Fulfillment* (Boston: Twayne, 1980), Ibn Ṭufayl in Lenn E. Goodman, *Ibn Tufayl's Hayy bin Yaqzan* (3rd edition, Los Angeles: Gee Tee Bee, 1991; first published 1969), and Ibn Rushd in Simon van den Bergh, *Averroes: The Incoherence of the Incoherence* (London: Luzac & Co., 1954).

One anthology that contains a sizeable section devoted to translations of Islamic philosophy is Ralph Lerner and Muhsin Mahdi, eds., *Medieval Political Philosophy* (Ithaca: Cornell University Press, 1963), though over two-thirds of it is devoted to medieval Jewish and Christian philosophy. Another anthology of medieval philosophy that contains selections from Islamic texts is Arthur Hyman and James Walsh, eds., *Philosophy in the Middle Ages* (2nd edition, Indianapolis: Hackett, 1983).

A few important Islamic philosophical texts have recently been translated in a dual-text series, notably Michael E. Marmura, *Al-Ghazālī: The Incoherence of the Philosophers* (Provo, Utah: Brigham Young University Press, 1997), Charles Butterworth, *Averroes: Decisive Treatise and Epistle Dedicatory* (Provo, Utah: Brigham Young University Press, 2002). Several of Fārābī's central works have been reliably translated, including F. W. Zimmermann, *Al-Farabi's Commentary and Short Treatise on Aristotle's*

De Interpretatione (Oxford: Oxford University Press, 1981), Richard Walzer, *Al-Farabi on the Perfect State: Abū Naṣr al-Fārābī's Mabādi' Ārā' Ahl al-Madīnah al-Fāḍilah* (Oxford: Clarendon Press, 1985), Muhsin Mahdi, *Alfarabi's Philosophy of Plato and Aristotle* (2nd edition, Ithaca: Cornell University Press, 1969), and Charles E. Butterworth, *Alfarabi: The Political Writings. "Selected Aphorisms" and Other Texts* (Ithaca: Cornell University Press, 2001). For translations of works by Ibn Sīnā, see S. C. Inati, *Remarks and Admonitions, Part One: Logic* (Toronto: Pontifical Institute for Medieval Studies, 1984) and Nabil Shehaby, *The Propositional Logic of Avicenna* (Dordrecht: Reidel, 1973). Besides those mentioned above, two of Ibn Rushd's translated works are Charles E. Butterworth, *Averroes' Middle Commentary on Aristotle's Categories and De Interpretatione* (Princeton: Princeton University Press, 1983) and Charles E. Butterworth, *Averroes' Three Short Commentaries on Aristotle's "Topics," "Rhetoric," and "Poetics"* (Albany: State University of New York Press, 1977).

Secondary literature in English

The most comprehensive and accessible secondary source on Islamic philosophy remains M. Fakhry, *A History of Islamic Philosophy* (2nd edition, New York: Columbia University Press, 1983). A helpful two-volume anthology with thematic as well as single-author entries is S. H. Nasr and O. Leaman eds., *History of Islamic Philosophy*, vols. I and II (London: Routledge, 1996). Oliver Leaman has written two recent introductions to Islamic philosophy, *An Introduction to Classical Islamic Philosophy* (2nd edition, Cambridge: Cambridge University Press, 2002) and *A Brief Introduction to Islamic Philosophy* (Cambridge: Polity Press, 1985). A complete bibliography of books and articles is Hans Daiber, *Bibliography of Islamic Philosophy*, vols. I and II (Leiden: Brill, 1999).

Three of the authors represented in this volume have recently been the subjects of monographs in a single series: Ian Richard Netton, *Al-Fārābī and his School* (London: Routledge, 1992), Lenn E. Goodman, *Avicenna* (London: Routledge, 1992), and Dominique Urvoy, *Averroes* (London: Routledge, 1991). For other books on the philosophers represented in this volume, see for example Muhsin Mahdi, *Alfarabi and the Foundations of*

Islamic Political Philosophy (Chicago: University of Chicago Press, 2001), H. A. Davidson, *Alfarabi, Avicenna, and Averroes on Intellect* (Oxford: Oxford University Press, 1992), Miriam Galston, *The Political Philosophy of Alfarabi* (Princeton: Princeton University Press, 1990), Dimitri Gutas, *Avicenna and the Aristotelian Tradition* (Leiden: Brill, 1988), Barry Kogan, *Averroes and the Metaphysics of Creation* (Albany: State University of New York Press, 1985), and Majid Fakhry, *Averroes* (Oxford: OneWorld, 2001).

An account of the translation movement from Greek into Arabic that provided part of the impetus for the development of the Islamic philosophical tradition can be found in Dimitri Gutas, *Greek Thought, Arabic Culture* (London: Routledge, 1998). An analysis of the early theological debates that furnished a backdrop for the emergence of Islamic philosophy is H. Wolfson, *The Philosophy of the Kalam* (Cambridge, Mass.: Harvard University Press, 1976). Other wide-ranging works on selected aspects of Islamic philosophy include W. M. Watt, *Islamic Philosophy and Theology* (2nd edition, Cambridge: Cambridge University Press, 1985), Nicholas Rescher, *The Development of Arabic Logic* (Pittsburgh: University of Pittsburgh Press, 1964), F. E. Peters, *Aristotle and the Arabs* (New York: New York University Press, 1968), Seyyed Hossein Nasr, *An Introduction to Islamic Cosmological Doctrines* (Boulder, Col.: Shambhala, 1978), and Majid Fakhry, *Islamic Occasionalism* (London: Allen & Unwin, 1958). However, much of the relevant secondary literature is to be found in journal articles, in such journals as *Arabic Sciences and Philosophy*, *Journal of the American Oriental Society*, *International Journal of Middle East Studies*, *Journal of the History of Philosophy*, among others. Short introductions to some of the major figures and topics can also be found in various entries in Edward Craig, ed., *Routledge Encyclopedia of Philosophy* (London: Routledge, 1998).

For general works on Islamic civilization, see Marshall G. S. Hodgson, *The Venture of Islam* vols. I, II, and III (Chicago: University of Chicago Press, 1974), Albert Hourani, *A History of the Arab Peoples* (New York: Warner Books, 1992), Fazlur Rahman, *Islam* (2nd edition, Chicago: University of Chicago Press, 1979), and Tarif Khalidi, *Classical Arab Islam* (Princeton: Darwin Press, 1985), all of which contain vital background material on Islamic philosophy. For some insights into the way in which medieval Islamic philosophers influenced modern intellectual debates in the Arab world, see the first chapter of Albert Hourani, *Arabic Thought in the Liberal Age 1798–1939* (2nd edition, Cambridge: Cambridge University Press, 1983). Finally, an indispensable general reference work for all things Islamic is H. A. R. Gibb *et al.*, eds., *Encyclopedia of Islam* (Leiden: Brill, 2003), abbreviated as *EI* in the footnotes to this volume.

Note on the translation

All translations are made from the published Arabic editions listed below rather than from original manuscripts. Most of these editions are reliable and accurate; however, one or two (particularly Ghazālī and Ibn Ṭufayl) contain minor typographical errors, which I have taken the liberty to correct. (In the case of Ghazālī, I have checked the edition against another, which is based on it but which corrects the main typographical errors: al-Ghazālī, *al-Munqidh min al-Ḍalāl*, ed. Farīd Jabr, Bayrūt: al-Lajnah al-Lubnānīyyah li-Tarjamat al-Rawā'iᶜ, 1969.) Only two are critical editions in the true sense (Fārābī, Ibn Rushd), though all are based on more than one manuscript and indicate variant readings, at least on occasion. In the case of one of the texts (Ibn Sīnā), I have also relied on the variant manuscript readings that are noted in a previous translation by Fazlur Rahman, which itself relies on five manuscripts and two published editions. Generally, I have not marked the points at which I have followed variant manuscript readings or corrected minor typographical errors. I have indicated variant readings only on the rare occasions when they are my own suggestions and do not derive from any of the manuscripts cited in the published editions. Moreover, I have not always followed the punctuation marks and paragraph breaks indicated in these editions, on the assumption that this is generally the work of later editors and is subject to modification. With the exception of the Fārābī text, the paragraphs of which are sequentially numbered, the page numbers of the Arabic editions of these texts have been preserved in the translations; they are enclosed in square brackets in bold font. Moreover, all references to the translations in the notes and introduction make use of these bracketed page numbers. Additions to the text are indicated in square brackets, but only when they involve important substantive additions, not when they are clearly implied by the sense and are needed for ease of comprehension. Translations from the Qur'ān and Ḥadīth are my own, though I have consulted several existing translations of the Qur'ān. The system of transliteration adopted is based on that of the *International Journal of Middle Eastern Studies.*

Abū Naṣr al-Fārābī, *Kitāb al-Ḥurūf*, ed. Muḥsin Mahdī, Dār al-Mashriq: Bayrūt, 1970

Abū ᶜAlī Ibn Sīnā, *Kitāb al-Najāt fil-Ḥikmah al-Mantiqīyyah wal-Ṭabīᶜīyyah wal-Ilāhīyyah*, ed. Mājid Fakhrī, Dār al-Āfāq al-Jadīdah: Bayrūt, 1985

Abū Ḥāmid al-Ghazālī, *Al-Munqidh min al-Ḍalāl wal-Mūṣil ilā dhil-ᶜIzzah wal-Jalāl*, ed. Jamīl Ṣalībā and Kāmil ᶜAyyād, Dār al-Andalus: Bayrūt, 1988

Abū Bakr Ibn Ṭufayl, *Ḥayy bin Yaqẓān*, ed. Albert Naṣrī Nādir, Dār al-Mashriq: Bayrūt, 1993

Abū al-Walīd Ibn Rushd, *Tahāfut al-Tahāfut*, ed. Maurice Bouyges, Dār al-Mashriq: Bayrūt, 1992

Al-Fārābī, *The Book of Letters*

108. The capacities for dialectic, sophistry, and for the uncertain or dubious philosophy[1] must precede the capacity for the certain philosophy, which is demonstrative philosophy, since one becomes aware of demonstrations after these others [i.e. dialectic and sophistry]. Religion, if rendered human, comes after philosophy, in general, since it aims simply to instruct the multitude in theoretical and practical matters that have been inferred in philosophy, in such a way as to enable the multitude to understand them by persuasion or imaginative representation, or both.[2]

109. The arts of theology and jurisprudence come after philosophy in time and are dependent upon it. If a religion is dependent upon an uncertain or dubious ancient philosophy, the theology and jurisprudence that are dependent upon it will be in accordance with it. Or rather, they will be of a lower [standard], especially if the religion had corrupted the things it took from either or both of these philosophies, substituting images and similes for them. In this case, the art of theology takes these similes and images for certain truth and seeks to verify them with arguments. It sometimes happens that in legislating theoretical matters, a more recent [religious] lawgiver has imitated one who preceded him, who took these theoretical matters from an uncertain or dubious philosophy. If the more recent lawgiver takes the similes and images imaginatively represented by

[1] The uncertain philosophy (*al-falsafah al-maẓnūnah*) is what Fārābī later calls dialectical philosophy, while the dubious philosophy (*al-falsafah al-mumawwahah*) is what he later calls sophistical philosophy (see section 110).

[2] Fārābī later acknowledges that religion can precede philosophy if a nation imports religion from another nation (see section 148).

the first lawgiver, which were in turn taken from that philosophy, to be the truth rather than similes, he will seek to represent them imaginatively using similes. Then, the theologian in his religion will take these similes for the truth. Thus, what is studied by the art of theology in this religion is further from the truth than the first religion, since it seeks merely to verify each simile of a thing that it assumes to be the truth, or that is falsely represented as the truth.

110. It is clear that the arts of theology and jurisprudence come after religion, and that religion comes after philosophy. Also, the capacities for dialectic and sophistry precede philosophy, and dialectical philosophy and sophistical philosophy precede demonstrative philosophy. Philosophy as a whole precedes religion, just as the user of tools precedes the tools. Dialectic and sophistry precede philosophy, just as the nourishment of the tree precedes the fruit, or the flower of the tree precedes the fruit. Religion precedes theology and jurisprudence just as the master who uses the servant precedes the servant and the user of tools precedes the tools.

111. Since religion teaches theoretical things only by imaginative representation and persuasion, and since its followers are acquainted with these two methods of instruction to the exclusion of others, it is clear that the art of theology, which is dependent upon religion, is only aware of the persuasive things and verifies religion only by persuasive methods and arguments, in particular if it seeks to verify the similes of truth as though they were true. Persuasion proceeds either by premises that are effective and commonly held as preliminary opinions,[3] or by semblances[4] and similes; in general, by rhetorical methods, whether arguments or matters that follow from them. Thus, the theologian limits himself to the theoretical matters that he verifies using shared preliminary opinions. He shares this with the multitude. He may also revise the preliminary opinion, but he only revises the preliminary opinion using something else that is also preliminary opinion. The utmost justification he attains is in negating an opinion dialectically. In this, he differs from the multitude somewhat. In addition, he makes the purpose of his life what can be of benefit. He also differs from the multitude in that respect. Moreover,

[3] Arabic: *bādi' al-ra'y*, i.e. opinions commonly held rather than demonstratively proven.
[4] Literally, hidden things (*ḍamā'ir*).

since he is the servant of religion, and since religion has the position that it does with respect to philosophy, the position of theology with respect to philosophy is such that it is in some sense also a servant to it, through the mediation of religion. For it only advocates and seeks for the verification of what has been verified first in philosophy by demonstration, using what is commonly accepted as preliminary opinion among all, so that instruction is common to all. The theologian also differs from the multitude in this respect. That is why it is assumed that he is of the select, not the multitude. It should be known that he is also of the select, but only in comparison to the people of that religion, whereas the philosopher is select in comparison to all people and to the nations.

112. The jurist resembles the man of practical wisdom. They differ merely in the preliminary opinions they use in inferring the correct opinion in the deduction of particulars. Thus, the jurist uses as principles acquired premises transferred from the founder of the religion in the deduction of particulars, whereas the man of practical wisdom uses as principles premises commonly accepted among all and premises drawn from his experience. That is why the jurist is one of the select in relation to a certain specific religion and the man of practical wisdom is one of the select in relation to all.

113. Therefore, the select without qualification are those who are philosophers without qualification. All others who are considered of the select are only considered as such because they bear a resemblance to the philosophers. For example, anyone who is granted or undertakes political leadership, or is fit to assume it, or is being prepared to undertake it, renders himself one of the select, since he bears a certain resemblance to philosophy, one of whose parts is the leading practical art.[5] Similarly, the skilled person among the practitioners of each practical art renders himself among the select in view of the fact that he goes to great lengths to revise what is taken by the practitioners of that art in its apparent [meaning]. It is not only the skilled person among the practitioners of each art who describes himself as such, but the practitioners of a practical art may also describe themselves as select in comparison to those who are not practitioners of that art, since they speak of and study their

[5] That is, the art of political governance (*al-ṣināʿah al-raʾīsah al-ʿamalīyyah*).

art using the things pertaining to that art, while others speak of it and study it using preliminary opinion and what is common to all in every art. In addition, physicians describe themselves as being of the select either because they undertake to manage the ill and diseased, or because their art shares natural science with philosophy, or because they need to go to great lengths to revise the preliminary opinions in their art more so than other arts due to the danger and damage that people may be exposed to from the slightest error that they may commit, or else because the art of medicine uses many other practical arts such as the art of cookery and the art of amulets,[6] and in general all arts that benefit human health. All of the above resemble philosophy in some respect, but none of them should be described as select except metaphorically. For only the philosophers should be taken to be select in the first instance, in point of excellence, and without qualification, followed by the dialecticians and the sophists, then the [religious] lawgivers, and finally the theologians and jurists. The public and the multitude are those we have specified as such, whether or not they include someone who has undertaken political leadership or is fit to assume it.

114. It is clear that the public and the multitude precede the select in time. Likewise, the shared cognitions, which are the preliminary opinions of all, precede the practical arts and the cognitions that pertain to each art, which are collectively the common cognitions. The public and the multitude are the first to originate and come to be. They come to be in a specific abode and country and have by nature specific forms and characters in their bodies. Their bodies have definite qualities and compositions, and their souls are disposed towards and prepared for cognitions, conceptions, and images to specific degrees both quantitatively and qualitatively – making them easier for them. Moreover, their souls are affected by certain affections in specific ways and degrees both qualitatively and quantitatively, and these will also be easier for them. Their organs are disposed to move in specific directions and in certain ways, which will also be easier for them than others.

115. A human being who is left alone at the point at which he acquires his first nature will arise and move towards that which it is easiest to move

[6] Reading *al-ḥirz* for *al-ḥird* (a type of animal disease), which makes no sense in this context.

towards by nature and in the manner that is easiest. His soul undertakes to know, think, conceive, imagine, and intellect whatever he is most intensely disposed towards by nature, for that is what comes most easily to him. He moves his body and organs to whatever position and in whatever manner he is most intensely and perfectly disposed towards by nature, for this too is easiest for him. The first time he acts in this way, he acts through a capacity that is in him by nature and a natural attribute, not by prior habituation nor by art. If he repeats an action of one kind many times he will acquire a habitual attribute, either moral or artificial.

116. If a human being needs to acquaint another with what is in his mind or his intention, he will first use a sign to indicate what he wants from whomever he seeks to make understand, provided the other person is in a position to see his sign; later on he will use sound. The first sounds are calls, for that is how one who is being made to understand realizes that he is intended to the exclusion of others. This takes place when one restricts oneself to signaling to perceptibles in order to indicate what is in one's mind. After that, various sounds are used to indicate each and every thing that had previously been indicated by signaling to that thing and its perceptibles. Each specific thing signified is given some specific sound, which is not used for anything else, and so on.

117. It is clear that these sounds are produced simply by the breath striking a part or parts of the throat or parts of the inside of the nose or lips. These are the organs struck by the breath. The first to strike is the power that causes the breath to be emitted from the lung and the throat cavity, and gradually to the edge of the throat, which lies next to the mouth and nose and what is between the lips. The tongue then receives the breath and pushes it to each part of the inner parts of the mouth and to each part of the base of the teeth and the teeth, striking each of these parts. Each part against which the tongue pushes the breath produces a specific sound when struck by the breath. The tongue moves the sound through the air from one part to another of the base of the mouth, producing many specific successive sounds.

118. Clearly, the tongue moves first only to the part to which movement is easiest. Those who are in one abode and have similar characters in their organs will have tongues that naturally move to the exact same parts inside

the mouth, and these species of movements will be easier for them than to other parts. The people of another abode and country, who have organs with different characters and compositions, will be naturally suited to have their tongues move to some parts inside the mouth more easily than to others, which are different from the parts to which the tongues of the people of the first abode had moved. Hence, the sounds that they use as signs to indicate to each other what is in their minds will differ, which were originally signified by pointing to things and their perceptibles. This is the first reason for the variation in languages among the nations. These first sounds are the letters of the alphabet.

119. Since these letters, which are the first to be made into signs, are limited in number, they are insufficient to indicate everything that happens to be in their minds. Thus, they are required to combine them by putting some of them together in succession, letter by letter. This results in expressions made up of two or more letters, which are then also used as signs for other things. The first letters and expressions are signs for perceptibles that can be pointed to and to intelligibles derived from[7] perceptibles that can be pointed to. For each universal intelligible has particulars that differ from the particulars of another intelligible. Thus, many different sounds originate, some of which are signs for perceptibles, which are labels, and others of which indicate universal intelligibles that have perceptible particulars. Each sound is only understood to indicate a certain intelligible when one and the same sound is repeatedly applied to a particular that is being pointed to and to everything that resembles it with respect to that intelligible. Then a certain other sound will also be used for another particular falling under a different universal and to everything resembling it with respect to that intelligible.

120. That is how the letters of that nation and the expressions arising from those letters first originate. They originate first among some group or another. It so happens that one of them uses a sound or expression to indicate something when addressing someone else and the hearer memorizes it. Then the hearer uses the same expression when addressing the first inventor of that expression. In this case, the first hearer will have followed the example [of the inventor] and will have fallen in with it, in

[7] Alternatively, dependent upon (*tastanid ilā*).

such a way that they will have agreed upon that expression and acted in concert. They then use it to address others until it spreads through a certain group. Then whenever something originates in the mind of one of them, which he needs to convey to one of his neighbors, he invents a sound and indicates the thing to his friend. The friend hears it from him and then each of them memorizes it and they make it a sound indicating that thing. Sounds continue to originate one after another among some group or another of the people of that country, until someone begins to manage their affairs and to bring into being what they need in terms of sounds for the remaining things, for which indicative sounds have not yet happened to have been invented. Such a person is the author of the language of that nation. From that point on, he manages their affairs until expressions are laid down for all the things they need in the exigencies of life.

121. The first of these expressions are those of the common preliminary opinions that they have cognized and what is perceived of the common perceptibles pertaining to theoretical matters, such as the sky, planets, earth, and what is on it. These are followed by the things they inferred from these, then the actions resulting from the capacities that are theirs by nature, then the attributes resulting from habituation to these actions, both moral and artificial, and the actions resulting from them once they have become attributes by habituation. After that, they invent expressions for what they have cognized from experience step by step, then expressions for what is inferred from what is cognized from experiences common to all of them, then expressions for those things that pertain to each practical art, including tools and other things, and then expressions for what is derived from and is present in each art. In this way, expressions are provided for whatever the nation needs.

122. If the natures of the people of that nation are balanced and the nation tends towards intelligence[8] and knowledge, they naturally demand from those expressions – without intending to – that they imitate the meanings they are made to indicate. They make them so that they most closely resemble meanings and what exists. Their souls naturally[9] endeavor to

[8] In the sense of cleverness rather than intellect (*dhakā'*).

[9] Literally, their souls will rise with their natures (*nahaḍat anfusuhum bi-fiṭarihā*).

order these expressions according to the order of the meanings, as far as this is possible with expressions. Efforts are made so that their cases are inflected similarly to the cases of the meanings. If no one else happens to do so, those who manage their affairs in legislating their expressions will do so.

123. It will be clear from the outset that there are certain perceptibles apprehended by sense perception that contain similarities and differences. The similar perceptibles are in fact similar to one another with respect to a single intelligible meaning that they have in common, which is held in common by all things that they are similar to; and what is intelligible in one is intelligible in the other. This intelligible, which is predicable of many, is called the "universal" and the "general meaning." As for the perceptible itself, each meaning that is [applicable to] one and is not a common adjective for many things and is not similar to any other thing, is called a "particular" and "individual."[10] All universals are called "genera" and "species." Hence, some expressions are expressions indicating genera and species – in general, universals – and others indicate particulars and individuals. Meanings differ in generality and specificity. If expressions are to be made similar to meanings, the articulation of one meaning that generalizes over numerous things would be through one single expression that generalizes over those numerous things. Meanings differing in generality and particularity would have expressions differing in generality and particularity, and disparate meanings would have disparate expressions. Just as, among meanings, there are meanings that remain exactly the same while accidents succeed one another, so also among expressions there are fixed letters and letters that act as though they were changing accidents occurring in the same expression, with each changing letter corresponding to a changing accident. If a single meaning remains fixed, while accidents change in succession, it is articulated by means of a single expression that remains fixed while letters change, with each letter indicating each change. If meanings are similar in terms of a certain accident or disposition[11] which they hold in common, they are articulated using expressions of a similar shape and having similar endings and beginnings. Each of its endings or beginnings is a single letter and is made to indicate

[10] These two expressions have been translated in the singular rather than the plural (*ashkāṣ* and *aʿyān*) for the sake of agreement with the rest of the sentence.

[11] Alternatively, state or condition (*ḥāl*).

that accident. Thus, an order of expressions is needed that takes care to articulate meanings using expressions that resemble those meanings.[12]

124. Such great pains are taken to demand order and to make expressions resemble meanings that a single expression is [sometimes] made to indicate meanings with different essences when they are similar in some other respect and in their effects,[13] albeit very distant. This results in ambiguous expressions.

125. Then the resemblance of expressions to meanings becomes clear to us and we invent expressions to imitate the meanings that are not being articulated. It is required that expressions be invented that generalize over numerous things *qua* expressions, just as among meanings there are meanings that generalize over things with numerous meanings. This results in homonymous expressions. These homonymous expressions are such that they do not each indicate a common meaning. Similarly, expressions are invented that are different qua expressions, just as there are different meanings. This results in synonymous expressions.

126. The same thing occurs in the combination of expressions, for the act of combining expressions is similar to the combination of composite meanings, which are indicated by these composite expressions. Composite expressions are given things enabling them to connect with one another when these expressions indicate composite meanings that connect to one another. Care is taken that the arrangement of expressions is equivalent to the arrangement of meanings in the soul.

127. At some point expressions settle on the meanings that they have been made to signify, such that there are one-to-one, one-to-many, or many-to-one [relations] between them. After expressions have become affixed to the meanings whose essences they indicate, people then proceed to abrogate rules in expressing themselves and to use their expressions figuratively.

[12] This passage is somewhat obscure, but one possibility is that Fārābī is setting up an analogy between words and meanings, whereby words are composed of essential letters and accidental letters, just as meanings can include essences and accidents. A near English equivalent would be words such as "glow," "gleam," "glisten," "glimmer," and so on, all of which contain the "fixed letters" "gl," which may be said to correspond to the "essential" meaning (to shine or sparkle), as well as "changing letters," which may be said to correspond to various accidents.

[13] Literally, realization or manifestation (*adā'ihā*).

Meanings are articulated in words other than those first assigned to them. A word that was once fixed to a meaning and indicated its essence is now made to articulate something else, so long as there is some relation between them, however slight, whether due to a distant resemblance or some other thing, and without that word being fixed to that second meaning and indicating its essence. This marks the origin of metaphors, figurative language, and the substitution of an expression for one meaning for declaration of the expression of another meaning that follows it, when the second can be understood from the first. This is also the origin of the expressions for many meanings that are used to declare the expressions for other meanings, if they are such as to be associated with the first meanings when the second are understood whenever the first are. Moreover, articulation expands by the multiplication of expressions and their substitution for one another, as well as their arrangement, and enhancement. That is the point at which the rhetorical [capacity] first originates, followed gradually by the poetical.

128. Eventually, there are those who grow up among them habituated to utter their letters, the words made up of those letters, and the statements composed of those words, in such a way that they cannot overcome their habituation and such that nothing is uttered other than what they have been accustomed to use. This is made possible by their habituation to them in their souls and on their tongues, so that they cannot cognize anything else, to the point that their tongues are incapable of uttering any other expression, any formation of expressions other than the one that has established itself in them, and any order of statements other than the ones they have been habituated to. This is what has established itself on their tongues and in their souls by habit, based on what they have taken from their predecessors, who in turn took it from their predecessors, and so on up to those who first set it down for them by perfecting what all these predecessors had laid down for them. This is what is eloquent and correct in their expressions, and these expressions are the language of this nation, and whatever diverges from them is foreign[14] and incorrect.

129. Clearly, the intelligible meanings of this nation are entirely rhetorical, since they are all arrived at by preliminary opinion. Their premises,

[14] Alternatively, incorrect Arabic (*a'jam*).

expressions, and arguments are all rhetorical at first, for the rhetorical ones precede the rest. Over the course of time, events occur that put them in need of rhetorical speeches or portions of speeches. These develop gradually until rhetorical art becomes the first of the syllogistic arts to originate among them. With its development, or thereafter, begins the use of similes and imaginative representations of meanings, which elucidate meanings or replace them, resulting in poetical meanings. This [practice] continues to grow until poetry originates gradually, giving rise to another syllogistic art, poetic art, which stems from the natural inclination of human beings to seek order and organization in all things. The rhythms of expressions are orderly, well composed, and organized relative to the time uttered. In due course, the art of poetry also[15] arises. Hence, these two syllogistic arts, which are the popular syllogistic arts, originate among them.

130. Moreover, they engage in rhetoric and poetry in order to relate reports about past and current matters that they need to be informed of. Reciters of speeches and poems originate among them, as well as memorizers of the reports that are related therein. These people will be the eloquent and fluent people of the nation; they will also be the first sages and managers of that nation, and the authorities on the language of that nation. They are also the ones who combine expressions for the nation that had not been combined before that time, and they make them synonymous with some of the commonly known expressions. They apply themselves keenly to this and multiply such expressions, giving rise to specialized expressions, with which they acquaint one another and learn from one another, passing them down from one generation to the next. In addition, they also attend to the things that fall under genera or species for which words may not yet have been invented. If they become aware of [new] occurrences,[16] they will create words for them. The same goes for things that were not required with necessity beforehand, and for which words did not happen to have been invented. They compose words for these things as well. The other people of the nation will not be acquainted with these words, so all these will be considered specialized expressions. These experts are the people who scrutinize the expressions of this nation and repair

[15] That is, in addition to rhetoric proper, which is the first rhetorical art to arise.

[16] Alternatively, accidents (*aʿrāḍ*).

what is defective among them. They also look into whatever is difficult to utter among what was first set down, and simplify it; they render harmonious whatever is dissonant. In addition, there are some composite expressions that accidentally become difficult to utter, but which the originators of the language were not aware of, or which had not occurred accidentally in their time. In either case, when these experts become acquainted with or aware of their dissonance, they devise ways of making matters easier and rendering them harmonious. They also examine the possible types of combinations and orders of expressions. They scrutinize those expressions that are the most perfect indicators of the combination and order of meanings in the soul, and they investigate them and take particular notice of them. They set the rest aside, not using them unless necessary. The expressions of the nation then become more eloquent than before, and that is when their language[17] is perfected. These things are then taken by the younger generation from the previous one, in the manner in which they heard them from the older generation. They are nurtured on these expressions and are habituated to them with their educators, until they become thoroughly established in them and they are unable to utter anything but the most eloquent of their expressions. The younger generation memorizes the speeches made and poetry recited by the older generation, along with the histories and morals that they contain.

131. They continue to transmit what has been memorized until the material they seek to memorize becomes excessive and unmanageable. At this point, they need to think of ways of simplifying their task, and writing is discovered. At first, writing is disorderly, but it is gradually rectified with the passage of time, until it is made to imitate, resemble, and approximate expressions as nearly as possible. This process is comparable to the older one of making expressions resemble meanings as nearly possible.[18] They use writing to set down in books what is difficult to memorize, what they cannot ensure not to forget over the course of time, what they seek to safeguard for future generations, and what they seek to teach and convey to those distant from them in other countries and abodes.

[17] Literally, language and tongue (*lughatuhum wa lisānuhum*).

[18] That is, written expressions are made to resemble spoken expressions, as spoken expressions are made to resemble meanings.

132. Subsequently, it can be seen that the art of linguistics begins to originate gradually, as people[19] become eager to memorize individual indicative expressions, having memorized poems, speeches, and composite statements. Thus, they endeavor to separate these expressions after having combined them, or want to collect them by listening to members of their community. They listen to those who have a reputation for using the most eloquent expressions in their rhetorical discourse and those who have occupied themselves with memorizing speeches, poems, and histories, or those who have heard them from such people. They hear these expressions from each of these people over a long period of time, and transcribe what they hear and commit it to memory.

133. For this purpose, one needs to know from whom the language of that nation ought to be acquired. We say that it ought to be acquired from those whose habits, in the course of time, have become so firmly established in their tongues and their souls that they are fortified against imagining or uttering any other letters than their own. They are also unable to acquire or utter expressions other than those composed of their own letters. Such a person has not heard anything but his own tongue and language; or else he has, but his mind avoids imagining it and his tongue avoids uttering it. As for those people whose tongues acquiesce in uttering any letter they wish of those external to their own letters, any expression composed of letters other than their own, and any statement composed of expressions other than their own, one cannot ensure that such a person's tongue does not utter what is extrinsic to their originally established habits. He becomes habituated to what his tongue utters and his articulation diverges from that of the nation, resulting in error, solecism, and ineloquence. If, in addition to this, such a person has mingled with people of other nations and has heard their languages or has uttered them, he will be yet more prone and apt to commit errors. One cannot ensure that whatever is present in his habit does not pertain to a nation other than the one to which he belongs. Moreover, there are those who are fortified against uttering and acquiring the letters and expressions of other nations by being protected from what they had not been originally habituated to, in terms of violating the shapes and inflections of their expressions. But if such people often mingle with other nations and hear their letters and

[19] In singular in original, i.e. as a person becomes eager, etc. (*yatashawwaq insān*).

expressions, one cannot ensure that they will not change their original habits and that what they hear from these others will not become established in them. In such cases, what one hears from these people will also be untrustworthy.

134. In every nation, those who inhabit the wilderness in houses of hair or wool, tents, and encampments[20] are more averse and less prone to abandon what has become established in them by habit. They are more apt to fortify their souls against imagining the letters and expressions of other nations, and to fortify their tongues against uttering them. People of other nations are more likely not to mingle with them due to their wildness and roughness. The inhabitants of towns, villages, and mud houses are more impressionable and their souls are more compliant to understanding, conceiving, and imagining what they have not been habituated to, and their tongues to utter what they have not been habituated to. Therefore, whenever nations contain both groups, it is better to take the language[21] of the nation from the inhabitants of the wilderness, and preferably those among them who inhabit the interior parts of their country. For those who inhabit the peripheries are more likely to mingle with neighboring nations, so that their language mixes with those others, and they are more likely to imagine the linguistic barbarisms of their neighbors. If they deal with them, the others will need to speak in a language foreign to their own, and their tongues will not acquiesce to pronounce many of their letters, so that they will resort to articulating them insofar as they are able and will omit what they find difficult. Their expressions will be harsh and unattractive, and will contain an accent and barbarisms acquired from the languages of others. Then, if the people of this nation are given to hearing many errors from their neighbors from other nations, and if they become habituated to understand them as being correct, one cannot ensure that their habit will not change. That is why the language should not be acquired from them. If there are no inhabitants of the wilderness in the nation, then the language is taken from those whose abodes are in the innermost regions.

135. You can verify this by contemplating the case of the Arabs in this regard. They include inhabitants of the wilderness and inhabitants of

[20] Reading *akhbiyah* for *aḥsiyah* (small amounts of water), which makes no sense in this context.
[21] In plural in original, indicating perhaps the totality of usage of the entire community.

cities. They were most preoccupied with this matter [i.e. linguistics and the collection of the pure form of the language] between the years 90 and 200 AH [708–816 AD]. Those who undertook that task in their cities were the inhabitants of al-Kūfah and al-Baṣrah in the land of Iraq. They learned their language and the eloquent part of it from the inhabitants of the wilderness rather than the town dwellers, and especially from the people of the interior regions and from the wildest and roughest of them, and the least submissive and compliant, namely [the tribes of] Qays, Tamīm, Asad, and Ṭayy, followed by Hudhayl. These include most of those from whom the language of the Arabs was taken.[22] Nothing was taken from the rest because they were on the peripheries of their country and mingled with other nations. They were characterized by the speed with which their tongues complied with the expressions of surrounding nations, including Ethiopians, Indians, Persians, Assyrians, and the peoples of Syria and Egypt.

136. Their single expressions, both specialized and common, are acquired first, until they are completed; then they are memorized or written down. Then come all their composite expressions, including poems and speeches. After that, one who studies them begins to contemplate the resemblances among both the single and composite expressions. The types of resemblances are recorded, as well as the modes of resemblance[23] in each type, and what falls under each type. At that point, the soul originates universals for them and universal rules. When universals and rules for expressions originate, he [i.e. the one who studies them] will need expressions to articulate these universals and rules, so that they can be learned and taught. At that point, he does one of two things. He either invents or composes expressions from their letters that have never before been uttered, or else he transfers expressions from those that they had used to indicate other meanings, either haphazardly and not for any reason, or for some particular reason. Each of these [practices] is possible and widespread. But it is better to phrase rules using words that have meanings that most closely resemble those rules. One should look into which of the original meanings most closely resembles each rule pertaining to expressions, so that the universal and the rule can be named using the word for that meaning. Following this pattern, all the universals and rules

[22] Literally, transferred (*nuqila*).

[23] Literally, that in which it resembles (*bi-mādhā tatashābah*).

can be named using what resembles them among the original meanings for which they had words.

137. At this point, they transform their tongue and language in the form of an art. This makes it possible for it to be taught and learned in speech, and for causes to be adduced for all that they say. In addition, if there are universals and rules pertaining to the scripts that they use to write their expressions, they are all recorded so that they may seek to discourse about them, teach them, and learn them in speech. Thus, the expressions used at that point to articulate those rules become expressions in the second imposition,[24] while the original expressions are expressions in the first imposition. The expressions in the second imposition are transferred from the meanings that they used to indicate.

138. Five arts thus arise among them: the art of rhetoric, the art of poetry, the capacity to memorize and recite their reports and poetry, the art of linguistics, and the art of writing. Rhetoric is the ability to persuade the multitude about the pursuits of the multitude, to the extent that they can cognize them, using premises that are effective among the multitude according to preliminary opinion, and using expressions of the first imposition in the way in which the multitude is habituated to using them. The art of poetry imaginatively represents these same things in speech. The art of linguistics consists of the expressions that indicate those very same meanings in the first imposition.

139. Specialists in these arts are considered of the multitude, since the concepts[25] in their arts are in no instance theoretical matters, and they do not involve the art that is the leader of all arts without qualification [viz. philosophy]. It may be possible for them to have leaders and leading arts, which are the arts that enable them to manage their affairs, including arts that preserve the arts that they pursue, so that each of them can achieve the purpose for which he pursues it and is not hindered in so doing. This also

[24] The distinction between expressions in the "first imposition" (*al-waḍ*ᶜ *al-awwal*) and "second imposition" (*al-waḍ*ᶜ *al-thānī*) draws on an Aristotelian tradition that distinguishes between the object language and the grammatical metalanguage, respectively. Expressions in the first imposition are those like "table," "justice," etc., whereas expressions in the second imposition are those like "noun," "verb," and so on.

[25] The term *ma*ᶜ*nā* (plural *ma*ᶜ*ānī*), which has been translated as "meaning" up to this point, is translated here and in the rest of the text as "concept" for greater fluency.

includes arts that enable their leader to use them in their respective arts to achieve his purpose from them and what he desires for his soul by way of money or power. The leader's position with respect to them is that of the leader of the farmers. For the leader of the farmers has the ability that enables him to use the farmers and the ability to advise them concerning farming, so that they may achieve their purposes in their respective types of farming, or so that he can achieve his purposes and aims by means of their types of farming. For this reason, he is also considered one of them. The leader of the multitude and the manager of their affairs follows the same pattern with regard to the use of the multitude in the practical arts, the preservation of their arts, and in general, his use of them in these arts, whether for their souls, for his soul, for them, or for him. He is also one of them, since his utmost goal is also their goal in his art, which is also their art in genus and species, except that it is the most sublime art of that genus and species. Thus, the leaders of the multitude, who preserve for them those things that make them the multitude and use them with respect to the things that make them the multitude, are also of the multitude. That is because the goal of the leader in preserving it for them and using them in it is also their goal, that it be achieved for himself alone and that it be achieved for them, so he is one of them. Therefore, the leaders of the multitude who are as we have described them are also of the multitude. This is one more art belonging to the multitude. It is also a popular art, though its practitioners and specialists render themselves of the select. Thus, the kings of the multitude are also of the multitude.

140. If the practical arts and all other popular arts that we mentioned have been exhaustively investigated, souls yearn to be cognizant of the causes of perceptible things in the earth, upon it, surrounding it, and everything else that is perceivable and apparent in the sky. They also yearn to be cognizant of many of the things inferred in the practical arts, such as shapes, numbers, pictures in mirrors, colors, and so on. Someone arises to search for the causes of these things. He first uses rhetorical methods in examining them, in verifying the opinions for himself and in teaching others, and in verifying them upon reviewing them, because these are the syllogistic methods that they are aware of first. Thus originates the examination of mathematical matters and of the natural world.[26]

[26] Literally, nature (*al-ṭabīʿah*).

141. Those studying these matters will continue to use rhetorical methods [at first], so their opinions will diverge and factions will disagree. Their rhetorical discourse to one another increases, containing opinions that each of them verifies for himself and revisions by each of the others. Each of them then needs, when he is challenged by what he perceives to be an opposing opinion, to justify the method he uses and to endeavor to make it such that it cannot be opposed or that it can only be opposed with difficulty. They continue to strive and to try the most justified methods until, after some time, they discover the dialectical methods. They distinguish the dialectical methods from the sophistical methods, which were previously used by them indiscriminately. For rhetorical methods hold them in common and mix them up. At this point, the rhetorical methods are rejected and the dialectical methods are used instead. Since sophistical methods resemble dialectical methods, many people use sophistical methods in examining opinions and in verifying them. Later, people settle on using dialectical methods in investigating, examining, and verifying theoretical matters; sophistical methods are set aside and are only used in times of crisis.

142. These dialectical methods will continue to be used until dialectical discourse is perfected, and it becomes clear by dialectical methods that they are not themselves sufficient to produce certainty. The examination of mathematical methods and the science[27] of certainty commences at this point. In the course of this process, people will have discovered the mathematical methods, which will have almost been perfected or have neared perfection. The difference between the methods of dialectic and the methods of certainty[28] comes into sight, and they are distinguished somewhat. Meanwhile, people are inclined towards the study of the science of political affairs, which are those matters based on the principle of volition and choice. They examine them using dialectical methods mixed with the methods of certainty, after dialectical methods have been justified to the greatest extent possible and have almost become scientific. Things proceed in this manner until philosophy attains the condition it was in at the time of Plato.

[27] Alternatively, knowledge (*ʿilm*). [28] That is, demonstrative methods.

143. They continue to be engaged in these matters until things become settled where they were during Aristotle's time. Theoretical science[29] is completed, the mathematical methods are all distinguished, theoretical philosophy and universal practical[30] philosophy are perfected, and they cease to contain any object of examination. It becomes an art that is only[31] learned and taught, and it is taught both to a select audience and commonly to all. Select instruction proceeds by demonstrative methods only, whereas common instruction, which is public, proceeds by dialectical, rhetorical, or poetical methods. However, the rhetorical and poetical methods are more appropriate for use in teaching the multitude those things about which opinion has settled, while demonstration is the correct method concerning theoretical and practical matters.

144. After all this, there will be a need for lawgiving[32] to teach the multitude those theoretical matters that have been inferred, concluded, and verified using demonstration, and those practical matters that have been inferred using the capacity for practical wisdom. The art of lawgiving consists of the ability to represent imaginatively[33] what is difficult for the multitude to conceive of the theoretical intelligibles. It also consists in the ability to infer each of the beneficial political actions in attaining happiness, and the ability to persuade with respect to all the theoretical and practical matters that the multitude should be taught using all persuasive methods. If laws of each of these two types are established and they are augmented with the methods by which the multitude is persuaded, taught, and educated, religion will have come into being. Through religion, the multitude are taught, educated, and given all that is needed to attain happinesss.

145. A group may then originate who contemplate what religion encompasses. If this group includes someone who considers what the founder of

29 Alternatively, scientific speculation (*al-naẓar al-ʿilmī*).

30 Reading *al-ʿamalīyyah* for *al-ʿāmmīyyah* (common or general). This fits better with what Fārābī says later about the difference between jurisprudence (*fiqh*) and theology (*kalām*): jurisprudence deals with particular practical matters, while theology deals with theoretical matters as well as universal practical matters (see section 145).

31 It is not clear what the force of "only" (*faqaṭ*) is here; the contrast is perhaps with arts that continue to be objects of investigation or examination, not just instruction.

32 That is, religious lawgiving (*waḍʿ al-nawāmīs*).

33 Literally, the ability of the excellence of representing imaginatively (*bil-iqtidār ʿalā jūdat al-takhyīl*).

the religion has openly declared concerning particular practical matters, takes this as given, and seeks to infer from this what the founder did not openly declare – always following his example in adopting his declared purpose in inferring these things – the art of jurisprudence will originate. Meanwhile, if a group aims to infer what the founder of the religion has not openly declared concerning theoretical matters and universal practical matters, or something other than what he has openly declared – following his example concerning what he has openly declared – another art will originate, namely the art of theology. If it so happens that there is a group that wishes to invalidate what is in this religion, the practitioners of theology will need a capacity to advocate that religion, to refute those who oppose it, and to refute the errors with which it is sought to invalidate what is openly declared in the religion. At this point, the art of theology will be perfected. The arts of both these capacities will therefore arise. It is clear that this can only occur through the common methods, namely the rhetorical methods.[34]

146. In this order, the syllogistic arts originate in nations, when these arts originate from their own native intelligence.[35]

147. If a religion is dependent upon a philosophy that has been perfected after all the syllogistic arts have been distinguished from one another, in the manner and order that we have claimed, the religion will be a valid one with the greatest excellence. However, if the philosophy has not yet become demonstrative, certain, and endowed with the greatest excellence, and if its opinions continue to be verified using rhetorical, dialectical, or sophistical methods, it is not impossible that all or most of it might contain false opinions unawares. This would be an uncertain or dubious philosophy. If a religion that depends upon this philosophy is founded some time thereafter, it will contain many false opinions. Then, if many of these false opinions are taken and their similes are put in their place – as religion does with those things that are difficult or difficult to conceive for the multitude – these opinions will be yet further from the truth. It will

[34] It is not clear why Fārābī equates the common methods with the rhetorical and omits the dialectical, which is the method of both theology and jurisprudence. Even though dialectic as a whole may arise through rhetoric, this still does not explain this apparent identification of the common with the rhetorical.

[35] That is, when they are not imported from other nations.

be a corrupt religion, and they will be unaware of its corruption. It will be even more corrupt if a lawgiver arrives afterwards and does not take his religion's opinions from the philosophy that happens to exist in his times, but takes them instead from the opinions contained in the first religion, which he takes to be true. He will then acquire it, adopt its similes, and teach them to the multitude. If yet another lawgiver arrives after him and is dependent upon the second lawgiver, he will be yet more corrupt. A valid religion only occurs in a nation in the first way mentioned; a corrupt religion occurs among them in the second way. In either case, religion originates only after philosophy, either certain philosophy, which is true philosophy, or uncertain philosophy, which is assumed to be philosophy though it is not in reality. This is the case when it originates among them from their own genius, natures, and souls.

148. Alternatively, a religion may be transferred from one nation that possessed this religion to another nation that does not possess a religion; or a religion belonging to a nation may be rectified by addition, subtraction, or some other change, and given to another nation, which is then educated, taught, and managed according to it. This would make it possible for religion to originate in this nation before philosophy, and before even dialectic and sophistry. A philosophy that does not originate in a nation as a result of their own genius, but is rather transferred to them from another group that had it before them, would make it possible for philosophy to originate among them after the religion that is transferred to them.

149. A religion may depend upon a perfect philosophy, [although] its theoretical matters may not be contained in it as they are in philosophy, because rather than using the expressions that express them, it may substitute their similes, either in whole or for the most part. This religion may be transferred to another nation without their being cognizant that it is dependent upon a philosophy, or that it contains similes of theoretical matters verified[36] by certain demonstration. They may be silent on this count and the second nation may assume that the similes encompassed by that religion are truths and that they are the theoretical matters themselves. If, after that, the philosophy on which the religion depends for its excellence is itself transferred to them, one cannot ensure that that religion

[36] Reading *ṣuḥḥiḥat* for *ṣaḥḥat* (to be or become true).

will not be in conflict with the philosophy and that its adherents will not oppose it and cast it aside. The practitioners of that philosophy will also oppose that religion if they do not know that it consists of the similes of what is contained in philosophy. Once they know that they are similes of its contents, they themselves will not oppose it, but the adherents of the religion will oppose the practitioners of that philosophy. Philosophy and its practitioners will not have authority over that religion or its adherents, but will rather be cast aside and its practitioners marginalized, and the religion will not gain much support from philosophy. One cannot ensure that philosophy and its practitioners will not be greatly harmed by that religion and its adherents. That is why the practitioners of philosophy, in order to protect themselves, may have to oppose the adherents of the religion at that point. They take care not to oppose the religion itself, but rather only to oppose their assumption that religion is in conflict with philosophy, and they make efforts to rid them of this assumption by seeking to make them understand that what their religion contains are similes.

150. If a religion depends upon a corrupt philosophy, and if valid demonstrative philosophy is then transferred to a nation, this philosophy will be opposed to that religion in every respect, and religion will be totally opposed to philosophy. Each of them will wish to eliminate the other. Whichever triumphs and becomes established in the souls will eliminate the other; or rather whichever conquers that nation will eliminate the other from it.

151. If dialectic or sophistry are transferred to a nation that has a settled religion, which has become established in them, each of them will be harmful to that religion and will disparage it in the souls of its believers. For the capacity of each acts to confirm and invalidate one and the same thing. That is why the use of dialectical and sophistical methods concerning the opinions that have become established in the soul regarding religion have a tendency to dislodge it and to implant doubts concerning it, according it the position of something that has not been verified and that awaits verification. Otherwise, it will have the effect of instilling perplexity concerning it, giving rise to the assumption that neither it nor its contrary are valid. That is why lawgivers have forbidden dialectic and sophistry, imposing the strictest ban upon them. The same goes for kings who have been appointed to preserve religion, whatever religion it may

be, who exert themselves to ban adherents from pursuing either dialectic or sophistry and issue dire warnings concerning both.

152. As for philosophy, some groups have sympathized with it, while others have defamed it, and yet others have ignored it. Some groups have forbidden it, for one of two reasons. First, because their nation is not capable of being taught explicit truth and theoretical matters as such. Due to the natures of its people, the purpose of the nation, or the purpose desired from it, the nation cannot be acquainted with the truth itself, but can be educated only by means of similes of the truth. Or else, the nation may be such as to be educated by actions, deeds, and practical matters only, and not by theoretical matters, or only by a small portion of them. Second, they have forbidden it because the religion that the lawgiver has given them was a corrupt and ignorant[37] one, from which he did not seek happiness for them but for himself, wanting to use it exclusively for his own happiness. Thus, the lawgiver feared that if he allowed them to look freely into philosophy, the nation would discover the corruption of the religion and the corruption of what he sought to establish in their souls.

153. It is apparent that in every religion opposed to philosophy, the art of theology in it will also be opposed to philosophy, and its practitioners will be opposed to the practitioners of philosophy, to the same extent that this religion itself is opposed to philosophy.

154. If a religion originates in a nation that had no religion before, and if that religion had not been the religion of another nation, it is clear that the laws[38] of that religion would not have been known in that nation, and therefore they will not have words for them. Thus, if the founder of that religion needs to set down words for these laws, then he must either [1] invent words that were not known among them before him, or else he must [2] transfer words for the things that have words among them that are most similar to the laws that he has laid down. If they had another religion before that, then he might use the words of the laws of that first religion and transfer them to what is similar to them in the laws of his religion. If his religion or part of it is transferred from another nation, then he might

37 The term *jāhilīyyah* is commonly used to denote the pre-Islamic era.

38 The term *sharā'i'* is usually associated with the laws of Islam in particular, rather than the term *nawāmīs*, which is used elsewhere in the text to denote religious law.

use the words of what was transferred of their laws to indicate them, after changing these expressions in such a way that their letters and structure become the letters and structure of his nation, in order to facilitate their utterance among them. If dialectic and sophistry originate among them, and if the people of the nation need to enunciate concepts that they have discovered, for which they hitherto had no words, since they were not known among them before, then they either invent expressions out of their own letters, or else they transfer the words for the things that are most similar to them. Similarly, if philosophy originates, then the people of the nation necessarily need to give utterance to concepts that were not known among them before, and they must take one of the two courses mentioned.

155. If philosophy has been transferred to them from another nation, then the people must examine the expressions that were used by that first nation to articulate the concepts of philosophy, and to know which of the concepts shared by both nations are transferred [i.e. from popular, nonphilosophical concepts] in the first nation. If they are acquainted with them, then they must take the expressions of their nation that are used to express the same popular concepts, and use those words for the philosophical concepts. They may find that there are philosophical concepts for which the first nation transferred words for popular concepts unknown to the second nation, and for which they have no words. If those same concepts resemble other popular concepts known to the second nation and for which they do have expressions, then it is better to cast aside the words of the first nation and to look for those that are most similar among their own popular concepts. They should take those expressions and use them to designate the philosophical concepts. If concepts are found for which the first nation used words for the most similar popular things in accordance with their imagination of things, and if those philosophical concepts are most similar among the second nation to different popular concepts in accordance with *their* imagination of things, then it is better not to use the same words in the second nation that were used in the first nation, and it is better not to use them in the speech of the second nation. If there are concepts for which the second nation does not even have similar popular concepts in the first place – though this is almost never the case – then they must do one of three things: [1] invent words from their own letters, or [2] homonymously express other concepts with them in some

way or another, or [3] they must use the expressions of the first nation after they are altered in such a way as to enable the second nation to utter them with ease. This concept will be very strange to the second nation, for they would not have had it before, or anything similar to it. It may so happen that a philosophical concept resembles two popular concepts, and that each of them has a word in the two nations. If it resembles one of them more than the other, and if it is designated by the word for that which most resembles it in the first nation, then it must be designated by the word for that which most resembles it in the second nation.

156. The philosophy that now exists among the Arabs has been transferred to them from the Greeks. Those who transferred it have endeavored, in designating the concepts present in it, to follow the courses that we have mentioned. We find some who exaggerate and go too far to express them all in Arabic. This leads them into homonymy. For example, they have given the following two concepts one word in Arabic: they have named *isṭaqis* [Greek *stoikheion*] *al-ʿunṣur*, and they have also named *hayūlā* [Greek *hulē*] *al-ʿunṣur*. *Isṭaqis* is not to be named *al-māddah* or *hayūlā*. Sometimes they use *hayūlā*, and sometimes they use *al-ʿunṣur* in place of *hayūlā*.[39] However, the words they have left in Greek are few. Those philosophical concepts that were designated in the first way are those of which it can be said that they are acquired, in the sense that they are concepts indicated by the expressions of both nations. If the popular concepts from which they were transferred to philosophical concepts have words shared by all nations, these philosophical concepts are acquired, in the sense that they are indicated by expressions of all nations. Those that were designated in the other ways are acquired, in the sense that they are indicated by expressions of the second nation only.

157. Philosophical concepts ought to be acquired that are either not originally indicated by an expression but simply in terms of being intelligible, or if they are taken as being indicated by expressions they must be taken as indicated by the expressions of any nation. These expressions should

[39] Fārābī implies that it is sometimes preferable to transliterate Greek philosophical terms rather than translate them, since two different Greek terms, *stoikheion* (element) and *hulē* (prime matter) have been translated by a single Arabic term, *ʿunṣur*, causing some confusion. Instead, he seems to advocate transliterating Greek *hulē* as Arabic *hayūlā* and Greek *stoikheion* as Arabic *isṭaqis*, though he also mentions the option of translating the former as *māddah* (matter) and the latter as *ʿunṣur* (element).

be retained when they are being uttered in times of instruction because of their resemblance to the popular concepts from which the expressions have been transferred. They may be confused with one another and it may give rise to the illusion that they are numerically identical with the popular concepts and that they are in agreement in their expressions. That is why one group is of the opinion that they should not be expressed using expressions for their similes, but that it is better to invent words for them, which had not been used by them to indicate anything before that, composed from their letters according to their habits in shaping their expressions. But these respects of similarity have a certain utility when teaching a novice in an art in making him understand these concepts quickly, since they are articulated using expressions that express similar concepts, with which he was acquainted before being initiated into the art. But one must guard against being led into equivocation, in the same way that one guards against homonymous words.[40]

[40] The last paragraph has been omitted, since it is difficult to understand without the benefit of the final section of the text.

Ibn Sīnā, *On the Soul*

[202] Of the rational soul

The faculties of the human rational soul can also[1] be divided into a practical faculty and a theoretical[2] faculty. Each of these faculties is called by the homonymous term "intellect." The practical faculty is a principle that moves the human body to the particular actions that are specific to it, by deliberation, in accordance with common opinions that are specific to it. It is related[3] to the animal faculty of appetite, to the animal faculty[4] of imagination and estimation, and to itself. It is related to the animal faculty of appetite in that dispositions originate there that are specific to humans, which dispose it to quick actions and affections,[5] such as timidity, shame, laughter, crying, and similar things. It is related to the animal faculty of imagination and estimation insofar as it uses it to discover measures pertaining to the realm of generation and corruption, and to discover the human arts. It is related to itself in that, along with the theoretical intellect, it generates the **[203]** commonly held opinions, for example that lying is repugnant, injustice is repugnant, and similar premises, which are

[1] That is, analogously to the animal soul, which also has two parts (the locomotive and cognitive faculties).

[2] Literally, knowing (*ʿālimah*).

[3] The phrase *bil-qiyās* (by a relation) seems redundant here, so it has not been translated.

[4] Ibn Sīnā here uses the singular, even though he generally regards the faculties of imagination (*al-mutakhayyilah*) and estimation (*al-mutawahhimah*) as two different faculties. They are two of the five faculties associated with the five internal senses, which also include: common sense (*al-ḥiss al-mushtarak*) or phantasy (*fanṭāsīyā*), representation (*al-khayālīyyah*), and recollection (*al-ḥāfiẓah al-dhākirah*). For details, see introduction above, p. xxi.

[5] The verb "affect" and noun "affection" are used to translate the terms *infaʿala* and *infiʿāl*, respectively, but the adjective "passive" is used to translate the corresponding adjective *munfaʿil*.

clearly distinguished from the pure intellectual [premises] in the books of logic.

This faculty [i.e. the practical faculty] should be the one to dominate all the other bodily faculties, in accordance with what is necessitated by the judgments of the other faculty mentioned [i.e. the theoretical faculty], so that the practical faculty is not affected by the bodily faculties at all. Rather the bodily faculties must be affected by the practical faculty and must be subjugated to it, to prevent the origination in it of submissive dispositions from the body, which are acquired from physical things and are termed vicious character traits. Instead, the practical faculty must not be passive at all and must not be led but must dominate, thereby possessing virtuous character traits. It is possible that character traits may also be ascribed to the bodily faculties. But if the bodily faculties are dominant then they will have an active form and the practical faculty will have a passive form, and the same thing will give rise to a character trait in the practical faculty and in the bodily faculties. However, if the bodily faculties are subordinated, then they will have a passive form, while the practical faculty will have an intrinsic active form [thereby also giving rise to two character traits], or else there will be one character trait with two aspects.[6]

Upon examination, moral characteristics pertain to the practical faculty, for the human soul, as will become apparent in due course, is a single substance, which is related[7] to two realms,[8] one of which lies below it and the other lies above it. In accordance with each realm, it has a faculty by means of which the relation with that realm is organized. The practical faculty is the faculty that is related to the realm that lies below it, namely to the body and its governance. As for the theoretical faculty, it is the faculty that is related to the realm that lies above it, being affected by it, benefiting from it, and receiving from it. It is as though each one of our souls has two aspects: one aspect – which must not be receptive at all to effects of a bodily nature – must be directed towards the body and another aspect must be directed towards the higher principles. This

[6] The passage beginning "It is possible that . . ." is hard to interpret, but Ibn Sīnā seems to be saying that there can be a nonrational moral characteristic ascribed to bodily faculties; this can either be regarded as a separate trait or a different aspect of the same trait as the corresponding trait ascribed to the practical intellect. As Fazlur Rahman points out, the origin of the doctrine is Aristotelian, whereby there are instinctive virtues attributable to the bodily faculties, which can either be regarded as two different species of virtue from the same genus or preparatory for moral virtue, as matter is to form. See Fazlur Rahman, *Avicenna's Psychology* (Oxford: Oxford University Press, 1952), pp. 86–7.

[7] Omitting *wa qiyās* (and relation), which is redundant here.

[8] Literally, two sides (*janbatayn*).

latter aspect must always be receptive to what lies there and be affected by it.

Of the theoretical faculty and its ranks

The theoretical faculty is a faculty that has a tendency to be imprinted with the universal forms that are abstracted from matter. If they are abstract in themselves then it is imprinted with them as is, and if not, it renders them abstract by abstracting them from matter, leaving them without any attachment to matter at all, as will be shown **[204]** later. This theoretical faculty will have [different] relations to these forms, since anything that has a tendency to be receptive to something else may either be potentially or actually receptive to it.

"Potential" is used in three senses, according to priority and posteriority. [1] "Potential" is applied to absolute disposition, from which nothing has emerged into actuality, and nothing has occurred through which it will emerge, such as an infant's potential to write. [2] Such a disposition is also termed "potential" if what has occurred to a thing is simply what will enable it to arrive at acquiring the action without mediation, for example the potential of the boy to write, when he has been brought up to know the pen, writing implements, and the elements of letters. [3] Such a disposition is also termed "potential" if the instrument has been perfected and has become perfectly disposed, such that the agent can act whenever he wants, without the need for acquisition. Rather it is sufficient merely for the agent to intend the action, for example the potential of a writer who has perfected the art when he is not [actually] writing. The first potential is called "absolute potential" and "material potential," the second potential is called "possible potential," and the third potential is called "habit." Sometimes the second is called "habit" and the third is called "perfect potential."

Thus, the theoretical faculty is sometimes related as absolute potential to the abstract forms[9] mentioned above; this potential belongs to the soul that has not yet received any of the perfection that is its due, at which point it is called "material intellect." The potential that is called the "material intellect" is present in every individual of the species. It is called "material" simply by comparison with prime matter,

[9] Reading *ṣūwar* (plural) for *ṣūrah* (singular), which makes more sense here.

which does not have any of the forms in itself, but is the object of all forms.

At other times, it is related in some way to the possible potential, namely when, of its perfections, the first intelligibles have occurred in the material potential, through which and by means of which one attains the second intelligibles. By the first intelligibles, I mean the premises in which belief occurs not by acquisition, and which the believer feels that he could not possibly have gone without believing at any time. These would include, for example, our belief that the whole is greater than the part, or that things equal to the same thing are equal to one another. As soon as this degree of intellect occurs in someone, it is called "habitual intellect." It is possible to call this "actual intellect" in relation to the first, because the first cannot reason[10] about anything in actuality, whereas the second can reason, when it actually begins to use syllogisms.

[205] At other times, it is related in some way to the perfect potential when the acquired intelligible forms have also occurred in it after the primary intelligibles, though it is not acquainted with them and does not consult them in actuality. Rather, it is as though they are stored in it, and it can be actually acquainted with them when it so wishes and can reason about them, reasoning that it can reason about them. At that point, it will be termed an "actual intellect," for it has reasoned and can reason when it so wishes without the effort of acquisition, even though it can be termed a potential intellect in comparison to what comes afterwards.

At yet other times, it is related to absolute actuality, when the intelligible form is present in it, it is acquainted with it and reasons about it in actuality, and reasons that it reasons about it in actuality. At that point, it will become an acquired intellect, for as will become clear, the potential intellect becomes actual only due to an intellect that is always actual.[11] If a potential intellect connects with the intellect that is always actual in some way, it will be actually imprinted with a type of form that is externally acquired.

Thus, these are the ranks of potentialities that are called theoretical intellects. At the stage of the acquired intellect, the animal genus is perfected, including the human species. At that point, the human potential

[10] The verbs *ʿaqala* and *taʿaqqala* are usually translated here by the verb "to reason," rather than the archaic "to intellect," though this obscures the connection with the noun form *ʿaql*, which is usually translated "intellect" rather than "reason" in this text.

[11] This is what is termed the Active Intellect (*al-ʿaql al-faʿʿāl*) in what follows.

will have become comparable to the first principles[12] of the whole of existence.

On the means by which the rational soul acquires knowledge[13]

You should know that there are variations in learning,[14] whether it occurs by means of someone other than the learner or by means of the learner himself. Some learners are closer to the formation of conceptions, since their disposition, which is prior to the disposition mentioned above,[15] is stronger. If that human being is disposed to be perfected in and of himself, this strong disposition is called "intuition." This intuition may be so strong in some people that it does not need great effort, education, or instruction to connect to the Active Intellect. Rather, it will be extremely disposed to do so, as though the second disposition has occurred in it, or rather as though it is cognizant of everything by itself, which is the highest degree of this disposition. This state of the material intellect must be called a "holy intellect," which is of the same genus as the habitual intellect, except that it is very refined and is not shared by all people. It is not unlikely that the actions ascribed to the holy spirit will emanate to the imagination also, due to their strength and superiority, and the imagination will **[206]** also imitate it with sensory and auditory examples in discourse, in the manner previously mentioned.[16]

This is verified by the fact that it is well known and apparent that intelligible matters that are attained by acquisition, are acquired only by arriving at the middle term in a syllogism. This middle term can be arrived at in two ways. Sometimes it is arrived at by intuition, which is an action of the mind by virtue of which it discovers the middle term by itself, and cleverness is just the faculty of intuition. At other times, it is arrived at by instruction, though the origin of instruction is intuition, for these things end necessarily with intuitions, since the masters of those intuitions discovered them and conveyed them to learners. Thus, it is

12 On the first principles (*al-mabādi' al-awwalīyyah*), see note 66 below.

13 Alternatively, the sciences (*al-ʿulūm*).

14 Alternatively, the acquisition of knowledge (*taʿallum*).

15 Presumably, Ibn Sīnā means: prior to the highest stage, namely the acquired intellect. Later, he states that it is of the same genus as the habitual intellect (see below).

16 The reference seems to be to an earlier section of this work, in which he explains the functions of the imagination.

possible for intuition to occur to a human being by himself and for the syllogism to come together in his mind without a teacher. This varies both quantitatively and qualitatively: quantitatively because some people can intuit a greater number of middle terms, and qualitatively because some people can intuit in a shorter time. Since this variation is unlimited, being always capable of increase and decrease, and since it ends on the side of deficiency with someone who has no intuition at all, it must therefore end also on the side of excess with someone who has an intuition in all inquiries or most of them, or with someone who has an intuition in the quickest and shortest times. It is possible for someone to have a soul bolstered[17] by intense purity and closeness of connection to the rational[18] principles, to the point that he is ablaze with intuition. What I mean is that he will be receptive to the inspiration of the Active Intellect in all things, and the forms contained in the Active Intellect will be imprinted in him concerning all things, either all at once or nearly so. This imprinting will occur not by conforming to convention[19] but rather in an orderly manner that includes the middle terms. Conformist[20] beliefs concerning those matters that are cognized only together with their causes are not certain and rational. This is a kind of prophecy, or rather the highest of the prophetic faculties,[21] and this faculty is most worthy of being called a "holy faculty." It ranks highest among the human faculties.

On the ranking of faculties in terms of ruling and serving

Now consider and examine the manner in which some of these faculties rule others, and how some serve others. You will find that the acquired intellect, or rather the holy intellect, is the ruler served by all the others, and it is the utmost goal. It is followed by the actual intellect, which is served by the habitual intellect **[207]**, and the material intellect is entirely disposed to serve the habitual intellect. Then the practical intellect serves all these, because the bodily relation exists, as will become clear, for the perfection of the theoretical intellect and its purification, and the practical intellect governs that relation. Then the practical intellect is served by

[17] Compare Qur'ān [2:87]: "We have bolstered him with a soul of such purity . . . ," with reference to Jesus, who is considered a prophet in the Islamic tradition.
[18] Alternatively, intellectual (*ʿaqlīyyah*).
[19] Alternatively, following authority (*taqlīdan*); reading *taqlīdan* rather than *taqlīdīyyan*.
[20] Alternatively, conventional or authority-based (*taqlīdīyyāt*).
[21] Alternatively, powers (*qiwā*).

the faculty of estimation, and estimation is served by two faculties, one preceding it and one subsequent to it. The faculty that is subsequent to it is the one that preserves what it conveys,[22] and the faculty that precedes it includes all the animal faculties. Then, the faculty of imagination is served by two faculties that serve it in different ways, for the appetitive faculty serves it by carrying out its commands because it impels it to move, while the faculty of representation[23] serves it by being receptive to the combination and separation of its forms.

These two faculties rule over two groups. The faculty of representation is served by phantasy,[24] which is in turn served by the five senses. As for the appetitive faculty, it is served by desire and anger, and desire and anger are served by the locomotive faculty that pervades the muscles, and this is where the animal faculties end. Then the animal faculties as a whole are served by the vegetative faculties, first and foremost, the reproductive faculty. The faculty of growth serves the reproductive faculty, and the nutritive faculty serves them all. After that, the four natural faculties serve these: the faculty of digestion serves it in one respect, retention in another, assimilation in a third, and excretion in a fourth respect. And all of them are served by the four qualities [i.e. elements]. However, cold serves heat, and dryness and wetness serve them both. This is the last level of faculties.[25]

On the difference between apprehension[26] by sensation, representation, estimation, and the intellect

It seems that every apprehension involves acquiring the form of what is apprehended. If what is apprehended is material, then it is simply the acquisition of a form abstracted from matter in some way. However, the types of abstraction differ and their degrees are varied. A material form accidentally possesses states and things that do not pertain to it by its

[22] This is the faculty of recollection, one of the faculties associated with the five internal senses (see note 4).

[23] The faculty of representation is one of the faculties associated with the five internal senses (see note 4).

[24] The faculty of phantasy (*fanṭāsiyā*, Greek *phantasia*), also known as the common sense (*al-ḥiss al-mushtarak*), is one of the faculties associated with the five internal senses (see note 4).

[25] Alternatively, powers or potencies (*qiwā*) in this context, to include the four elements.

[26] In this section, Ibn Sīnā is using apprehension (*idrāk*) as a catch-all term for perception and other forms of cognition.

essence, insofar as it is that form. Sometimes it is extracted[27] with all or some of its attachments and at other times it is extracted entirely, being abstracted from matter and from whatever depends on it because of its relation to matter. For example, the **[208]** human form and quiddity[28] is a nature that is necessarily equally shared by all individuals of the species. It is one thing in terms of its definition, but being accidentally present in one individual or another, it becomes multiple. It is not multiple with respect to its human nature. If human nature were necessarily multiple, then "human" would not be predicated of what is numerically one. If humanness were present in Zayd because it is his humanness, then it would not exist for ᶜAmr. Thus, one of the accidents that occur to the human form with respect to matter is multiplicity and divisibility. In addition to these accidents, other accidents occur to it, for if it exists in some matter then it will occur with a certain quantity, quality, place, and position. All these are extrinsic to its nature, for if it were by virtue of being human that it had such a measure of quantity, quality, place, and position, then it would necessarily be the case that every human would share these attributes[29] with every other. And if human beings had some other measure or type of quantity, quality, place, and position in virtue of their humanness, then each person would have to share them.

Thus, the human form in essence is not accompanied necessarily by any of these dependents. These dependents must necessarily be accidents due to matter, because the matter that is coupled with the form is such that these dependents depend upon it. Sense perception acquires this form from matter along with these dependents and along with its relation to matter. If that relation ceases, then the acquisition is annulled, for sense perception does not extract the form from the matter abstracted from all its dependents, and it is unable to retain that form if matter is absent. It is as though sense perception does not extract form from matter completely, but also requires the presence of matter for that form to remain present in it.

As for the faculty of representation, it renders the extracted form more free from matter. It does so by acquiring it from matter in such a way

[27] Ibn Sīnā seems to use *nazᶜ* (extraction) here and elsewhere as a rough synonym for *tajrīd* (abstraction); but I have maintained the distinction in the translation.

[28] The term *māhīyyah*, usually translated "quiddity," is the noun form of the phrase *mā hūwa* (what it is); roughly speaking, it can be considered interchangeable with the term "essence" (*dhāt*).

[29] Literally, meanings or concepts (*maᶜānī*).

that it does not require the existence of matter in order to exist in the representation. For if matter is absent or annihilated, then the form will still exist securely in the faculty of representation, but the form is not abstracted from all material dependents. Recall that sense perception does not completely abstract the form from matter, nor does it abstract it from the dependents of matter. By contrast, representation does abstract it completely from matter **[209]**, but it does not abstract it at all from the dependents of matter, for the form that occurs in representation is the same as the sensory forms, having some quantity, quality, and position. It is quite impossible to represent a form that is such that all individuals of that species can share in it, for the represented person will be like some person or another, and it is possible for there to be existing and represented persons who are not like that human being as represented in representation.

As for the faculty of estimation, it somewhat exceeds this degree of abstraction, for it grasps concepts that are not material in essence, even though they may accidentally exist in matter. That is because shape, color, position, and the like cannot but pertain to corporeal matter, but goodness, evil, approval, disapproval, and the like, are all immaterial in themselves, but may accidentally exist in matter. The proof that these things are immaterial is that had they been material in essence, then goodness, evil, approval, and disapproval could not be intelligible except as accidents of a body; however, they may be intelligible as such [i.e. not as existing in matter]. Thus, it is clear that these things are in themselves immaterial, and are merely accidentally material. The faculty of estimation grasps and apprehends such things. Therefore, it apprehends immaterial things and acquires them from matter. This act of extraction is more comprehensive and closer to simplicity than the other two [viz. perception and representation]. Nevertheless, it does not abstract the form from [all] the dependents of matter, because it acquires it as a particular and with respect to each specific matter, in relation to it, in connection with perceptible forms that are conditioned by the dependents of matter, and because it acquires it with the participation of the faculty of representation.

As for the faculty that contains the retained forms, either the forms of existents that are completely immaterial and cannot be accidentally material, or the forms of existents that are immaterial but may be accidentally material, or the forms of material existents that are however freed of material attachments in every respect, it is clear that it apprehends the forms by acquiring them in such a way that they are abstracted from matter in every respect. This is apparent when it comes to what is essentially abstracted from matter. As for what exists in matter, either because its existence is material or because it is accidentally so, it acquires it by abstraction in such a way that it extracts it from matter in every respect, as well as from the dependents of matter. Thus, for example, when it comes to the form of "human," which can be applied to many, with many taking on a single nature **[210]**, it separates it from all material quantity, quality, and position, then it abstracts it from all that to make it suitable to be applied to all.

That is how the apprehension of the judge of sense perception differs from the judge of representation, estimation, and intellect. And that is the point[30] we intended to convey in the argument[31] of this chapter.[32]

Elaboration of the claim that the substance that is the receptacle for the intelligibles is immaterial[33]

Furthermore, we state that the substance that is the receptacle for the intelligibles is neither a body nor does it subsist in a body such that it is a faculty of the body or a form of the body, in any way. For, if the receptacle of intelligibles were a body or some magnitude or another, then the receptacle of forms would either be [1] an indivisible part of it, or [2] would inhere in a divisible part of it.

[1] Let us determine first whether it could be an indivisible part. I say that this is impossible, by the following argument. An [indivisible] point is a limit of some kind that cannot be distinguished in position from the line or magnitude[34] that ends at that point, and nothing can be imprinted upon it without that imprint being in a part of that line. Just as a point is not separate in essence but is rather an essential part of what is essentially a magnitude, so also it is possible to say that, in a sense, a part of something inheres in a point if it inheres in **[214]** the

[30] Literally, meaning or concept (*maʿnā*). [31] Literally, discourse (*kalām*).

[32] A section has been omitted here, in which Ibn Sīnā attempts to show that every faculty that perceives particulars must have a bodily organ. He argues that, even though imagination represents a further stage of abstraction than sense perception, it must also have a bodily organ.

[33] Literally, abstract (*mujarrad*). [34] Presumably, a line segment.

magnitude of which it is a part. It [i.e. the thing that inheres in it] therefore becomes accidentally a magnitude, and similarly, it becomes accidentally limited by that point. If the point is separate and receives something or another, then it would have a distinct essence, and the point would thus have two sides, one of which would be adjacent to the line from which it is distinct, and another side opposite to it. As such, it would be separated from the line, and the line would have another limit that touches it. That point would then be the limit of the line, not the first one, and the same would apply to it. This would lead us to the conclusion that points are iterated in a line, either finitely or infinitely. But this has been shown elsewhere to be clearly impossible, since points do not constitute a line by being iterated. It has also been shown clearly that a point does not have a distinct and specific position. [One can show that an iteration of points does not constitute a line by] referring to a part of the line. Consider the two points that surround one point on both sides. There are two alternatives: [a] The middle point creates a barrier between them so that they do not touch, which entails by the insight of the primary intellect that each one of them touches something specific of the middle point, and this would then divide the middle point, which is impossible.[35] [b] Alternatively, the middle point would not prevent the two surrounding points from touching. Then the intelligible form would inhere in all points, and all of them would be like one point. This one point has been placed in such a way that it is separate from the line. The line has on one side something that separates it from the point, another limit that separates it from the point. That point would then have a different position than the first point. However, all the points have been supposed to share the same position. This leads to a contradiction.[36] Therefore, the statement that the receptacle of intelligibles is an indivisible part of the body has been refuted.

[2] It remains that, if the receptacle of the intelligibles is a body, that body is something divisible. Suppose that there is an intelligible form that

[35] That is, if A, B, and C are adjacent points on a line, the first alternative is that A touches B and B touches C, but A does not touch C. Then A and C would touch different parts of B, which implies that the middle point B is divisible (*contra hypothesi*).

[36] That is, if A, B, and C are adjacent points on a line, the second alternative is that A touches B, B touches C, and A also touches C. But if all adjacent points on a line touch one another, then they are really all one point; moreover, the same could be said of all points on that line. But then one cannot speak of the endpoint of a line that is distinct from the rest of the line (*contra hypothesi*).

inheres in something divisible. If we suppose it to be something divisible in some way or another, then the form would also be accidentally divisible. Then, its two parts would either be [a] similar or [b] dissimilar. [a] If they are similar, how could their conjunction be something different from either of them – unless it is something occurring in them [when taken together] such as an increase in magnitude or number, not [a difference in] the form itself? But then the intelligible form would have a certain shape or a certain number. However, the intelligible form does not have a shape, since it would then be representational rather than intelligible. A clearer argument is as follows: It is impossible to say that **[215]** each of the two parts is in itself complete in meaning, for if the second part does not enter into the meaning of the whole, then we should ascribe the entire meaning of the intelligible to the first part from the outset, not to both parts. And if it does enter into the meaning, it is quite clear that the first part alone does not indicate the meaning completely. [b] If the two parts are dissimilar, let us investigate how the intelligible form might have dissimilar parts. The only possibility is that the dissimilar parts are the parts of the definition, namely the genera and differentiae. However, this leads necessarily to impossibilities. For example, since every part of the body that is the receptacle of the intelligibles is potentially infinitely divisible, so also the genera and differentiae must be potentially infinite. But it has been determined that the essential genera and differentiae of a single thing are not potentially infinite. Moreover, it is not that an imaginary division distinguishes between genus and differentia. Rather, it is surely the case that if there were a genus and differentia that were capable of being distinguished in the receptacle, then that distinction would not be merely a question of an imaginary division. Instead, the genus and differentia would have to be actually infinite. But it has been determined that the genera, differentiae, and parts of the definition of a single thing are finite in every respect. If they were actually infinite, they could not be conjoined in the body in such a fashion, for that would necessitate that a single body be separable into infinite parts.

Again, consider another argument. Let the division of the receptacle be made in some manner that results in the genus on one side and the differentia on the other. If we had changed the manner of division, then half the genus and half the differentia might fall on one side of the divide, or the genus might fall on the side of the differentia and vice versa. Thus, our imaginary supposition would switch the position of the genus and the differentia, displacing each to the opposite side based on the will of an extrinsic volitional agent. Indeed, that is not all, for it is possible to effect a division within each division [i.e. dividing the genus into parts and the differentia into parts]. However, not every intelligible can be divided into simpler intelligibles, for some intelligibles are the simplest of all and are the principles of combination for all the other intelligibles. They do not have genera and differentiae, are not quantitatively divisible, nor are they divisible in meaning. Therefore, the parts **[216]** that are imagined to be in the receptacle cannot possibly be dissimilar in meaning from each other and from the whole, when in fact the whole results from their conjunction.

Since it is not possible for the intelligible form to be divided or to inhere in an indivisible part of a magnitude, and since the intelligible form must have a receptacle within us, it is clear that the receptacle of intelligibles is a substance that is not a body, nor a bodily faculty. Otherwise, that would make the receptacle divisible like a body and it would be subject to all the impossibilities mentioned above.[37]

We can demonstrate this using another demonstrative proof, as follows. The intellectual faculty is what abstracts intelligibles from a definite quantity, place, position, and the other categories. We must examine the essence of that form, to determine in what sense[38] it has been abstracted from its position. Is it an abstraction relative to the thing from which it is acquired? Or relative to the thing that acquires it? That is, is the intelligible essence abstracted from its position while it is in external existence, or from its conceived existence while it is in the intelligent substance? It is impossible for it to be abstracted in external existence; thus, it remains that it is separated from position and place while it exists in the intellect. Therefore, when it exists in the intellect, it will not have a position and cannot be qualified[39] by partition or division or any similar concept. Hence, it is impossible for it to be in a body.

Moreover, if the unitary indivisible form is imprinted in divisible matter with dimensions, and it is of things that are indivisible in meaning, then either [1] none of the parts that the matter is supposed to have by virtue

[37] A section heading has been omitted here, since what follows clearly belongs to the same topic.

[38] Literally, how (*kayf*), or in what manner.

[39] Literally, cannot be signified (*ishārah*).

of its dimensions is related to the single indivisible intelligible essence that has been abstracted from matter, or [2] it is related to each one of its supposed parts, or [3] it is related to some parts and not others. If [1] none of the material parts is related, then necessarily the whole thing is not related. If [2] some of them are related and not others, then those that are not related to it are not part of its meaning at all. And if [3] all the supposed parts are related in some way, then either each supposed part is related to: [a] the essence as a whole, or [b] a part of the essence. [a] If each supposed part is related to **[217]** the essence as a whole, then the parts are not the parts of the intelligible concept, but rather each of them is a single intelligible in its own right, or indeed, the intelligible itself, and it will be actually intelligible an infinite number of times at once. [b] If each part is related differently to the essence, the essence must then be divisible in the intellect. However, it has been posited to be indivisible, so this leads to a contradiction. Moreover, if each part is related to something different in the essence than every other part, the divisibility of the essence is all the more apparent, and this is irrational.

This shows that the forms that are imprinted in matter are merely similar[40] to the particular divisible things, and that every part of them is related either actually or potentially to some part of those things. Moreover, something that is multiple with regards to the parts of its definition has a unity with respect to its completeness, which is indivisible. How can that unity of definition, insofar as it is a unity, be imprinted in something divisible? If it could, the same would occur to it as we mentioned above to the parts of the definition of the nonmultiple thing.

In addition, it may be determined that the supposed intelligibles about which the rational faculty can reason one by one in actuality are potentially infinite, and none have precedence[41] over any others. It has also been verified that something that is capable of a potentially infinite number of things cannot possibly have a receptacle that is a body or a bodily faculty. This has been demonstrated in the *Physics*.[42] Thus, it is impossible for the essence that receives the intelligibles to subsist in a body at all, nor is it possible for its action to be in a body or through a body.

[40] Reading *ashbāh* for *ashbāḥ* (apparitions).

[41] It is not clear what Ibn Sīnā means by saying that none has precedence (*awlā*).

[42] Possibly, the second section of *Kitāb al-Najāt*, which deals with physics or natural science.

The intellectual faculty does not reason by means of the bodily instrument[43]

If the intellectual faculty were to reason by means of a bodily instrument, and its specific function[44] were to take place only by using that bodily instrument, then it would follow that it could not reason about itself or the instrument, nor could it reason that it reasons. For there is no instrument between it and itself, there is no instrument between it and the instrument, and there is no instrument between it and its own reasoning. Yet, it reasons about itself, reasons about the instrument that is called its instrument, and reasons that it reasons. Therefore, it reasons by means of itself, not by means of an instrument.

Moreover, there are only the following alternatives. The intellect reasons about its instrument due to the existence of something both in it and in its instrument. That could be: [1] the form of the instrument itself, [2] a numerically different form of the same instrument, or **[218]** [3] the form of a different instrument. [1] If the intellect reasons about its instrument due to the existence of the form of its instrument, then the form of its instrument is in its instrument, and it is therefore always in the intellect by commonality. Therefore, it must always reason about its instrument, since it reasons due to the incidence of the form in it.[45] [2] If it is due to the presence of a numerically different form, then different things that share a definition either differ in their matter, or in universality and particularity, or because one is abstracted from matter and the other is present in matter. In this case, there is no difference in matter for the matter is the same, and no difference between abstraction and existence in matter, since both are in matter.[46] Moreover, there is no difference in specificity and generality, since one of them only gains particularity because of the particular matter and the dependents that accrue to it with respect to the matter in which it exists, and this concept is not specific to one of them rather than the other. [3] It cannot be due to the existence of another intelligible form, different from the form of its own instrument, for this

43 Throughout this section, by bodily instrument (*al-ālah al-jasadīyyah*), Ibn Sīnā means a part of the body or a bodily organ. Earlier in this same text, he specifies the location of some psychological faculties (e.g. imagination) in particular regions of the brain.

44 Alternatively, action (*fiʿluhā*).

45 Ibn Sīnā clearly rejects this alternative based on the fact that the intellect does not always reason about its own instrument.

46 Presumably, this is the matter of the alleged bodily instrument that enables the intellect to reason.

impossibility is more apparent. Suppose that the intelligible form that inheres in the receiving substance enables it to reason about the thing whose form it is or what is related to that thing, so that the form of what is related to it becomes part of that form. This intelligible form is not the form of that instrument, nor is it the form of something essentially related to it, because the essence of that instrument is a substance. We merely acquire and consider the form of its essence,[47] and the substance itself is not related to it.

This is also an impressive demonstration that it is impossible for apprehension[48] to apprehend an instrument that is its own instrument in apprehension. That is why sense perception only perceives external things; it does not perceive itself, its instrument, or its perception. Similarly, the faculty of representation does not represent itself, its action, or its instrument. Rather, when it represents its own instrument, it does not represent it in such a way that the representation is necessarily specific to it and nothing else. It is possible for perception to provide it with the form of its instrument. But in that case, this will be an imitation of a representation obtained from perception and not related by it to anything else in such a way that had it not been its own instrument it would not have been able to represent it.[49]

Another argument that confirms and convinces us of this is that the faculties that apprehend by the imprinting of forms in their instruments are fatigued by continuous action. That is because instruments are fatigued by continuous activity[50] and their compositions[51] are corrupted, which are their substance and nature. Powerful things that are difficult to apprehend also weaken them, and may indeed corrupt them so that they are afterwards unable to apprehend weaker matters **[219]**, due to the fact that they are preoccupied with being affected by what is more difficult. For example, strenuous and repeated perceptibles weaken perception and may even corrupt it, as bright light does for vision or loud thunder does for hearing. While apprehending strong perceptions, it is unable to apprehend

47 That is, when we reason.

48 That is, the faculties of cognition (*al-mudrik*), which include the external and internal senses.

49 The meaning is somewhat obscure, but perhaps Ibn Sīnā is saying that for the faculty of representation really to represent its own instrument, it would be required to relate the representation to the instrument in some way, not just to entertain some representation or other relayed by sense perception.

50 Literally, motion (*ḥarakah*).

51 Alternatively, their admixtures (*mizājahā*), i.e. the particular compositions of the four humors that constitute their physical makeup.

weak ones. Thus, someone who sees an intense light cannot at the same time or shortly thereafter see a weak light, one who hears a loud sound cannot at the same time or shortly thereafter hear a soft sound, and one who tastes something intensely sweet cannot afterwards taste something more weakly sweet. With the intellectual faculty, the reverse is the case. Constant reasoning and conceiving of powerful things endows it with the strength and facility to receive weaker things afterwards. If it sometimes experiences fatigue and weakness, that is because the intellect relies on the faculty of representation, which uses an instrument that fatigues and ceases to serve the intellect. If it were due to some other thing, then it would happen always [or] in most cases, but the opposite is the case.

Moreover, the faculties of all the parts of the body begin to weaken after the completion of the process of growth and development, which occurs before or around the age of 40. However, in most cases, the intellectual faculty becomes stronger after that point. If it were one of the bodily faculties, then it would always have to weaken at that point. However, that is necessitated only in some cases and when it meets certain obstacles, not in all cases. Therefore, it is not one of the bodily faculties.

Some are under the illusion that the soul forgets its intelligibles and ceases to perform its function when the body is sick or with the onset of old age, and that this is caused by the fact that its function can only be fulfilled by means of the body. That opinion is neither necessary nor true. For after having determined that the soul reasons by means of itself, we must seek the cause of this doubting objection. If it were possible to conjoin the two views without contradiction, namely that the soul functions[52] by itself, and that it loses its function and ceases to function with the illness of the body, then we would not need to consider this objection. [But it is not possible, so we must consider it.]

We reply as follows. The soul has a function relative to the body, namely governing, and a function relative to itself and its principles, namely reasoning. These two functions are in opposition and are mutually exclusive: if it becomes preoccupied with one of them, it disregards the other, and it is difficult for it to combine the two. Its bodily preoccupations are perception, imagination, desire, anger, fear, sorrow, and pain. You can know that [the soul cannot combine bodily preoccupations and intellectual ones by considering the following]: if you think about an intelligible

[52] Alternatively, the soul has an action (*fiʿlan*).

[220], all of these bodily preoccupations are disabled – unless they prevail and compel the soul to return to them. You also know that perception prevents the soul from reasoning, for if the soul applies itself to the perceptible realm it is distracted from the intelligible realm, when the instrument of the intellect or the intellect itself has not been afflicted with any harm in any respect. You also know that the cause of that is the preoccupation of the soul with one function rather than another. That is why the functions of the intellect are disabled during illness. Had the intelligible form been annihilated or corrupted due to the bodily instrument, the return of the instrument to its former state would require it to acquire the intelligibles all over again. However, that is not the case, for the soul may resume its thinking at once.[53] Thus, what was restored had existed in it in some way or another; it was merely distracted from it.

The difference between these two aspects of the soul's functions is not the only thing that necessitates mutual exclusivity among its functions. The multiplicity of functions within each of the two aspects may necessitate the very same thing. For example, fear distracts one from hunger, desire blocks anger, and anger diverts one from fear. The cause in all these cases is the same: the soul's total preoccupation with one thing. Thus, if something does not perform its function when it is preoccupied with something else, it is not necessary that it cannot perform unless that thing exists.[54]

We could clarify this topic further, but protracted examination of a subject after attaining sufficiency may cause us to encumber the discussion with what is not strictly needed. The principles that we have affirmed show clearly that the soul is not imprinted in the body nor does it subsist by means of the body. Rather, the soul must become specific to the body by virtue of having a particular disposition to be attracted to governing a particular body, along the lines of an essential concern that is specific to it.

[53] Literally, resume its (former) state at once, by reasoning about everything it had reasoned about (previously) (*ʿāqilah li-jamīʿ mā ʿaqalathu bi-ḥālihi*).

[54] In other words, it is not necessary that it cannot perform its function unless something exists to satisfy it (e.g. hunger distracts one from fear, but it is not necessary that hunger be completely satisfied by food in order for one to experience the fear again). Here, the point seems to be that it is *total* preoccupation with one function that diverts one from other functions, and that one is able to combine psychological functions to some extent, provided no single function is all-consuming.

On the assistance given by the bodily faculties to the rational soul

Furthermore, we say that the bodily faculties assist the rational soul in some ways. For example, sense perception provides it with particulars. Four things occur to the soul due to these particulars. First, the soul extracts single universals from the particulars, by abstracting their meanings from matter and material attachments and dependents, all the while attending to similarities and differences, essential [221] existence and accidental existence. In this way, the principles of conception originate in the soul, with the assistance provided by the use of the faculties of representation and estimation. Second, the soul finds relations among these single universals, such as negation and affirmation. Whenever it is self-evident that a combination yields negation or affirmation, the soul accepts it; and whenever it is not clear, it sets it aside until the discovery of the middle term. Third, it acquires the empirical premises, as follows. It discovers through perception a predicate that is judged to be necessarily related to a subject negatively or affirmatively, or to forbid it or to follow from it, to be affirmatively or negatively connected, to be affirmatively or negatively opposed, or not to forbid it.[55] This is to be found not just in some cases or half the time, but rather always, so that the soul can be assured that it is of the nature of this predicate to be related in this way to the subject, and that it is of the nature of the subject to entail the predicate or to negate its essence necessarily, not arbitrarily. Such a belief is based on perception and reason.[56] It is based on perception because these matters have been observed, and on reason because had it been arbitrary, it would not have been present in all or most cases. An example would be our judgment that scammony is by nature a laxative for bile. We have perceived this many times, and have reasoned that had it not been so by nature but arbitrarily, then it would have been the case only sometimes. Fourth, the soul assents to reports due to extensive recurrent corroboration. The human soul is assisted by the body in acquiring these principles for conception and assent. Once it acquires them, it returns to itself. If the lower faculties happen to preoccupy it later, they will distract it from its function or will hamper its function if they do not distract it outright. Thereafter, it will

[55] Some of these logical terms are unclear, but it seems that "connected" (*ittiṣāl*) denotes a relation of implication, and "opposed" (*ʿinād*) denotes a relation of exclusive disjunction.

[56] Literally, syllogism (*qiyās*).

not need them in pursuing its specific function, except when it comes to matters for which the soul specifically needs to return to the imaginative faculties[57] once again to discover an additional principle to the ones it had acquired, or to assist it in conjuring up a representation. This happens often at the beginning,[58] but less so with time.

If the soul is perfected and strengthened, it will devote itself exclusively to its functions, and the perceptual, imaginative, and other bodily faculties will divert it from its function. An analogy for this would be as follows. A human being may need a riding animal and instruments to arrive at a certain destination. When he reaches that destination and something happens to cause him to leave it, the causes that helped him to arrive at the destination will themselves become a hindrance. Moreover, the demonstrative proofs we have put forward showing that the receptacle of intelligibles, that is the rational soul, is neither a body nor a bodily faculty, relieve us from supplying further **[222]** evidence for the subsistence of the soul by itself without needing the body. However, this is attested also by its action.

On the proof of the origination of the soul

We say that human souls are the same in species and concept. If they existed before the body, they must either have multiple essences or be one essence. However, it will be shown that it is impossible for them to have multiple essences or to be one essence, and thus, that it is impossible for them to exist before the body. We will begin by showing the impossibility of their being numerically multiple. We say that the difference among souls before the existence of bodies is either with respect to their quiddity and form, or with respect to their relation to the element [i.e. the matter to which they are related]. Matter is multiple in space, each part of which is occupied by matter; it is multiple in time, each soul being originated in matter at one specific moment in time; and it is multiple with respect to the causes that divide it. The souls are not different in quiddity and form, since their form is one. Therefore, they must differ with respect to the receptacle of the quiddity, or in terms of the body to which the quiddity is specifically related. Before the origination of the body, the soul is simply pure quiddity,

57 It is not clear why Ibn Sīnā uses the plural here, but he may mean the faculties of imagination and representation.

58 That is, at the beginning of intellectual activity.

so that souls cannot differ from one another numerically. Quiddity does not admit essential difference – this is absolutely applicable to everything. Those things whose essences are merely concepts, are multiple in species only with respect to their receptacles,[59] effects, some relation to these, or their times. But if they are originally abstract, they are not different with respect to the things mentioned, so it is impossible that there be difference and multiplicity in them. Therefore, it is false that souls are numerically multiple in essence before entering bodies.

I state that it is also impossible for souls to be numerically one before the origination of the body, for when two bodies come into being, two souls will come to be in those bodies. Consider two alternatives: [1] The two souls are two parts of that one [preexisting] soul. That would mean that one thing that has no magnitude or size is potentially divisible, which is clearly false given the principles affirmed in the natural sciences. [2] The soul that is numerically one will be in two bodies, which again does not require much effort to show that it is false. Hence, it has been determined that a soul originates every time a body originates that is suitable to be used by it. The originated body **[223]** will be that soul's domain and instrument. Moreover, the disposition of the substance of a soul that is originated with a body – the body that warrants its origination from the first principles[60] – will have a natural tendency to occupy itself with that body, to use it, to concern itself with its states, and to be attracted to it. This disposition renders the soul specific to that body and naturally diverts it from contact with all other bodies besides it, unless mediated by its own body. If the soul is found to be individualized, the principle of individualization must result from the dispositions that appoint it to that individual. These dispositions determine the soul's specificity for that body and the suitability of the body and soul for mutual improvement, though that state and suitability are hidden from us. The principles of complementarity originate in the soul by means of the body, and it supplements them by its nature, not by means of the body. After separating from the body, each soul will have become a separate essence due to the difference in the matters in which they were present, as well as the differences in their times of origination, and the different dispositions of their various different bodies, which must differ in their states.

[59] Omitting *ḥawāmil*, which seems synonymous with *qawābil* (receptacles) in this context.
[60] Presumably, the separate or immaterial causes (see note 66 below).

The soul does not die with the body, nor is it corrupted

We say that the soul does not die with the body nor is it corrupted at all. It does not die with the death of the body because everything that is corrupted is corrupted by the corruption of something else, upon which it is dependent[61] in some way. And everything that is dependent on something in some way is either dependent on it in such a way that it [1] is coexistent with it, [2] is subsequent to it in existence, or [3] precedes it in existence essentially but not temporally.

[1] If the dependence of the soul on the body is that of coexistence, and if this dependence is essential rather than accidental to the soul, then each is essentially related to the other, and neither the body nor the soul is a substance. However, both are substances. If it is accidental rather than essential, then if one of them is corrupted, the accidental relation between them ceases, though the essence of the other is not corrupted. [Thus, in that case, the soul would not be corrupted with the corruption of the body.]

[2] If it is dependent in such a way that it is subsequent to it in existence, then the body would be the cause of the existence of the soul. There are four causes, so the body will either be [a] the efficient cause of the soul, endowing it with existence; [b] the material[62] cause by way of composition, as the elements are for bodies, or **[224]** by way of simplicity, as copper is for a statue; [c] the formal cause; or [d] the final cause. [a] It is impossible for [the body] to be the efficient cause of the soul, since body insofar as it is body, is not an agent[63] at all but acts merely through its faculties. If it were to act through its essence rather than its faculties, then every body would perform the same actions. Furthermore, all bodily faculties are either accidents or material forms, and it is impossible for accidents or forms that subsist in matter to give existence to an immaterial self-subsisting essence or to give existence to an absolute substance. [b] It is also impossible for it to be a material cause, for we have shown and proven demonstratively that the soul is not imprinted in the body in any way. Thus, the body is not informed with the form of the soul, neither by simplicity nor by composition, such that parts of the body are combined and mixed[64] in certain ways so that the soul is imprinted in them. [c, d] Moreover, it is impossible for the body to be a formal or final cause of

[61] Alternatively, to which it is attached (*mutaʿalliq*).

[62] Literally, receptive (*qābilīyyah*) cause.

[63] Alternatively, does not act (*lā yafʿal*).

[64] That is, the humors of the body are mixed (*tamtazij*).

the soul; rather, it would be more apt for it to be the other way around. Therefore, the dependence of the soul on the body is not that of an effect on an essential cause. In fact, the body and temperament[65] are an accidental cause of the soul. For if the matter of a body originates that is suitable to be the instrument and domain of the soul, the separate[66] causes give rise to a particular soul. At that point, a particular soul will originate from them, since it is impossible for a particular soul to be originated without a cause that specifies the origination of one soul rather than another. In addition, it is impossible for numerical multiplicity to originate in it, as we have shown, and every created thing that has not yet come into existence must be preceded by matter that has a disposition to receive it or to be related to it in some way, as has been shown in the other sciences.[67] Moreover, had it been possible for a particular soul to originate without an instrument through which it is perfected and acts, its existence would be aimless and nothing is aimless by nature. However, if the disposition for the relation and the receptivity of the instrument have both originated, then it is necessary for something, the soul, to originate at that point from the separate causes. It is not the case that if the origination of something is necessary [with the origination of another], then its annihilation is necessary with the annihilation of the other. That is only the case if the essence of that first thing subsists by and in the other thing.

It is possible for some things to originate as a result of others and for the latter to be annihilated while the former remain, so long as their essences do not subsist in them, especially if what endows them with existence is something other than what merely became disposed to gain from their existence. What endows the soul with existence is not a body nor a bodily faculty, as we have shown, but must rather be another substance that is not a body. If its existence by that substance and the body takes place only at the time at which it becomes worthy of existence **[225]**, then it is not dependent for existence itself on the body, nor is the body a cause of it, except accidentally. Thus, it is not permissible to say that the dependence between them is such that it necessitates that the body precedes the soul as essential causes do.

[65] Literally, mixture (*mizāj*), i.e. of humors.

[66] Also referred to as the immaterial causes (*al-ʿilal al-mufāriqah*) or the first principles (*al-mabādi' al-awwalīyyah*), these are the intelligences associated with the ten celestial spheres, which emanate ultimately from God. The last of these is the Active Intellect, from which human souls emanate.

[67] Perhaps in the section of *al-Najāt* devoted to the natural sciences.

[3] As for the third division we mentioned at the outset, namely that the soul is dependent on the body such that it precedes it in existence, then it must[68] precede it essentially but not temporally – for it is not separate from it temporally. This type of precedence is precedence in essence: whenever the precedent comes into existence it necessarily endows existence to the essence of the subsequent. In this way, the precedent could not exist if we suppose that the subsequent has been annihilated, not because supposing that the subsequent is annihilated necessitates the annihilation of the precedent, but rather because the subsequent could not have been annihilated unless something had naturally occurred to the precedent that annihilated it, thereby annihilating the subsequent. Thus, it is not that the supposition of the annihilation of the subsequent necessitates the annihilation of the precedent, but rather it necessitates the supposition of the annihilation of the precedent itself, because the subsequent can be supposed to be annihilated only if something has occurred[69] to the precedent itself to annihilate it.

If this is the case, the annihilating cause must occur in the substance of the soul, thereby corrupting the body; it is not at all the case that the body is corrupted by a cause that is specific to it. However, in fact, the corruption of the body takes place because of a cause that is specific to it, owing to a change in its temperament or composition. Therefore, it is false that the soul is dependent on the body such that it precedes it in essence, and that the body is definitely corrupted by a cause that is proper to it. Hence, this dependence does not obtain between soul and body.

If that is so, then all forms of dependence have been refuted, and the only remaining alternative is that the soul is not dependent for its existence on the body, but is rather dependent for its existence on the other[70] principles, which are not subject to transformation or annihilation. Moreover, the soul cannot be corrupted at all, for I state that nothing else can annihilate it in any way. That is because everything that has a tendency to be corrupted by some cause has the potentiality of corruption and, before being corrupted, has the actuality of persistence. It is impossible for one thing to have both the potentiality of corruption and the actuality of persistence in the same respect. Rather, its disposition to be corrupted is not due to the cause of its persistence. The concept of potentiality is

[68] Reading *fa-lā budd* rather than *fa-immā* (either), which does not appear to make sense here.
[69] Alternatively, something has occurred accidentally (*ʿaraḍa*).
[70] That is, the separate or immaterial causes.

opposed to the concept of actuality, and the relation of this potentiality is opposed to the relation of that actuality, because one is related to corruption and the other is related to persistence. Thus, these two concepts stand for two different states in one thing. We say that it is possible for composite things **[226]** and simple things that subsist in these compounds to combine the actuality of persistence with the potentiality of corruption; however, simple things that are separate in essence cannot combine these two features.

I state that in another absolute sense, it is impossible for these two concepts to be combined in one thing with a unitary essence. That is because everything that persists and has the potentiality of corruption also has the potentiality of persistence, since its persistence is not necessary. If it is not necessary then it is possible, and possibility is the nature of potentiality. Thus, it will have the potentiality of persistence in its substance. It is obvious that the actuality of persistence in it must not be the same as the potentiality of persistence in it. Therefore, the actuality of persistence will occur to something that has the potentiality of persistence in it. That potentiality will not actually pertain to a certain essence, but rather to something that occurs to its essence enabling it to persist in actuality, which is not the reality of its essence. This implies that its essence must be composed of: [1] something that, if it is found in it, will enable its essence to exist in actuality, which is the form in everything; and [2] something to which that actuality has occurred and from whose nature is found its potentiality, namely its matter. If the soul is absolutely simple and is not divisible into matter and form, it will not be receptive to corruption. If it is composite, let us set aside the compound and examine the substance that is its matter, specifically discoursing about the matter itself. We state that this matter can either always be divided in this way indefinitely, which would prove the point, but which is impossible; or else this thing, which is the substance and basis of the soul, will not be annihilated. Then our discourse will be about this thing that is the basis and origin, not about something that is a combination of it and another thing. It is obvious that everything that is simple and not composite, or is the origin and basis of something composite, will not combine the potentiality of persistence with the potentiality of annihilation in relation to its essence. If it has the potentiality of annihilation, then it is impossible for it to have the actuality of persistence. And if it has the actuality of persistence and existence, then it does not have the potentiality for annihilation. Thus, it is clear that the substance of the soul does not contain the potentiality for corruption.

As for corruptible beings, they are composite and conjoined, and the potentiality of corruption and persistence are not in the concept[71] by virtue of which the composite is unitary, but are rather in the matter, which has the potentiality to receive two contraries. Hence, there is no potentiality of persistence or potentiality of corruption in the corruptible compound, and thus they are never combined in it. As for matter, it either persists not by a potentiality [227] that disposes it to persist – as some people think – or it persists by a potentiality by virtue of which it persists and has no potential to be corrupted, but rather the potentiality of corruption by something else originates in it. The potentiality of corruption for simple things in matter is due to the matter, not to their own substance. The demonstrative proof that necessitates that every being is corruptible due to the finitude of the potentialities for persistence and annihilation, is only applicable to what consists of matter and form. In matter, there is both the potential for a form to persist in it as well as a potential for it to be corrupted. Thus, it is clear that the soul is definitely not corruptible, which is what we intended to show in our discourse.

Refutation of reincarnation

We have shown that souls originate and are multiple only when bodies are disposed to receive them. The disposition of bodies necessitates that the existence of the soul emanates to them from the immaterial causes. It is apparent, therefore, that this does not come about arbitrarily or by chance, which would make it the case that the existence of an originated soul does not take place because this body's temperament warrants an originated soul to govern it, but rather that a soul exists and a body just happens to exist with it. In that case, the multiplicity of souls would not have an essential cause at all, but rather an accidental one. We know that essential causes precede accidental ones in existence. If that is so, every body warrants, with the origination of its temperament, the origination of a soul for it; it is not that some bodies do and others do not, for the individuals of a species do not differ in terms of the things by which they

[71] Here, Ibn Sīnā seems to be using the term "concept" (*maʿnā*) roughly interchangeably with "form."

subsist. If we suppose that a soul is reincarnated in multiple bodies, while every body in itself warrants a soul to be originated for it and is dependent on it, then one body would have two souls at once. Moreover, the relation between soul and body is not such that the soul is imprinted in the body, as we have already said, but rather such that the soul is occupied with the body, to the point that the soul is aware of that body and the body is affected by that soul. Every animal is aware[72] of being one soul, which is what governs the body and makes it function. If there were really another soul of which the animal is not aware, which is not aware of itself and is not occupied with the body, then it would have no relation to the body, for the relationship can only be of that kind. Therefore, there is no reincarnation of any kind. This much is sufficient for those who desire brevity, though one could expand greatly on this topic.

[228] On the unity of the soul

We state that the soul is one essence and that it has many faculties. If the faculties of the soul were not combined in one essence, sense perception having a separate principle, anger another, and each of the other faculties a separate principle, then when something appears in perception, one of two things would occur. [1] That same concept would arise in anger, desire, and so on, which would mean that the faculty of anger would also perceive, imagine, and so on, each faculty issuing in actions of different types.[73] [2] Alternatively, perception and anger would be combined in one faculty, and they would not therefore be separated in two different faculties that are not capable of being combined. Since these functions of the soul are occupied with one another and convey their effects to one another, then either each one of them is capable of being transformed when the other is, or else one thing would be capable of combining these faculties, to which all of them would lead and which would receive what arises in each. However, the first division is impossible, because each faculty has a function that is specific to it, in relation to the thing of which it is said to be a faculty, and it is not the case that every faculty is suitable for every function. Thus, the faculty of anger, insofar as it is the faculty of anger, does not perceive, and the faculty of perception, insofar as it is the faculty of perception, does not become angry. That

72 Alternatively, is self-aware (*yastashʿir nafsahu*).

73 Literally, genera (*ajnās*).

leaves the second division, which states that the faculties all lead to one principle.

One might object that the faculty of anger is not affected by the perceptible form, but rather that when the faculty of perception perceives a perceptible, this is necessarily accompanied by the effect of anger from the faculty of anger, though it is not affected by the perceptible form. The reply to this is that this is impossible because if the faculty of anger is affected by the faculty of perception, that is due to one of two things. [1] It is either because some influence has arrived at it from the faculty of perception, which is the influence of that perceptible. That would mean that it has been affected by that perceptible, and everything affected by a perceptible, insofar as it is a perceptible, is a perceiver. [2] Or else, it has been affected by the faculty of perception, but not with respect to that perceptible. Then, anger will not really result from that perceptible. However, we have supposed that it is from that perceptible. That is a contradiction.

Moreover, we sometimes say, "When I perceived such-and-such, I became angry." Since this is a true statement, it is one thing that perceived and then became angry. That one thing is either the human body or the human soul. If it is the human body, then it would either be the totality of its organs or some of its organs. But it cannot be the totality of its organs, for it does not include the hand **[229]** or the foot. It also cannot be two different organs, one of which perceived and the other became angry. For then it would not really be one thing that perceived and then was angry. It is also not the case that one bodily organ – according to someone who makes such a statement – is the object of both perception and anger. Rather, the truth is that the statement "I perceived and then became angry" means perhaps that something within us perceived and something within us was angry. But the intention of one who utters, "I perceived and then became angry," is not that this occurs to two things within us, but rather that the very thing to which perception conveyed this concept then became angry. Therefore, either the [literal] meaning of this statement is false, or else the truth is that the one who perceived and was angry is one thing. But since this statement is obviously [literally] true, then the thing to which perception conveys its perceptible is the very thing that becomes angry. And since it has such a position, even if it is a body, it does not have this position insofar as it is a body. Instead, it has it by virtue of having a faculty that makes it suitable for the combination of these two things. This faculty is not physical, and it must therefore be a soul.

Thus, the subject that combines these two, perception and anger, is not the totality of our body, nor two of our organs, nor one organ insofar as it is physical. The only remaining alternative is that what combines them is a soul in itself, or a body insofar as it has a soul in reality. Thus, the soul is what combines them, and that soul is the principle for all these faculties. It must be attached to any organ in which life is generated. It is impossible for an organ to have life without a faculty of the soul having some attachment to it. It is also impossible that the first thing that attaches to the body is not this principle but a faculty that originates subsequent to this principle. This being the case, the organ that attaches to this principle must be the heart.[74] This opinion of the Philosopher [Aristotle] is opposed to that of the divine Plato.

This is the source of some doubt,[75] since we find that the vegetative faculties are found in plants, where there is no perceptive soul nor a rational soul; moreover they are also in animals, where there is no rational soul. Thus, each of them [i.e. the vegetative, perceptive, and rational souls] is a different faculty that is not attached to the other. What we must know to resolve this doubt is that elemental bodies are prevented by their purely contrary nature from receiving life. The more you endeavor to destroy pure contrariety and bring a body towards the center that has no contrary, the more similar it becomes to the **[230]** celestial bodies, and it becomes worthy to that extent of receiving the potentiality of life from the separate governing principle. Moreover, the closer it comes to the midpoint [i.e. of the four elements], the more it becomes receptive to life. Eventually, the goal is reached, and it becomes impossible for it to come closer to centrality and to be more destructive of the contrary extremes. At that point, it receives a substance that is very similar in one respect to the separate[76] substance, just as the celestial substances received it and were connected with it. Then, at this juncture, what originated in this body before the presence of this substance in it

[74] That is, because it is the first organ to be created.

[75] Ibn Sīnā is here considering an objection to his claim that the soul is unitary. The objection states that, since the animal and vegetative souls are found separately in animals and plants respectively, the human soul must consist of three separable parts: vegetative soul, animal soul, and rational soul.

[76] Alternatively, immaterial (*mufāriq*) here and throughout this section.

will originate in it both from the separate substance as well as from this substance.[77]

An analogy with this in the natural sciences would be as follows. Imagine in place of the separate substance a fire, or indeed the sun, and in place of the body an entity that is affected by fire, say a sphere. Then the vegetative soul would correspond to being heated by the sun, the animal soul would correspond to being illuminated by it, and the human soul to igniting a fire in it. We state that a body that is affected as the sphere is may not be in a position with respect to what affects it to receive illumination, lighting, and igniting a fire in it, but may be in a position only to be heated and nothing else. Alternatively, it may be in a position to be heated by it, and may also be transparent or translucent, or related to it in such a way that it can be powerfully lit, so it will be heated by it as well as illuminated by it. Then the light that is cast upon it from the sun will also be the principle of heating, as is that separate principle itself, for the sun heats by radiation. If the sphere's receptivity is yet greater, and there is something within it that is capable of igniting by means of the cause that has the tendency to burn with its potentiality or radiation, then it will burst into flame, and the flame will have given rise to a body that resembles the separate substance in some respect.[78]

That flame will also be, along with the separate principle, the cause of both illumination and heat. If it were to remain on its own, illumination and heating would continue. In addition, it is possible that the heating might have existed on its own, or only the heating and illumination, in which case, what is subsequent [i.e. the flame] would not be a principle from which the precedent [i.e. heating and illumination] emanates. But if all three effects, heating, illumination, and fire, are combined, then everything that has been supposed to be subsequent [i.e. the flame] is also a principle for the precedent [i.e. heating and illumination], from which the precedent emanates.[79]

77 This paragraph relies on a theory according to which the temperament or composition of the human body is the most balanced of all animate beings, being centrally located between the four elements. As such, it is most worthy of receiving life (cf. Ibn Ṭufayl [29, 70–2]).

78 Perhaps Ibn Sīnā means that the flame will have given rise to a body that resembles the sun in some respect, which corresponds to the separate substance in the analogy.

79 The sense seems to be that first comes heating, illumination, (precedent) then fire (subsequent), and when all three are present, the fire leads in turn to heating and illumination, so what was supposed to be precedent will also be subsequent, which is analogous to the process that is initiated by the Active Intellect in the human soul.

That is how the faculties of the soul should be conceived. It has become clear for us from this analogy that the soul exists with the body, and does not originate from a body but from a substance that is an immaterial form.

[231] On using the states of the rational soul to infer the existence of the Active Intellect, and on explaining It in some respect

We state that the theoretical faculty in humans also emerges from potentiality to actuality by the illumination of a substance that has such an effect upon it. That is because nothing can emerge from potentiality into actuality without something that endows it with actuality; it cannot do so by itself. The actuality[80] with which the theoretical faculty is endowed is the form of the intelligibles. Hence, there is something that endows the soul with the form of the intelligibles, and imprints them upon it from its own substance. Thus, this entity must have the form of the intelligibles essentially, and it is therefore essentially an intellect. If it were merely a potential intellect there would be an impossible infinite regress, or else the regress would be blocked by something that is an intellect in substance, and is what causes everything that is a potential intellect to become an actual intellect. This cause will be sufficient on its own to render potential intellects into actual intellects. This is what is called the "Active Intellect," in comparison with the potential intellects that emerge into actuality, just as the material intellect is called the "passive intellect" in relation to it, and the faculty of representation is called another "passive intellect" in relation to it. The intellect that exists between the Active Intellect and the passive intellect is called the "acquired intellect." The relation of this Active Intellect to our souls, which are potential intellects, and to the intelligibles, which are potential intelligibles, is the same as the relation of the sun to our vision, which is a potential perceiver, and to colors, which are potential perceptibles. Thus, if such an effect, which is radiation, makes contact with the potential perceptibles, it makes them into actual perceptibles and makes vision into an actual perceiver.

The same applies to the Active Intellect, from which emanates a power that flows to imagined things, which are potentially intelligible, rendering them actually intelligible and rendering the potential intellect into an actual intellect. And just as the sun is itself perceived and is also a cause of

[80] Literally, action (*fiʿl*).

rendering something potentially perceptible into something actually perceptible, so also this substance [i.e. the Active Intellect] is itself intelligible and is also a cause of rendering all the intelligibles, which are potentially intelligible, actually intelligible. However, what is essentially intelligible is also essentially an intellect, for what is intelligible in essence is a form abstracted from matter, especially if it is abstract in itself, not abstracted by means of something else. This entity is also an intellect in actuality, so it is always actually intelligible in essence, and an intellect in actuality.

Al-Ghazālī, *The Rescuer from Error*

[77] Praise be to God, with whose praise every epistle and treatise begins, and blessings upon Muḥammad, the chosen one, prophet, and messenger, and upon his kin and companions who guide one from error.

You have asked me, my brother in religion, to convey to you the aim and secrets of the sciences, as well as the confusing intricacies of creeds, and to relate what I have endured in extricating truth from the mayhem of factions, with their differing approaches and methods, and how I have ventured to raise myself from the depths of conformity to the heights of insight. You have also asked me to relate, first, what I gleaned from theology; second, what I gathered[1] from the methods of the Instructionists,[2] who hold that truth is apprehended solely by conforming to the instruction of the imām; third, what I criticized of the methods of philosophizing; and finally, what I endorsed of [78] the method of mysticism. You have asked me to convey the nuggets of truth that I uncovered in the midst of my investigation into the doctrines of humanity, what diverted me from the spread of knowledge in Baghdād despite the large number of students, and what led me to resume teaching in Nishapur after a long absence. Therefore, I will hasten to comply with your demand, having determined the sincerity of your request, and will relate this to you, asking God for assistance, support, success, and refuge.

May God Almighty guide you and allow truth to lead you: you should know that the differences among people in sects and religions, and the

[1] Reading *iḥtawaytuhu* rather than *ijtawaytahu* (despised).

[2] The Instructionists (*Taʿlīmīyyūn*) are the Ismāʿīlīs, an Islamic sect who believe in "authoritative teaching in religion, which could be carried out only by a divinely chosen imām in every age after the prophet" (*EI* entry on Ismāʿīlīyya).

divergences among the masters[3] of various creeds, factions, and methods, is a deep ocean in which many have drowned and from which only a few have been saved. Each faction claims that they are **[79]** saved, and "each is content with what they have" [cf. Qur'ān 23:53, 30:32]. This was predicted by the Prince of the Messengers (the blessings of God be upon him), for he is the truthful and sincere one, who said: "My community will be divided into seventy-three factions, one of which will be saved." His prediction has almost come true.

I have persisted, ever since the prime of my youth and my tender years – all the way from my adolescence, before reaching the age of 20, until the present day, when I am over 50 – to plumb the depths of this ocean and to plunge into it boldly, not with diffident cowardice. I have attempted to penetrate every obscurity, grapple with every problem, tackle every predicament, examine the beliefs of every faction, and investigate the hidden creed of each sect **[80]**. I have done so in order to distinguish the honest person from the liar, and the orthodox from the heretic. I never let an esotericist go by without wanting to ascertain his esotericism, nor do I pass up an exotericist without wanting to know the outcome of his exotericism.[4] I never meet a philosopher without seeking to understand the underlying nature of his philosophy, a theologian without making an effort to become acquainted with the aim of his theology and dialectic, a mystic without aspiring to find the secret of his mysticism, an ascetic without scrutinizing the aim of his ascetic worship, and a blasphemous atheist[5] without prying **[81]** into the reasons behind the audacity of his atheism.

The thirst for apprehending things as they really are has been my preoccupation and principle from a very early age. It is part of my God-given instinct and nature, a matter of temperament not of choice or invention. Hence, I was freed from the bonds of conformity and my inherited beliefs were shattered while I was just a boy, since I observed that Christian boys grew up only to be Christians, Jewish boys only to be Jewish, and Muslim boys only to be Muslim. I also heard the Ḥadīth[6] attributed to the Prophet

[3] The Arabic term *imām* is being used in a loose sense here, not in the narrow sense of prayer leader.

[4] An esotericist (*bāṭinī*) is one who ascribes figurative meanings to certain Qur'ānic passages, and an exotericist (*ẓāhirī*) is one who insists on a literal reading.

[5] Literally, a Manichean denier of the attributes of God (*zindīqan muʿaṭṭilan*). However, Ghazālī seems to use both Arabic terms rather loosely, applying them sometimes to blasphemers or atheists in general.

[6] A Ḥadīth is a saying attributed to the prophet Muḥammad.

of God (may he be blessed by God) that states: "Every child is born in the natural state; his parents make him a Jew, Christian, or Magian." I was therefore inwardly moved to seek out the reality of this original nature, as well as the reality of the beliefs acquired out of conformity **[82]** to parents and teachers. I also sought to distinguish among these conformist beliefs about which there are disagreements in differentiating true from false, beginning with the instilled beliefs. I said to myself: "Since I seek to know things as they really are, I must first seek out the reality of knowledge itself." It became apparent to me that certain knowledge is that in which what is known is laid bare in such a way as to leave no room for doubt, and is unaccompanied by the possibility of error or illusion, to the point that the mind[7] cannot even conceive it. Rather, what is secure from error should be so closely associated with certainty, that if someone tried to show that it was false by turning stone into gold or a stick into a snake, for example, that would not make it doubtful or refute it. Thus, if I came to know that ten is greater than three, and someone said to me: "No, three is greater than ten, in proof of which I will turn this stick into a serpent," then went on to do so in plain view, I would not as a result of that come to doubt what I was cognizant of. The only outcome would be wonderment at how he is able to perform such a feat. As to doubt concerning what I know, there is none. Thus, I knew that whatever I did not know in this manner and was not certain of in this way was untrustworthy and insecure knowledge; and every knowledge that is insecure is not certain knowledge.

[83] Then I searched the sum of my knowledge and found myself devoid of knowledge characterized by this attribute, apart from sensory beliefs and necessary beliefs.[8] I said: "Now, after despair has set in, I have no hope of solving problems except with regard to what is evident, which are sensory beliefs and necessary beliefs. Hence, I must safeguard them first to make certain of my confidence in sensory beliefs and my security from error when it comes to necessary beliefs. Is it of the same kind as my former trust in conformist beliefs and the trust that most people have in theoretical beliefs?[9] Or is it a justified trust, which is neither deceptive nor confused?" **[84]** I proceeded in real earnest to contemplate sensory beliefs

7 Literally, the heart (*al-qalb*); but see Ghazālī's remarks on the "heart" at [151].

8 Ghazālī calls them, quite simply, "sensories" (*al-ḥissīyyāt*, or *al-maḥsūsāt*) and "necessaries" (*al-ḍarūrīyyāt*).

9 Alternatively, speculative beliefs or speculations (*naẓarīyyāt*).

and necessary beliefs, to see whether I could make myself doubt them. After a lengthy process of doubt, my mind did not allow me to maintain my trust in sensory beliefs either, and began gradually to cast doubt on them, saying: "Where does this confidence in sensory beliefs come from? The strongest sense is vision, which looks at a shadow and sees that it is stationary, and judges that there is no motion. But then as a result of experience and observation, after an hour, it is cognizant that the shadow is indeed moving. Moreover, it finds that it did not move suddenly, all at once, but rather incrementally atom by atom, in such a way that it was never actually stationary. Likewise, vision looks at a celestial body and sees that it is small, around the size of a dinar, but then geometrical proofs indicate that it is in fact larger than the earth in size. In this and other such sensory matters, the judge of sensation makes its judgments, but the judge of reason[10] then judges it to be false and disproves it irrefutably." So I said: "My confidence in sensory beliefs has also been annulled. Perhaps one can only trust the rational beliefs,[11] which are among the first principles, such as the statements, 'Ten is greater than three,' 'Negation and affirmation cannot coexist in the same thing,'[12] and 'The same thing cannot be both originated and eternal, or existent and nonexistent, or necessary and impossible'" **[85]**. The sensory beliefs replied: "How can you be sure that your confidence in rational beliefs is not like that in sensory beliefs? You trusted in me, but the judge of reason disproved me. Were it not for the judge of reason, you would have continued to believe me. Perhaps behind rational apprehension there is another judge who, if he were to manifest himself, would disprove the judgment of reason, just as the judge of reason manifested himself to disprove the judgments of sense perception. The fact that such an apprehension has not manifested itself does not indicate that it is impossible."

My mind hesitated a while before responding to that. Meanwhile, sense perception underscored the problem by referring to dreams, saying: "Do you not believe things in dreams and imagine situations that you believe to be permanent and stable, never doubting them while you are in that state? And do you not then wake up and come to know that all your

[10] In this text, the Arabic term *ʿaql* (often used to translate the Greek *nous*) is sometimes translated as reason and sometimes as intellect.

[11] It is clear from what follows that the rational beliefs (*al-ʿaqlīyyāt*) are the same as the necessary beliefs (*ḍarūrīyyāt*).

[12] Alternatively, something cannot be affirmed and denied at once.

imaginings and beliefs were baseless and futile? Why are you so sure that everything that you believe in your waking state on the basis of the senses or reason is true in relation to your current state? A state may arise that bears the same relation to your waking state as your waking state does to your dream state. By comparison to that state your waking state would be like sleep. If such a state were to occur, you would become certain that all the things conjured up by your reason were inconsequential imaginings. Perhaps that state is what the mystics hold to be their state, for they claim to have a vision in their states when they are immersed in themselves and lose awareness of their senses, which does not agree with these rational beliefs.[13] Or perhaps that state is death, for the Prophet of God (blessings be upon him) said: 'People are asleep, and when they die **[86]** they wake up.' Thus, perhaps the temporal life is slumber by comparison with the afterlife, and when you die things will appear differently to you from the way they do now. At that point, you will be told: 'We have removed your veil and your vision is now acute' [Qur'ān 50:22]."

When these notions occurred to me and made an impression on my mind, I sought a cure but found none. For they could only be rebutted with a proof, and a proof can only be constructed by combining the first [principles of] knowledge.[14] If these are not given, then it is impossible to arrange a proof. This disease defied all cure and lasted for almost two months, during which I embraced the sophistical[15] creed in actual fact, though not in speech nor expression. Eventually, God cured me of this disease and my mind was restored to health and balance. The rational necessary beliefs were once again accepted and trusted, both securely and certainly. This did not come about by composing a proof or by an arrangement of words, but rather by a light that God Almighty cast into my breast, which is the key to the greater part of cognizance. Whoever supposes that enlightenment[16] depends upon explicit proofs has **[87]** narrowed the expanse of God's mercy. The Prophet of God was asked about the meaning of "opening" in the Qur'ānic verse: "Whomever God desires to guide, He opens his heart to Islam" [Qur'ān 6:125]. He said: "It is a light that God Almighty casts into the heart." He was asked: "What

[13] For more on the state (*ḥāl*) of the Islamic mystics or Ṣūfīs, see below (especially [140–1]).
[14] Ghazālī has already stated that these include the necessary truths that he has rejected earlier.
[15] Though Ghazālī writes "sophistical creed" (*madhhab al-safsaṭah*), his arguments are more reminiscent of the ancient skeptics than the sophists.
[16] Literally, uncovering or removing the veil (as in the Qur'ānic passage quoted above).

is its sign?" He replied: "Aversion to the realm of conceit and devotion to the realm of eternity." He also said (blessings be upon him): "God Almighty created people in darkness then sprinkled them with his light." Enlightenment must be sought from that light, which flows from God's bounty at certain times and must be monitored closely. As the Prophet (peace be upon him) has said: "Your Lord sends breaths [of grace] in the days of your lifetime; put yourselves in their way" **[88]**. The intention behind these statements is that the utmost efforts should be made in seeking [knowledge], right up to the point that one ends up seeking what cannot be sought. For first principles are not sought but are present, and if what is present is sought it will be lost and will disappear. Moreover, whoever seeks what cannot be sought cannot be accused of falling short in seeking what can.[17]

[89] After God Almighty cured me of this disease by His grace and all-embracing generosity, I narrowed down the seekers of knowledge to four factions: (i) Theologians, who claim that they are the party of opinion and theoretical speculation; (ii) Esotericists, who claim that they are the party of instruction and are privileged to receive instruction from the infallible imām; (iii) Philosophers, who claim that they are the party of logic and demonstration; and (iv) Mystics, who claim that they alone are privileged to be in the presence[18] of God and are the party of vision and illumination. I said to myself: "Truth must not lie outside the purview of these four types, for they are the ones who follow the paths of truth-seeking. If truth eludes them all, then I have no hope of apprehending it, for there is no point in reverting to conformism once one has left it behind. It is a precondition of being a conformist **[90]** that the conformist not know that he is merely conforming. Once he comes to know that, the glass of conformity is fractured and the damage is irreparable. It cannot be reassembled using the techniques of restoration and renovation, but must rather be melted down in the fire and created all over again."

Without further ado, I prepared to travel this course of truth-seeking and to detail what these factions had accomplished, beginning with the

[17] This passage is somewhat obscure. Perhaps the sense is as follows: Ghazālī sought what could be sought right up to the point of seeking what cannot be sought (first principles). This is not a futile enterprise, since, given that he got this far, he can be said to have gone as far as one can go in seeking knowledge, and cannot be accused of not going far enough.

[18] Islamic mystics, or Ṣūfīs, have used various terms to denote a state of proximity to God, one of which is presence (*ḥadrah*), to which Ghazālī here refers.

science of theology, proceeding to philosophy, going on to esoteric instruction, and ending with mysticism.

[91] I began with theology, which I acquired and grasped intellectually by reading the works of the reputable authorities among the theologians and by writing some works of my own. I found it to be a science that fulfilled its purpose but not mine. Its purpose was to preserve the beliefs of the orthodox and to protect them from the misinformation of the heretics. By means of His messenger, God Almighty handed down to His worshippers [92] a doctrine that is the truth, which contains what is needed for their well-being in both religious and temporal matters, and cognizance of which is pronounced by the Qur'ān and Ḥadīth. Then the devil insinuated to the heretics certain things that were contrary to orthodoxy, which they eagerly embraced and with which they almost succeeded in confounding the party of the doctrine of truth. So God Almighty gave rise to the theologians and motivated them to advocate orthodoxy with systematic discourse that revealed the deceptions of the heretical innovators and their departures from accepted orthodoxy. That is how the science of theology and its practitioners arose. Some of the theologians have carried out what God Almighty appointed them to do and have defended orthodoxy admirably. They have fought on behalf of the doctrine received through the acceptance of prophecy and have corrected the innovations of the heretics. However, in doing so, they have relied on premises that they took over from their opponents, which their opponents are required to acknowledge either on the basis of conformity to tradition, or consensus of the community, or mere acceptance of the Qur'ān and Ḥadīth. Most of their endeavors consist in exposing the contradictions of their opponents and in criticizing the implications of their tenets. This was of little use for someone who only accepts necessary truths. Thus, theology was not sufficient for my needs and did not provide a cure for my disease. To be sure, as the art of theology developed and was practiced abundantly over a long period of time, the theologians aspired to defend orthodoxy [93] by investigating the reality of things, and examined substances, accidents, and their principles. However, since that was not the main purpose of their science, their discourse did not attain the ultimate goal in this regard and did not achieve the total elimination of the obscure perplexities to be found in the disagreements among humanity. I am not ruling out the possibility that this may have been achieved for others – indeed, I do not doubt that it was achieved for some – but the achievement will have been

tainted by conformity to tradition with respect to certain things that are not first principles. In any case, my purpose now is to set out my own case, not to deny that others have been cured by theology. Medications differ depending on the disease, and there are many medications that benefit one patient and harm another.

[94] After finishing with the science of theology, I moved on to the science of philosophy. I knew with certainty that one cannot understand the failings of a certain type of science unless one reaches the utmost limit of that science. One must become equal with the most knowledgeable of its practitioners, then exceed them and surpass their level, so that one is acquainted with the intricacies and confusions that even the practitioners themselves are not acquainted with. Only then is it possible to take someone's claims about its failings to be true. I found that none of the religious scholars[19] of Islam had devoted their concerted efforts to that end.

The discourses in the books of the theologians where they busied themselves with responding to the philosophers consisted of some stray convoluted statements, which were clearly contradictory and defective. No person of ordinary intellect would be duped by them, much less someone who claims mastery of the subtleties **[95]** of the sciences. I knew that refuting the creed before understanding it and becoming acquainted with its underlying nature was like taking a shot in the dark. Therefore, I forged ahead in earnest and exerted myself to acquire that science from books, simply by reading on my own without the help of an instructor. I did so during my free time, when I was not engaged in writing and teaching the religious sciences, for at that time I was charged with teaching and advising three hundred students in Baghdād. Thanks to God Almighty, I was able merely by reading philosophy during these stolen hours to reach the utmost limits of that science in less than two years. Then I devoted another year to further reflecting upon it after having understood it, returning to it, poring over it again, and reexamining its intricacies and confusions. In this way, I managed to acquaint myself indubitably with its ruses, deceptions, justifications, and illusions.[20]

Let me give you an account of the philosophers and the end result of the philosophical sciences. I found the philosophers to be divided into

[19] The term *ʿālim* (plural *ʿulamā'*), which can simply mean knowledgeable person, is widely used to denote a member of the class of scholars who, in the absence of a clergy, served as a kind of Islamic religious establishment.

[20] Literally, imaginative representation (*takhyīl*).

a number of categories, and the philosophical sciences to be split into a number of divisions. Despite their many subdivisions, they all carry the stigma of blasphemy and apostasy. Nevertheless, there are vast variations among the philosophers – most ancient, ancient, later, and more recent – in terms of their distance from and proximity to the truth **[96]**. You should know that, despite differences among the philosophers and notwithstanding the variety of philosophical creeds, they may be classified into three categories: materialists, naturalists, and theists.

The first type, the materialists, are an ancient faction who renounced the Creator, Governor, Knower, and Almighty. They claimed that the universe has always existed as it is without a creator, and that animals come from seed and seed from animals, and that this has always occurred and will occur forever. These are the atheists.

The second category, the naturalists, are a group of people who actively investigated the natural world, including the wonders of animals and plants. They delved deeply into the science of anatomy, dissecting the organs of animals and discovering there the marvels created by God Almighty and the wonders of His wisdom. This obliged them **[97]** to admit the existence of a wise Creator who is apprised of the goals of things and their purposes. No one can become acquainted with anatomy and the marvelous uses of organs without acquiring necessary knowledge of the perfection bestowed by the Artisan on the structures of animals, especially the structure of human beings. However, as a result of their intense investigations into nature, it became clear to these philosophers how efficacious a balanced temperament[21] was in sustaining the animal faculties. They assumed that the rational faculty in humans was also dependent upon the human temperament, and that it would be extinguished when the temperament expired, thereby ceasing to exist. Since, as they claim, it is irrational for the nonexistent to return to life, they concluded that the soul dies and does not return. Thus, they denied the afterlife, heaven and hell, judgment and restoration, and resurrection and reckoning, and they were left with no reward for obedience and no punishment for transgression. Unfettered by that, they proceeded to indulge themselves in sensual pleasures like grazing sheep. These are blasphemers also, since the basis of faith is faith in God and the Day of Judgment, and even though they do believe in God and His attributes, they renounce the Day of Judgment.

[21] Literally, mixture (*mizāj*); i.e. a balanced mixture of the four humors in the body.

The third category, the theists, consists of the less ancient of the three groups of philosophers, such as Socrates, who was the teacher of Plato, and Plato the teacher of Aristotle **[98]**, and Aristotle himself, who systematized logic for them, organized the sciences, rendered accurate what had been imprecise, and brought to maturity those of their sciences that were still in their infancy. The theists generally responded to the first two categories of philosophers, the materialists and naturalists, and in exposing their shortcomings relieved others of the task. "God spared the faithful from combat" [Qur'ān 33:25] due to the in-fighting of their opponents. Moreover, Aristotle refuted Plato, Socrates, and the other theists before them, in such a thoroughgoing fashion that he ended up dissociating himself from all of them. But he also retained some remnants of their blasphemous and heretical vices, which he was not able to shed. Hence, it is necessary to consider all the theist philosophers blasphemous, including their followers among the Islamic philosophers, such as Ibn Sīnā **[99]**, al-Fārābī, and others. None of the other Islamic philosophers transmitted the knowledge of Aristotle as did these two men. What was transmitted by others is so full of commotion and confusion as to bewilder the heart of the reader and prevent him from understanding – and what cannot be understood can neither be rejected nor accepted. The sum total of Aristotle's genuine philosophy, as transmitted by these two men, can be divided into three parts: what must be considered blasphemous, what must be considered heretical, and what must not be denied at all. I will show this in what follows.

[100] You should know that, for our present purpose, their sciences have six branches: mathematical, logical, metaphysical,[22] physical, political, and ethical.

(1) The mathematical sciences pertain to the sciences of arithmetic, geometry, and astronomy,[23] and none of them is relevant to religious matters, either by way of negation or affirmation. Rather, these are demonstrative matters that one cannot deny once one has understood them and become cognizant of them. Nevertheless, mathematics has given rise to two types of harm.

[22] Literally, divine (*ilāhīyyah*) sciences. However, Ghazālī does not mean theology, but rather the reference is to *al-ilāhīyyāt*, the philosophical study of divine matters, which is the term often used to denote metaphysics in general, or an important portion of metaphysics (which is also known more literally as *mā baᶜd al-ṭabīᶜah*, what comes after physics).

[23] Ghazālī seems to use *ᶜilm hay'at al-ᶜālam* to denote astronomy and *ᶜilm al-nujūm* to denote astrology in this text.

The first is that a person who examines mathematics comes to marvel at its subtleties and the compelling nature of its demonstrations, and because of this he takes on a favorable attitude towards the philosophers. He supposes that all their sciences are as clear as this science and that all their demonstrations are just as firm. Then, since he has heard of the philosophers' blasphemy, atheism,[24] and slackness when it comes to the religious law, he becomes blasphemous merely by conforming to the philosophical tradition **[101]**. He says: "If religion were true, it could not have escaped these mathematicians, given the scrutiny they give to their science." Moreover, if he is cognizant of what people say about the philosophers' blasphemy and renunciation of religion, he infers that truth lies in the renunciation and denial of religion. I have seen so many stray from the truth solely on this pretext without having any other grounds for doing so. One may say to such a person: "Someone who is proficient in one art need not be so in every art. Thus, one who is versed in jurisprudence and theology need not be versed in medicine, and one who is ignorant of rational[25] science may not be ignorant of grammar. For each art has its practitioners who have attained a degree of skill and distinction in that particular art, and who may well be obtuse and ignorant in other arts. The discourse of the ancient philosophers in mathematics is demonstrative, while in metaphysics it is merely conjectural. This can be recognized only by someone who has experienced it and delved into it." However, if this argument is conveyed to the person who becomes an apostate by conforming to philosophical tradition[26] and it is not accepted by him, he will instead be moved by the dominance of passion, vain desires, and a penchant for appearing clever to insist on his favorable attitude towards the philosophers in all the sciences. Because of this great harm, everyone who explores these sciences ought to be restrained. Even though the mathematical sciences are not concerned with religious matters **[102]**, they are among the principal[27] philosophical sciences, and the evil and malevolence of the philosophers infects those who study them. Few delve into them without losing their religion and slipping off the bonds of piety.

[24] Literally, denial of God's attributes (*taʿṭīlihim*).
[25] The Arabic term is *al-ʿaqlīyyāt*; presumably, Ghazālī has in mind here the philosophical sciences, including natural science (cf. [133], where these sciences are contrasted with the religious sciences).
[26] Omitting *wa* (and).
[27] Alternatively, they [supply] some of the principles of their sciences (*mabādi' ʿulūmihim*).

The second harm originates with an ignorant friend of Islam, who supposes that religion must be defended by denying every science attributed to the philosophers. He goes on to deny all their sciences and accuses them of ignorance, to the point that he denies what they say about the solar and lunar eclipses and alleges that it is contrary to religious law. When this comes to the attention of those who have become cognizant of these things by way of absolute demonstrations, they do not come to doubt their demonstrations, but rather come to believe that Islam is based on ignorance and a denial of absolute demonstrations, which just increases their love of philosophy and their aversion to Islam. Anyone who supposes that religion is to be defended by denying these sciences has committed a great offense against Islam. There is nothing in the religious law that either negates or affirms these sciences, nor is there anything in these sciences that concerns religious matters. The Prophet (blessings upon him) said: "The sun and the moon are two of the signs of God, and they are not eclipsed for anyone's death or life. If you see an eclipse, recollect God Almighty and pray to him in fear" **[103]**. There is nothing in this to deny the science of arithmetic in particular, which informs us of the orbits of the sun and moon, their conjunction, and their opposition. As for the saying of the Prophet (peace be upon him): "But when God manifests Himself to something, it submits to Him," this further addition to the above saying is not found at all in authentic collections of Ḥadīths.[28] That is the correct judgment concerning mathematics and its harm.

(2) The logical sciences are not in any way relevant to religion, either by way of negation or affirmation. Rather, they are the theoretical investigation of the methods of proof and syllogism, the conditions on the premises of demonstrations and their manner of combination, as well as the conditions on valid definitions and their manner of construction. Knowledge consists either of conception, cognizance of which proceeds by means of **[104]** definition, or assent, cognizance of which proceeds by means of demonstration. There is nothing here that ought to be denied. Rather, what the logicians say is of the same kind as what has been said about proofs by the theologians and other theoreticians, though the logicians differ in the expressions and terms they use, and they go much further in their

[28] It is not clear how this addition pertains to Ghazālī's present point and why he is keen to deny it. Perhaps this addition to the Ḥadīth, if authentic, would show a more direct link between religion and eclipses.

characterizations and distinctions. An example of their discourse in logic would be the statement: "If it is affirmed that every A is B, then that implies that some B is A," e.g., "If it is affirmed that every human is an animal, then that implies that some animal is a human." They express this by saying that the converse of a universal affirmative proposition is a particular affirmative proposition. What relevance does this have to the requirements of religion, that it should be renounced or denied? If it is denied, this will only make logicians take a dim view of the intellect of the person who denies it **[105]**, and indeed of the religion that is alleged to depend on such a denial. To be sure, the logicians are somewhat unfair in practicing their science, in that they assemble the conditions that are known necessarily to endow a demonstration with certainty, but since they are unable to satisfy these conditions when it comes to religious matters, they relax them to a great extent. Likewise, those who examine logic may admire its clarity and may suppose that the blasphemies reported of logicians are supported by similarly clear demonstrations. They might then promptly blaspheme before attaining the study of divine metaphysics. This harm also afflicts logic.[29]

(3) The science of physics is the investigation of the celestial realm and the planets, as well as what lies beneath them: the simple bodies, such as water, air, earth, and fire, and the composite bodies, such as animals, plants, and minerals. It also investigates the causes of their changes, transformations, and mixtures. As such, it is comparable to medicine, which investigates the human body, its principal and subsidiary organs, and the causes of the transformation of its temperament. Just as it is not one of the provisions of religion to deny the science of medicine, it is also not one of its provisions to deny the science of physics except with regard to the specific issues mentioned in our book, "The Incoherence **[106]** of the Philosophers" (*Tahāfut al-Falāsifah*). All other issues that should be opposed turn out on further contemplation to be subsumed under these. Our opposition in all these cases is based upon the knowledge that nature is subject to God Almighty and does not function by itself, but is rather an instrument for its Creator. The sun, moon, stars, and other natural entities are subject to His command and none of them acts in and of itself.[30]

[29] That is, as it does mathematics.
[30] Alternatively, of its essence and by its essence (*bi-dhātihi wa ʿan dhātihi*).

(4) Metaphysics contains most of the errors of the philosophers, for they are not able to fulfill the conditions on demonstrations that are set down in logic, and they therefore disagree considerably among themselves about metaphysical questions. Aristotle's position in metaphysics is close to that of the Islamic philosophers, as transmitted by al-Fārābī and Ibn Sīnā. The sum total of their errors can be reduced to twenty basic ones; they should be considered blasphemous on three counts and heretical on seventeen counts. We have composed the work "The Incoherence" (*al-Tahāfut*) in order to refute their positions on these twenty issues. The three issues on which they have opposed all Muslims are as follows. First, they state that bodies are not resurrected in the afterlife, but rather that reward and punishment are meted out simply to souls and that punishments are spiritual, not **[107]** corporeal. They are right to affirm the spiritual punishments, which are indeed present, but they are wrong to deny corporeal punishments, and have blasphemed against the religious law with this utterance. Second, they state that: "God Almighty knows universals not particulars," which is also clear blasphemy. Rather, the truth is: "An atom's weight does not escape Him in the heavens nor on earth" [Qur'ān 34:3]. Third, they assert that the world is preeternal and has always existed. No Muslim has ventured to make any of these pronouncements.

As for the other seventeen points besides these, such as their denial of God's attributes, their statement that God knows by His essence not by what is added to His essence, and similar things, their position is close to that of the Muᶜtazilites,[31] who ought not to be **[108]** considered blasphemous for such things. In our book "Criterion **[109]** of the Difference between Islam and Atheism" (*Fayṣal al-Tafriqah bayn al-Islām wal-Zandaqah*) we have made clear that it is a corrupt opinion that rushes to consider blasphemous any creed that is contrary to one's own.

(5) Their entire discourse in the political sciences is derived from the beneficial maxims relating to temporal matters and monarchical rule. They simply took them from the books of God that were revealed to the prophets and the maxims handed down by the precursors of prophets.

(6) In ethics, their entire discourse comes down to the enumeration of the attributes of the soul and its character,[32] the genera and species

[31] An Islamic philosophical and theological movement that originated in the eighth century AD (second century AH) that aimed to provide a rationalistic account of Islamic doctrine.

[32] Alternatively, its ethics (*akhlāqihā*).

of souls, and how to treat and tame souls. This is simply taken from the discourse of the mystics, who are preoccupied with the divine and who diligently recollect God Almighty, oppose passion, and tread the path to God by avoiding worldly pleasures. In the course of their spiritual exertion they have uncovered people's characters, defects, and their pernicious actions. Hence, they proclaimed these things, and the philosophers took this and intermingled it with their own discourse, in a bid to revamp and promote their falsehoods. Such groups, who are preoccupied with the divine, existed in the era of the philosophers **[110]**, as indeed in all other eras, since God does not allow the world to be empty of them, for they are the pillars of the earth. Mercy descends upon the people of the earth thanks to their blessings, as has been reported in the Ḥadīth of the Prophet (blessings upon him): "By virtue of them you will have rain, thanks to them you will have prosperity, and from them were drawn the people of the Cave."[33] They have been present in all previous eras, as mentioned in the Qur'ān. Two harms have resulted from the philosophers' blending of prophetic discourse and mystical discourse in their books, one pertaining to its acceptance and the other to its rejection.

The harm pertaining to its rejection is a considerable one, since a group of weak people thinks that the discourse set down in their books, which is mixed with falsehood, ought to be shunned altogether and not repeated, but rather denounced to everyone who repeats it. Since they heard this discourse originally from the philosophers, their weak intellects jumped to the conclusion that it was false simply because those who professed it were dishonest. It is as though someone hears a Christian make the statement: "There is no God but God, Jesus is the prophet of God," and goes on to deny it, saying: "This is the discourse of Christians." Such a person does not pause long enough to consider whether the Christian is blasphemous in virtue of this statement or in virtue of his denial of the prophecy of Muḥammad (blessings and peace be upon him). If he is only blasphemous with regard to this denial, he ought not to be opposed when it comes to something true in itself and different from his blasphemy **[111]**, even though it is also true according to him. This is a habit of weak intellects, who recognize truth on the basis of men, rather than men on the basis of truth. Instead, a rational person emulates the supremely rational

33 The reference is to Qur'ān Sūrah 18, which relates the story of a small group of righteous men who sought refuge from persecution in a cave and were saved from their pursuers by God.

ᶜAlī bin Abī Ṭalib[34] (may God be pleased with him) who said: "Do not recognize truth on the basis of men; rather, recognize the truth first, then you will recognize the holders of truth." Thus, the cognizant rational person recognizes the truth, and then examines the statement itself. If it is true, he accepts it regardless of whether the person who made the statement is a liar or an honest person. Indeed, he may even strive to seize the truth from the statements of those who are in error, knowing full well that gold is mined among dirt and sand. The moneychanger is none the worse for having put his hand into the counterfeiter's bag and extracting pure gold from among the fakes and forgeries, so long as his eyesight is to be trusted. However, the counterfeiter is to be prevented from doing business with the rustic villager, not with the sharp-eyed moneychanger; the clumsy beginner is to be barred from the seashore, not the proficient swimmer; and the boy is to be stopped from touching the snake, not the skilled snake charmer.

Since the assumption that predominates in most people is that of their own proficiency [112], skill, soundness of intellect, and perfect ability to distinguish truth from falsehood and guidance from error, it is necessary to shut the door to restrict the multitude from reading the books of those in error as far as possible. For they will not be safe from the second harm to be mentioned, even if they escape the first.

Some of the passages set down in our works on the secrets of the religious sciences have elicited objections from a group of those who have not inwardly mastered the sciences and have not penetrated the furthest goals of creeds. They have claimed that these passages are taken from the discourse of the ancient philosophers, even though some of them are the innovations of my mind (for it is not unlikely for two footprints to coincide), while others are to be found in religious books, and most coincide in meaning with what is found in the works of mysticism. Still, even if this discourse could be found only in the books of the ancient philosophers, why should it be shunned and discarded, if it is rational in itself, supported by demonstration, and not contrary to the Qur'ān and Ḥadīth? If we were to set the precedent that all truths that had ever occurred to a falsifier were to be avoided, then it would follow that much of the truth would have to be abandoned, including many verses from the Qur'ān, the sayings of the Prophet, the narratives of our [113]

34 The fourth caliph of Islām and son-in-law of the prophet Muḥammad.

ancestors, and the statements of sages and mystics. All these would have to be discarded simply because the author of the work "The Brethren of Purity"[35] (*Ikhwān al-Ṣafā*) mentioned them in his book, citing them in order to win over the hearts of the simple-minded to his falsehoods. This would also enable the falsifiers to wrest the truth from our hands simply by setting it down in their own books.

At the very least, a knowledgeable person should be distinguishable from a common ignorant person. Accordingly, honey should not be eschewed if it is found in the cupping glass and one verifies [114] that the cupping glass does not change the essence of honey. The natural distaste that one feels towards it is based on a widespread misconception that the cupping glass is made only for unclean blood. Thus, it is assumed that the blood is unclean because it is found in the cupping glass, not due to an attribute of its essence. If this attribute does not exist in honey, its presence in that container will not endow it with that attribute, and one ought not necessarily ascribe impurity to it. This is a mistaken illusion that prevails among most human beings. If you make a statement, attributing it to someone they think highly of, they will accept it even if it is false; and if you attribute it to someone they hold in disregard, they will reject it even if it is true. They always recognize the truth by the men rather than the men by the truth, and that is the epitome of error. That is the harm due to rejection.

The second harm is that of acceptance. Those who examine the books of the "Brethren of Purity" and others, on finding that they mix their own discourse with wise prophetic maxims and mystical statements, may approve of them, accept them, and adopt a favorable stance towards them. They will then also hasten to accept the falsehoods that are intermingled with them, due to the favorable stance adopted towards what they have seen and approved of. This amounts to a kind of enticement to falsehood.

On account of this harm, access to their books should be restricted because of the [115] deceit and danger that they contain. Just as one must protect unskilled swimmers from perilous shores, people must be shielded from reading philosophical books. And just as boys must be held back from touching snakes, people must be guarded against hearing the muddled statements of the philosophers. The snake charmer must

[35] This philosophical work, a compilation of the teachings of a group of Islamic scholars in the tenth–eleventh centuries AD (fourth–fifth centuries AH), contains a considerable body of cosmological and metaphysical doctrine influenced both by Aristotle and neo-Platonism.

not handle the snake in front of his young son, if he knows that he will emulate him and suppose that he is like him. Rather, he must urge him to be wary of the snake by being cautious and by refraining from touching it while he is in his presence. Those with secure knowledge[36] should proceed in a similar fashion. Furthermore, the proficient snake charmer who can handle the snake and distinguish between the antidote and the poison, extracting the antidote and neutralizing the poison, should not withhold the antidote from someone who needs it. Similarly, the astute and sharp-eyed moneychanger who puts his hand into the counterfeiter's bag, withdrawing the pure gold and rejecting the fakes and forgeries, should not deny the good and acceptable coins to those in need. The same applies to those with knowledge. In addition, if someone in need of the antidote finds it repugnant once he knows that it is extracted from the snake, which is the source of the poison itself, he must be made to recognize his mistake. A poor person in need of money who snubs the gold withdrawn from the counterfeiter's bag must likewise be alerted to the fact that his distaste for it [116] is pure ignorance and will be the cause of his being denied the benefit that he seeks. He must be made aware of the fact that proximity between the fake and the genuine does not render the genuine fake, just as it does not render the fake genuine. Similarly, proximity between truth and falsehood does not render the true false, no more than it renders the false true.

That is all that we wanted to say concerning the harms of philosophy and its confusions.[37]

[130] When I was done with these sciences, I turned my energies to the way of mysticism and came to know that their method is brought about by a combination of knowledge and practice. The objective of their knowledge is to overcome the obstacles found in the soul. They free the soul of blameworthy characteristics and malicious attributes in order to cleanse the heart of everything but God Almighty and adorn it with the recollection of God.

The knowledge associated with mysticism was easier for me than the practice. I began to acquire their knowledge by [131] reading their books, such as Abū Ṭālib al-Makkī's "Nourishment for the Heart" (*Qūt al-Qulūb*), the works of al-Ḥārith al-Muḥāsibī, and the selections handed

[36] This is a variant of *al-rāsikhūn fil-ʿilm*, a common Qur'ānic phrase meaning those secure in knowledge, or with thorough mastery of knowledge.

[37] A section of the text is here omitted, containing Ghazālī's critique of the Instructionists.

down to us from al-Junayd, al-Shiblī, and Abū Yazīd [132] al-Bisṭāmī (may God sanctify their souls), as well as other masters.[38] I did so until I had ascertained the underlying purpose of their science and had acquired what could be acquired of their way through teaching and oral instruction. It became apparent to me that what was most distinctive about them and specific to them was what could not be attained through teaching but rather through "tasting," the "state," and a "transformation of attributes."[39] There is a world of difference between knowing the definitions of health and satiety, their causes, and their preconditions, and actually being healthy and satiated. Likewise, there is a world of difference between being cognizant of the definition of inebriation, which denotes a state that comes about as a result of vapors rising from the stomach and overwhelming the sources of thought, and actually being inebriated. Indeed, the inebriated person is not cognizant of the definition of inebriation, for his knowledge while he is inebriated is nonexistent [133]. By contrast, the sober person knows the definition of inebriation and its basis, although he bears no trace of inebriation. Furthermore, a doctor who is in a diseased state knows the definition of health, its causes, and remedies, even though he is lacking in health. There is a similar difference between knowing the reality of asceticism, its preconditions, and its causes, and the soul's actually being in a state of asceticism and renunciation of the world.

I came to know with certainty that the mystics were the masters of states[40] rather than statements, and that I had acquired what I could by way[41] of knowledge. All that remained was what could not be attained through oral instruction and teaching, but only through tasting and conduct.[42] Thanks to the sciences that I had practiced and the various approaches I had taken in the course of my investigation into both the religious and rational sciences, I had acquired certain faith in God Almighty, prophecy, and the Day of Judgment.[43] These three foundations of faith had become entrenched in my soul, not [134] as a result of a specific and

[38] These are Ṣūfī masters or figures in Islamic asceticism.

[39] Ṣūfī terms denoting aspects of the mystical experience.

[40] The reference is to the mystical state (*ḥāl*, plural *aḥwāl*) of proximity to God.

[41] Alternatively, by the method (*ṭarīq*) of knowledge.

[42] Alternatively, following the mystical path (*sulūk*).

[43] Ghazālī seems to be saying that, in addition to the necessary truths (and sensory truths?) acquired by means of the light from God before his foray into the sciences, he also picked up the basic tenets of monotheism along the way, in the course of investigating theology and philosophy. Notice that they are acquired in a variety of ways and not as a result of one clear source, or on the basis of a single foundation.

explicit proof, but rather due to reasons, indications, and experiences, the details of which do not lend themselves to a brief summary. It had also become apparent to me that I had no hope of achieving happiness in the afterlife except through piety and by barring the soul from passion. The first step is to sever the heart's attachment to this world, by means of aversion to the realm of conceit, devotion to eternal life, and exertion of one's utmost efforts to God Almighty. This can come about only by turning away from fame and wealth, as well as by releasing oneself from all preoccupations and attachments. When I took note of my own situation, I found myself immersed in attachments, which closed in on me from all sides. Then I pondered my professional duties, the best of which were tutoring and teaching, and found that I was engaged in inconsequential sciences, which were of no benefit when it came to the pursuit of the afterlife. After that, I reflected upon the intention behind my teaching and found that it was not done in the service of God Almighty, but rather that its entire motivation was the pursuit of fame and the impetus behind it was the enhancement of reputation. I became certain that I was on the edge of a dangerous precipice and on the verge of hellfire, if I did not devote myself to rectify my situation.

[135] I reflected on the matter for some time, while I was still in a position to make a choice.[44] One day, I would be determined to leave Baghdād and walk out on my whole situation, and the next I would lose my determination entirely. I put one step forward then took another back. My desire to pursue the afterlife would take hold one morning, only to be dispersed by the forces of appetite by evening. The temptations of the temporal world enchained me and tugged at me to remain, while the voice of faith cried out: "Depart! Depart! You have only a short time left to live, you have a long journey ahead, and your knowledge and practice are all hypocrisy and illusion. If not now, when will you prepare for the afterlife? If you do not sever these attachments now, when will you do so?" At that point, my resolve would be renewed and I would become determined once again to escape and take flight. But then the devil would reappear, saying: "This is a passing phase. Do not succumb to it whatever you do, because it will be quick to lapse. If you give in to it and leave behind this extensive fame, this carefree prestigious position, and a settled situation

[44] As Ghazālī explains below, after a period of six months, it ceased to be a matter of choice.

that is uncontested by opponents, you may look back one day and find that it is not easy to return."

[136] For almost six months, starting in the month of Rajab 488 AH [July–August 1095 AD], I swung between the temptations of the temporal world and the call of the afterlife. Finally, by the sixth month, it ceased to be a matter of choice and became one of necessity, for God locked up my tongue and I became incapable of teaching. I would exert myself to lecture for even one day to satisfy the hearts of those around me, but my tongue would not utter a single word, and I would be completely incapable of doing so. Obstruction of the tongue eventually led to desolation of the heart, which in turn brought with it a breakdown of the faculty that digests and assimilates food and drink; I could not even keep down broth or digest a single bite. This led to a weakening of all my faculties and the doctors lost hope for a cure. They said: "This is an affliction of the heart that has spread to the temperament, so the only way to cure it is by revival of the heart and removal of the derangement."

When I became aware of my incapacity and the choice was really out of my hands, I sought refuge in God Almighty in dire need and utter desperation, and was answered by Him "who responds to the one in need when he calls upon him" [Qur'ān 27:62]. He made it easier for me to turn away from fame and wealth **[137]**, as well as from family, children, and friends. Outwardly, I expressed my resolution to go to Mecca to perform the pilgrimage, while arranging silently to travel to Syria, so that the caliph and all my friends would not be apprised of my decision to take up residence in Syria. To this end, I resorted to all manner of subterfuge when I left Baghdād, resolved never to return to it again. All the imāms of Iraq assailed me, since none of them would allow that there could be a religious reason for my leaving everything behind. They assumed that I had reached the highest religious position. "That is the sum of their knowledge" [Qur'ān 53:30]. After that, people were caught up in conjectures concerning my decision. Those who were far from Iraq assumed that I had received word that I was out of favor with the authorities. However, those close to the authorities noted that they were attached to me and pursued me, while I avoided them and was impervious to their words. Thus, they concluded: "This is a supernatural matter. Its cause can only be a spell cast upon the people of Islam and the community of religious scholars."

Finally, I left Baghdād, distributing what wealth I had and preserving only a small amount for my subsistence and the sustenance of my children. I was aided in this by the fact that a portion of the wealth of Iraq is earmarked for social welfare in the form of a religious endowment[45] for the Muslims. Nowhere else in the world have I seen such abundant wealth [138] for scholars to draw upon to support their families. Then I entered Syria and resided there for almost two years, occupying myself exclusively with isolation, solitude, spiritual exercises, and mystical devotion. I was engaged in purifying my soul, moral education,[46] and cleansing my heart for the recollection of God Almighty, in accordance with what I had read in the books of the mystics. Each day, I would withdraw to the Mosque of Damascus, ascend the minaret, and lock myself up there for the duration of the day. From there, I made my way to Jerusalem, where I would enter the Dome of the Rock every day and sequester myself. Then I was moved by the call to fulfill the duty of pilgrimage, derive blessings from Mecca and Medina, and pay my respects to the tomb of the Prophet (God's blessings be upon him). But first, I stopped to visit the Mosque of Abraham in Hebron (God's blessings be upon him) before proceeding to Ḥijāz.

Eventually, certain concerns and my children's pleas to return pulled me back to the homeland, though I thought that I would never go back. There, I also opted for isolation in an attempt to preserve my secluded state and to keep my heart pure for the recollection of God. Various eventualities, family duties, and the need [139] for subsistence tended to affect the nature of my goal and intrude upon my undisturbed solitude. But even though I could attain the pure state only from time to time, that did not extinguish my hope of achieving it. Obstacles would impede me, but I would always go back to it.

I remained in this state for ten years, and things were revealed to me during my solitary retreats that cannot be enumerated or detailed. This much I will mention, since it may be of benefit to others: I came to know with certainty that the mystics are exclusively the ones who pursue the course that leads to God Almighty. Their conduct is the best, their way is the most correct, and their characters are the most morally refined. Indeed, if one were to gather together the intellect of all rational persons,

[45] A religious endowment (*waqf*) is an Islamic institution set up to provide for needy individuals, institutions, etc.

[46] Alternatively, adopting an ethical or moral character (*tahdhīb al-akhlāq*).

the wisdom of the sages, and the knowledge of those religious scholars apprised of the secrets of religious law, they would be unable to find anything in the conduct and character of the mystics that could be changed for the better. All their activity, whether outward or inward, is obtained from the light of the lantern of prophecy, in comparison with which no light on earth is capable of illuminating.

On the whole, what can one say about their way? Purity, which is its first precondition, is the complete purification of the heart from everything but God [140] Almighty. The key to their way, which follows from this first step, just as prayer follows from sanctity,[47] is the complete absorption of the heart in the recollection of God. The final step is complete obliteration[48] in God. Or rather, that is the final step relative to these first steps, which can almost be considered matters of choice and acquisition. But upon closer inspection, this is just the beginning of the mystic way and what precedes it is just an entryway for those who pursue the way. From the very first step of the mystic way, enlightenment and visions begin. The mystics even see the angels and the spirits of the prophets when they are awake, hearing their voices and deriving benefit from them. Then the mystical state progresses from the level of visions of images and similitudes to levels about which it is difficult to give utterance. Any interpreter who has tried to articulate such a state has inevitably committed a clear error of expression, which cannot be guarded against. On the whole, it all concludes with a kind of proximity to God, which one group represents imaginatively almost as [141] transfiguration, while another group represents it as union, and yet a third group as attainment.[49] But all these are erroneous representations, whose errors we have exposed in the work "The Radiant Goal" (*al-Maqsad al-Asnā*). Rather, whoever has managed to attain that state must not say more than the following:

> I do not remember what happened,
> So assume the best, and do not ask for a report![50]

[47] Literally, a state in which certain things are forbidden (*taḥrīm*).

[48] Obliteration (*fanā'*) is a common Ṣūfī term to denote the experience of losing oneself in God.

[49] Transfiguration (*ḥulūl*), union (*ittiḥād*), and attainment (*wuṣūl*) are all metaphorical ways used in the Ṣūfī literature to describe the ultimate mystical experience. As Ghazālī explains, he finds fault with all three since they carry erroneous implications.

[50] Line from the poet Ibn al-Muᶜtazz (d. 908 AD).

Generally speaking, anyone who has not been granted the taste of this state apprehends **[142]** the reality of prophecy in name alone. Upon verification, it transpires that the exalted states of those who are close to God are in fact the beginning of prophecy. That was the initial state of the Prophet (the blessings of God upon him) when he first approached Mount Ḥirā', where he would isolate himself and worship so devotedly that the Arabs said: "Muhammad has fallen in love with his Lord."

This state can be verified by anyone through direct tasting once they have pursued the mystical road. As for those who have not been granted the taste of it, they can become certain of it through experience and testimony if they frequent the company of the mystics, and they will come to a certain understanding of these states by means of evidence. Those who frequent their company will acquire faith from them – for they are the group whose companions will never be damned. As for those who are not granted their companionship, they can come to know of the possibility of this state with certainty by means of demonstrative indications, as we have mentioned in one of the sections of the book "The Revival of the Religious Sciences" (*Iḥyā' ʿUlūm al-Dīn*), which is entitled "The Wonders of the Heart."

Verification by means of demonstration is knowledge. Taking on the state itself is tasting. Acceptance based on testimony and experience based on trust[51] is faith **[143]**. These are three degrees, for "God ranks in degrees those of you who have faith and those to whom knowledge is granted" [Qur'ān 58:11].

Behind these mystics is a group of ignorant people, who deny the basis of this and wonder at these words. They listen, mock, and say: "How strange, they're babbling deliriously!" They are the ones of whom God Almighty said: "Some of them will listen to you and after they leave you, they will say to those to whom knowledge has been granted: 'What did he just say?' They are the ones whose hearts God has sealed and they have followed their passions" [Qur'ān 47:16], for he has made them deaf and blind.

Among the things that became clear to me with necessity as a result of practicing the way of the mystics was the reality of prophecy and its properties. Next, I must point out the basis of prophecy, for there is a dire need for that.

[51] Literally, experience based on favorable presumption (*al-tajribah bi-ḥusn al-ẓann*).

[144] You should know that the human substance in its original natural state is created blank, innocent, and without any information concerning the domains[52] of God Almighty. These domains are many in number and cannot be enumerated by anyone but God Almighty. As He has said: "No one knows God's legions but He" [Qur'ān 74:31]. Human beings gather information about these domains simply by means of apprehension, and each type of apprehension was created for humans to be apprised of some domain of existents, where by "domains" we mean the genera of existents.

The first sense to be created in the human being is touch, by means of which he apprehends a genus of existents: heat, coldness, wetness, dryness, softness, hardness, and so on. Touch is absolutely incapable of apprehending colors and sounds, which are as though nonexistent in relation to touch [145]. Next, the sense of vision is created in the human being, which enables him to apprehend colors and shapes; and this is the most extensive realm of perceptibles. After that, hearing is imparted to him, and he hears sounds and pitches. Then, taste is created, and so on, until he transcends the sensory world and is endowed with discrimination. This occurs when he approaches the age of 7, at which point he enters a new stage of his existence. In this stage he apprehends things that are additional to the sensory world, which do not exist in the sensory world. Then he enters yet another stage, when the intellect is created in him, and he apprehends necessity, possibility, and impossibility, as well as other matters that were not present in the previous stages.

Beyond the stage of the intellect, there is another stage in which another eye is opened, by means of which he is able to see supernatural[53] things, the future, and other matters from which the intellect is isolated, just as the faculty of discrimination is cut off from apprehending the intelligibles, or the sensory faculty is from the objects of discrimination. Just as the person who is capable of discrimination will reject and shun the objects of the intellect, so also some persons of intellect have rejected and shunned the objects of prophecy. That is the height of ignorance, since their only [146] grounds for doing so is that it is a stage that they have not attained and does not exist for them. Thus, they assume that it does not exist in itself. If the blind person did not know about colors and

[52] Literally, worlds (*ʿawālim*).

[53] The Arabic term (*al-ghayb*) literally means the absent, but here and elsewhere it carries the connotation of supernatural or occult matters.

shapes through recurrent[54] testimony, and were they not reported to him from an early age, he would not have understood them nor would he have approximated them. God has given his creatures an approximation of the properties of prophecy by providing them with an exemplar, namely sleep. The sleeper apprehends the supernatural, whether explicitly or clothed in similes that can be uncovered through interpretation. If a person did not experience this for himself, he would have denied it. If he were told: "Some people fall in a dead faint, losing all sense of touch, hearing, and vision, and apprehend what is absent," he would have devised a demonstrative proof to show that it was impossible, saying: "The sensory faculties are the causes of perception. Whoever does not perceive things when these faculties exist and are present will be even less able and fit to perceive when they are suspended." This is a species of reasoning[55] that is belied by what actually exists and can be observed. Thus, just as the intellect is a stage for the human being, in which he acquires an eye that can see types of intelligibles that are isolated from the senses, so also prophecy denotes a stage in which he acquires an eye that sheds light upon the supernatural and other things that the intellect cannot apprehend.

One may doubt the very possibility of prophecy, or its **[147]** actual existence and incidence, or its occurrence to a particular person. The proof of its possibility is its existence. The proof of its existence is the existence of things that can be cognized in the world, such as the sciences of medicine and astrology, which cannot conceivably be obtained through reason.[56] Whoever investigates these sciences will come to know with necessity that they can be apprehended only by means of divine inspiration and assistance from God Almighty, and that there is no way to acquire them by experience. Some astrological predictions[57] pertain to things that happen only once every thousand years. How are such things to be obtained from experience? The same may be said for the properties[58] of medications. This demonstration makes clear that it is possible that there is a means of apprehending those things that cannot be apprehended by reason, which is what is meant by prophecy. It is not that prophecy is solely a way of denoting this means, but rather that apprehension of this

[54] The Arabic term (*tawātur*) often indicates a process whereby testimony is recurrently corroborated by numerous sources, especially in authenticating a Ḥadīth.

[55] Alternatively, analogy (*qīyāsī*).

[56] Alternatively, the intellect (*al-ʿaql*).

[57] Literally, judgments (*aḥkām*).

[58] Ghazālī later dwells on the properties (*khawāṣṣ* or *khāṣṣīyyāt*, singular *khāṣṣah* or *khāṣṣīyyah*) of medications that are allegedly unknowable by reason; see [162].

kind of thing, which lies outside the things that reason can apprehend, is one of the properties of prophecy. It has many other properties; what we have mentioned is a mere drop in the ocean. But we mentioned it because you have an exemplar of prophecy in what you apprehend during sleep, and you have sciences of the same kind as prophecy in medicine and astrology. These are the miracles of the prophets (God's blessings upon them), for there is no way that persons of intellect can attain them by dint of reason alone.

As for the other properties of prophecy, they can be apprehended only by tasting as a result of following the mystical way. You can understand the first property of prophecy only by means of an exemplar that you have been granted, namely sleep, without which you would not have believed in it. However, if the prophet has another property of which you do not have an exemplar, you would not even understand it, so how could you believe in it? Belief only comes after understanding, and this other exemplar of prophecy [148] occurs only after the early stages of the mystical way, when tasting occurs, according to the degree attained. At that point belief takes place of a kind that was not acquired though syllogism. Still, the first property of prophecy is sufficient for you to have faith in the basis of prophecy.

If you are in doubt as to whether a specific individual is a prophet or not, you cannot be certain unless you know his circumstances either by first-hand observation or by recurrent testimony. If you are cognizant of medicine and jurisprudence, you can recognize the jurists and doctors by observing their circumstances and listening to their statements even if you are not able to observe them directly. Also, you are capable of recognizing that al-Shāfiᶜī (may God have mercy upon him) is a jurist and that Galen is a doctor. You can recognize this in reality [149], not just by conforming to a tradition handed down by others, but simply by learning something about jurisprudence and medicine, and reading their books and works. That way, you can gain necessary knowledge about their circumstances. Similarly, if you understand the concept of prophecy and examine closely the Qur'ān and Ḥadīth, you will gain necessary knowledge that the Prophet Muḥammad (God's blessings upon him) is in the highest rank of prophecy. You may confirm this by experiencing what he has said concerning worship and its effect on cleansing the heart, as well as the validity of the following sayings: "Whoever practices what he knows will be endowed by God with what he does not know," "Whoever aids an unjust person will be overpowered by him, by God's will," and "Whoever reduces all his cares to a single one [i.e. worship of God], will be relieved by God of the cares of this world and the next." If you experience these things a thousand times or more, you will obtain necessary knowledge of Muḥammad's prophecy and will not doubt it.

This is the way to seek certainty in prophecy, not in the turning of a stick into a serpent or the cleaving of the moon. For if you rely only on such things, and do not assemble innumerable pieces of evidence, you may one day come to assume that they are magic or fantasy, or even that they might be confusion sent by God Almighty, who "confuses whom he wishes and guides whom he wishes" [Qur'ān 16:93, 35:8] **[150]**. Thus, the whole issue of miracles will be thrown back at you. If your faith in prophecy is based solely upon statements supported by the evidence of a miracle, then that faith will be broken by statements designed to render that miracle dubious and suspect. Let such exceptional occurrences be just one of the proofs and indications that figure in the totality of your theoretical speculation, so that you will come to have necessary knowledge whose grounds cannot be narrowly specified. You will be like someone who has heard a report recurrently corroborated by a whole group of people. The certainty associated with the report cannot be said to derive from a single specific statement, but rather in an indefinite way. Although it does not derive from anyone outside the group, it cannot be traced back to any single individual. That is robust knowledge-based faith. As for tasting, it is like firsthand observation[59] and is found only in the mystical way. This much concerning the truth of prophecy suffices for my present purposes. I will now go on to relate why there is a need for it.

[151] After dedicating myself to isolation and solitude for close to ten years, it became clear to me with necessity, due to innumerable reasons (tasting, demonstrative knowledge, and faith-based acceptance) that human beings are created with a body and a heart. By "heart" I mean the reality of a human's spirit where his cognizance of God is located, not the flesh and blood that he shares with corpses and animals. In addition, just as the body has health, which leads to its happiness, and disease, which leads to its ruin, so also the heart has its health and soundness, for he only is saved "who comes to God with a sound heart" [Qur'ān 26:89]. Moreover, the heart has its own disease that leads ultimately to its eternal

[59] The term Ghazālī uses is the same used for the mystical vision (*mushāhadah*), see e.g. [140].

otherworldly destruction; as the Almighty has said: "A disease is in their hearts" [Qur'ān 2:10]. Ignorance of God is the heart's destructive poison and disobedience of God through the pursuit of passion is its diseased affliction. Cognizance of God Almighty is its revivifying antidote and obedience to God by opposing passion is its therapeutic medicine. The only way **[152]** to effect a treatment that eliminates the disease and restores health is by administering medications, just as in the case of the body. The body's medications bring about the restoration of health by virtue of a property they have, which cannot be apprehended by the people of intellect by dint of reason, but must be acquired by conforming to the tradition of the doctors, who in turn take it from the prophets, who ascertain the properties of things on account of a property of prophecy. Likewise, it became clear to me with necessity that the effects of the medications of worship, in the proportions and measured quantities that have been set down by the prophets, are not to be apprehended by the people of intellect by dint of reason. Rather, in this case too, they must be taken by conforming to the tradition of the prophets who apprehended these properties thanks to the light of prophecy, and not by means of reason. Moreover, medications are combined in various combinations according to type and quantity – sometimes one ingredient is double another by weight – and the differences in quantity hold secrets pertaining to their properties. So also the acts of worship, which are medications for the afflictions of the heart, are composed of actions of various types and quantities. For example, in prayer there are twice as many prostrations as bows, and the morning prayers are half the afternoon prayers in quantity. These matters also hold secrets that pertain to their properties, which cannot be ascertained without the light of prophecy. It is sheer folly and ignorance to try to discover a kind of wisdom in these things by means of the intellect, or else to assume that they are arbitrarily given and not based upon a divine secret that specifically dictates them. Medications have certain basic ingredients as well as additional components that complement them and influence **[153]** the actions of their basic ingredients in specific ways. These latter correspond to the supererogatory acts and customary practices that complement the effects of the basic elements of worship.

Generally speaking, the prophets (peace be upon them) are the physicians of the diseases of the heart. The only benefit and function of the intellect is that it informed us of that fact. The intellect vouched for the truthfulness of prophecy and admitted its own inability to apprehend what is apprehended with the eye of prophecy. It led us by the hand and delivered us to prophecy, as blind people are delivered to their guides or the bewildered sick are delivered to their benevolent doctors. That is the extent of the progress and advancement of the intellect, for it is barred from going further, though it can understand what the doctor prescribes. These are things of which I became cognizant with a necessity comparable to that of direct observation during my period of isolation and solitude.

Meanwhile, I witnessed the weakening of belief in the very basis of prophecy, in the reality of prophecy, as well as in practicing what prophecy explains. I verified that these trends were widespread among **[154]** people and looked into the reasons for this apathy and weakening of faith, concluding that there were four such reasons: (i) a reason due to those who follow the Instructionist path; (ii) a reason due to those who delve into mysticism; (iii) a reason due to those who delve into the science of philosophy; and (iv) a reason due to the conduct of those considered by most people to be religious scholars.[60]

For a while, I pursued individual human beings in order to question those who fell short of observing religious law, asking them about their doubts and searching for their beliefs and deepest convictions. I would say: "Why has your observance lapsed? If you have faith in the afterlife and are not preparing for it, but are rather trading it for this life, then that is folly. You would not sell two things for the price of one, so why should you trade an infinite time for a limited number of days? Moreover, if you do not have faith in the afterlife, then you are a blasphemer, and had better seek faith. Look to the reason for your covert blasphemy and your overt defiance, namely your inward creed – though you do not proclaim it out of courtesy for the faith and respect for the religious law."

One would reply: "If I were really obliged to observe this aspect of religious law, **[155]** then it would be all the more fitting for the religious scholars to do so. But one renowned learned man does not pray, another drinks wine, and a third appropriates the funds allocated to religious endowments and to orphans. Moreover, one religious scholar accepts money from the ruler without regard to what is forbidden according to religion, and another takes bribes for being a judge and a witness." He would go on to multiply such examples endlessly. Another would claim to

[60] (i) and (iii) have been switched around, to conform to the order of exposition at [161].

have mastered the discipline of mysticism, alleging that he had attained a level that transcends the need for acts of worship. A third would appeal to other doubts commonly cited as pretexts by the profligate. These are the ones who have strayed from the path of mysticism. A fourth person, who had met with the esoteric Instructionists, would say: "Truth is manifold, the road is strenuous, and disagreements are rife. No creed is more worthy than another, for the proofs of the intellect are in conflict, there is no confidence in the opinions of the men of opinion,[61] and those calling for instruction judge haphazardly without supporting arguments. So how can I replace doubt with certainty?" A fifth would assert: "I do not do this on the basis of conformism but because I have read the science of philosophy and have apprehended the reality of prophecy, which **[156]** simply comes down to what is wise and beneficial. The purpose of the rituals of worship is to keep the multitude in check by preventing them from clashing and quarreling, and to restrain them from overindulgence of the appetites. Since I am not one of the ignorant multitude, there is no need for me to be confined by such legal constraints. Instead, I am one of the wise who follow wisdom and are enlightened by it, and this enables me to do without conformism." This is the utmost limit of the faith of those who study the creed of the theist philosophers, who learn this from the books of Ibn Sīnā and Abū Naṣr al-Fārābī. They are Muslims in appearance only. You may see one of them reading the Qur'ān, attending communal prayers, or paying lip service to religious law, while at the same time continuing to drink wine and indulging in all kinds of depravity and debauchery. If one says to such a person: "If prophecy is invalid, why do you pray?," he may reply: "For bodily exercise, in keeping with the custom of the land, and to preserve property and family." Alternatively, he may say: "The religious law is valid and prophecy is true." If you ask: "Why do you drink wine?," he will respond: "Wine was forbidden only because it leads to aggression and enmity, but my wisdom protects me against that and I drink only in order to sharpen my wits." Indeed, Ibn Sīnā even wrote **[157]** in a will that he would promise God Almighty to undertake a number of tasks, including extoling the greatness of religious regulations, observing the ritual acts of worship, and refraining from drinking for entertainment but

[61] The phrase "men of opinion" (*ahl al-ra'y*) may be used here to refer to the theologians (cf. *ahl al-naẓar*, the men of theory or speculation, a phrase often used to refer to the philosophers). Alternatively, it could be a reference to a school of religious law or jurisprudence that privileges individual judgment over the authority of tradition.

doing so only for medicinal and therapeutic purposes. This is the furthest that he has gone as regards purity of faith and commitment to worship, namely that he reserved wine-drinking for therapeutic purposes! This is the faith of those among them who claim to be believers. Some people have been deceived by these philosophers, and their deception has been aggravated by the weakness of those objecting to the philosophers, for they have objected strenuously to geometry, logic, and the other necessary sciences, which is a problem that has already been elaborated above.

When I observed that all types of people had had their faith weakened to this extent for these reasons, I found myself devoting myself to dispelling these doubts. Exposing these people was easier to me than drinking water, since I had delved extensively into their sciences and methods, namely the methods of the mystics, philosophers, Instructionists, and those considered to be religious scholars. I became convinced that this activity on my part was destined to occur at this particular time. What use were solitude and isolation when the disease had become so widespread, the doctors were sick, and the people had almost perished? But then I said to myself: "If you occupy yourself **[158]** with exposing this affliction and combating this darkness in this time of laxity and period of dishonesty, calling people to abandon their ways and pointing them to the truth, then all the people of your time will become hostile towards you. Since you can barely resist them, how can you live with them? This endeavor could succeed only if you lived in a more auspicious time in the reign of a more forceful and pious ruler."

Thus, I asked permission of God Almighty to continue in my solitude, on the pretext that I was unable to reveal the truth by way of argument. But God decreed that the ruler of the time was internally motivated, not externally induced, to issue an order requiring me to move to Nishapur to tackle this religious laxity. The ruler's resolve was such that, had I insisted on defiance, it would have led to a rift. It then occurred to me that the reason behind the permission that I had asked of God had been undermined. One's motive for maintaining solitude should not be laziness, relaxation, the preservation of one's dignity, or protection from harm by others. Why permit myself to be excused from the difficulty of dealing with humanity, when God Almighty has said: "In the Name of the Merciful and the Compassionate. Alif Lām Mīm. Did people suppose that they would be given leave to say, 'We have faith,' without being tested? But we have tested those who preceded them . . ." [Qur'ān 29:1–3]. Moreover, God

Almighty has addressed His Messenger **[159]**, who is the most beloved among his creatures, saying: "Messengers before you have been accused of lying, but they persevered through accusations and injuries until we sent them help. God's words cannot be changed, and you have been sent reports of the other messengers" [Qur'ān 6:34]. The Almighty also states: "In the name of God the Merciful and Compassionate. Yā' Sīn. By the Wise Qur'ān . . . Only warn those who heed the reminder and fear God in the absence"[62] [Qur'ān 36:1–11]. Then I consulted a group of people about this matter, among whom were the masters of hearts and possessors of visions.[63] They all agreed in advising me to end my isolation and to leave the *zāwīyah*.[64] To this were added many corroborating dreams from righteous people, all attesting that this move would constitute an auspicious and reasonable beginning, and that God had ordained it for the turn of the century. My hope was strengthened as a result of these testimonies and I took on a more favorable attitude towards the move. God Almighty has vowed to revive his religion at the beginning of each century, and He facilitated my move to Nishapur in order to carry out this important mission in the month of Dhū al-Qa^{c}dah 499 AH [July–August 1106 AD]. I had first left Baghdād in 488 AH [1095 AD], so my period of isolation lasted eleven years in all. This move was ordained by God and was one of His marvelous decrees, for it had not even entered my heart during the period of isolation, just as the **[160]** possibility of my initial departure from Baghdād and of walking out on my circumstances had never even occurred to me. God Almighty effects the conversion of hearts and circumstances, for "the heart of the faithful is between two fingers of the Merciful."[65]

I know that even though I returned to spread knowledge, I did not really return, for to return is to go back to what was. In earlier times, I had spread the knowledge that brings fame. That is what I called for in both word and deed, and it was my purpose and intention. But now, I spread the knowledge that brings about the rejection of fame, and by means of which one becomes cognizant of its insignificance. God knows, this is now my intention, purpose, and hope. Moreover, I aspire to reform myself and others, though I cannot tell whether I will reach my aim or whether I will perish before attaining my goal. However, I am certain of my faith and

[62] Alternatively, the unknown or occult (*al-ghayb*). [63] This is a clear reference to the Ṣūfīs.
[64] A Ṣūfī hospice or retreat. [65] A Ḥadīth attributed to the prophet Muḥammad.

vision that there can be no ability and no power without God the Exalted and Magnificent. I was not the one who made the move, but rather God moved me; and I did not act but rather He acted through me. I ask Him to reform me first, then to reform through me; to guide me and then to guide through me. I also ask Him to show me the real truth and to grant me to follow it, as well as to show me falsehood for what it is and to grant me avoidance of it.

[161] Let us return to the reasons for the weakening of faith, and let us mention the ways of guiding the weak and delivering them from their own destruction.

(i) Those who claim perplexity among the esoteric Instructionists may be cured by what we have written in the work *The Correct Balance* (*al-Qisṭās al-Mustaqīm*), which will not be elaborated further in this epistle.

(ii) The illusions of the party of profligacy have been narrowed down to seven types of doubt and these have been dispelled in my work *The Alchemy of Happiness* (*Kīmyā' al-Saᶜādah*).

(iii) As for those whose faith has been spoiled by the method of philosophy, to the point that they have denied the reality of prophecy, we have already asserted the truth of prophecy and its existence by necessity, and have cited as proof the existence of the sciences of the properties of medications, astrology, and others. Indeed, that was the purpose of the previous section. We used the properties of medicine and astrology as proof of prophecy because these are the philosophers' own sciences. We demonstrate prophecy to all those who have knowledge of some science or another by using examples drawn from their own science, whether it be astrology, medicine, physics, magic, or the science of talismans.

Moreover, those who affirm prophecy verbally and equate the principles of religious law with what is wise, are upon closer inspection blasphemous when it comes to prophecy. Instead, they have faith in a wise judge, born under a special ascendant star, who must be followed.[66] This bears no relation to prophecy at all. Rather, to have faith in prophecy **[162]** is to admit the affirmation of a stage beyond the intellect[67] in which an eye is

[66] It is not clear which doctrine Ghazālī is referring to here. Perhaps he is parodying the "proof of prophecy" offered by some philosophers, who make prophecy out to be a special rational ability on the part of some to derive through intuition (*ḥads*) what others infer using the intellect (see e.g. Ibn Sīnā's "Proof of Prophecy").

[67] Alternatively, reason (*al-ᶜaql*).

opened that apprehends specific things from which the intellect is barred, just as hearing is barred from apprehending colors, vision from apprehending sounds, and all the senses from apprehending the intelligibles. If such a person does not admit this possibility, we have offered a demonstrative proof of its possibility, indeed of its existence. If he does admit it, then he has effectively affirmed that there are things called properties,[68] about which the intellect is unable to reason[69] at all. Indeed, the intellect all but denies them and rules that they are impossible. For example, the weight of one *dāniq* of opium is a lethal poison because it coagulates the blood in the veins due to its extreme coldness. Those who claim to know physical science contend that compounds have a cooling effect only by virtue of containing two elements, water and earth, which are the cold elements. However, it is well known that many *raṭl*s of water and earth are insufficient to cool the inside of the body to this extent.[70] If a physicist who had not experienced this were informed of this fact, he would have said: "That is impossible. The proof of its impossibility is that opium contains the elements of fire and air, which do not increase coldness. Moreover, even if opium were entirely composed of water and earth, it would not necessitate such a strong cooling effect. Thus, if two hot elements are added to it, there is even less reason to think that it will." This is considered a demonstrative proof! Indeed, most of the philosophers' demonstrations in physics and metaphysics are based on this kind of reasoning. They conceive of things as they find them and **[163]** grasp them by the intellect, and whatever is unfamiliar to them is considered impossible. If veridical supernatural visions were not familiar [i.e. from dreams], and someone were to claim that the future[71] can be known when the senses are inactive, those deemed to have such intellects would deny this. To take another example, if one of them were told: "Could there be something in the world that is the size of a grain, which, if released in a town would devour the entire town and all its contents, eventually consuming even itself, that

68 Also known as "sympathetic qualities" (*khawāṣṣ*, singular *khāṣṣah*), these properties are a "recurring theme in magic and occult sciences indicating the unaccountable, esoteric forces in animate and inanimate Nature." This conception developed during the Hellenistic period and was taken up by some Arab and Islamic thinkers in the medieval era. (*EI* entry on "khāṣṣa").

69 Alternatively, around which the intellect is unable to function at all (*lā yadūr taṣarruf al-ʿaql ḥawālayhā aṣlan*).

70 The weights mentioned in this example are difficult to specify exactly, since they varied at different times and different places in medieval Islam. To the nearest order of magnitude, a *dāniq* was a fraction of a gram, while a *raṭl* was a kilogram.

71 Literally, the hidden or absent (*al-ghayb*).

is, leaving nothing in the whole town, not even itself?" He would respond: "That is impossible, a mere fable." But that is precisely the case with fire, and whoever had not seen fire would deny that this could take place if he were told about it. Most of the denials of the wonders of the afterlife are of this kind. We say to the physicists: "You have been obliged to admit that opium has a cooling property that is not within the realm of the possible, according to physics. Why not admit the possibility of properties among the religious principles that are capable of healing and purifying the heart, which cannot be apprehended by the wisdom of the intellect, but can be seen only by the eye of prophecy?" Indeed, they have admitted the existence of stranger properties in their books, for example the strange properties associated with the following figure, which has been tested in treating pregnant women who have difficulty in labor:

2	9	4
7	5	3
6	1	8

This is inscribed on two pieces of cloth, untouched by water, and the pregnant woman looks at them directly. Then she places them under her feet and the infant emerges immediately from the womb. They have admitted this and mentioned it in the works concerning wondrous properties. This figure consists of a square with nine compartments, each inscribed with a special number **[164]**, in such a way that each row, column, and diagonal adds up to fifteen.

Who could believe that and not be broad-minded enough to believe that the fact that the morning prayers contain two prostrations, the noon prayers four, and the evening prayers three, are due to properties not known through philosophical speculation,[72] and that the prayers are different because of the difference in the times of day? These properties can be apprehended only through the light of prophecy. The strange thing is that if we had expressed these things differently, as astrologers do, their intellects would have grasped the difference made by the differences in the times of day, for example if we had said: "The astrological judgment

[72] Alternatively, through the speculation of wisdom (*bi-naẓar al-ḥikmah*).

concerning the ascendant differs depending on whether the sun is in the middle of the sky, in ascension, or in declension." In preparing their horoscopes,[73] they base different medical treatments, lifespans, and times of death, on such differences. Moreover, there is no difference between the meridian and the sun's being in the middle of the sky, or sunset and **[165]** the sun's being in declension. Do they have any reason for believing such things besides the fact that they hear them expressed in an astrologer's terms? They continue to believe the astrologer even after experiencing his lies one hundred times. An astrologer might say to such a person: "If the sun is in the middle of the sky, a certain planet is in opposition to it, and a certain constellation is in the ascendant, then if you wear a new cloak at that time, you will be killed in it." That person would then refrain from wearing the cloak at that time, perhaps subjecting himself to extreme cold as a result, even though he has received this advice from an astrologer with whose lies he has been acquainted many times. How can someone be open-minded enough to accept such marvels and be obliged to admit that they concern properties of which some prophets are miraculously cognizant, yet deny similar things reported by an honest prophet, who is supported by miracles and has never been recognized to lie? Why will his intellect not allow the possibility?

A philosopher who denies the properties of the number of prostrations in prayer, the throwing of stones during the pilgrimage, the basic elements of the pilgrimage, and other rituals of religious worship, will be unable to discern any difference at all between these things and the properties of medications and stars. That philosopher might say: "I have experienced something of astrology and medicine, and have found parts of them to be valid. Thus, my mind was moved to assent to them and my heart lost all tendency to reject and resist them. As for the other thing [i.e. prophecy], I have not experienced it, so I do not know that it exists and cannot verify it, **[166]** though I do admit its possibility." I respond: "You do not restrict yourself to assenting to what you have experienced, since you also accept the reports of those who have experienced things and then you go on to conform to them. Listen, therefore, to the statements of the prophets,

[73] The term used is *tasyīrāt* (singular *tasyīr*), which is "a procedure used in astrology of artificial continuation of a planet or of an astrological house or any other definite part of the heavens to another star or its aspects, or other houses with the object of ascertaining the equatorial degree situated between these two places, the figure of which is used, by converting it into a definite period of time, to prognosticate the date of a future happening, either good or evil" (*EI* entry on "tasyīr").

who have experienced and had a vision of the truth in every aspect of the religious law. If you follow their path, you will apprehend some of that through direct vision."[74]

I would add that even if you do not experience it for yourself, your very intellect rules that you absolutely must assent and follow their lead. Suppose that there is a man who has reached adulthood and the age of reason without having experienced disease, and that the man then comes down with a disease. Suppose also that he has a benevolent father who is proficient in medicine and whose reputation concerning cognizance of medical matters has been familiar to him ever since he attained the age of reason. Then consider that the father has concocted a medication for the son, saying: "This is suitable for your disease and will cure your illness." What would his intellect dictate in this case, even if the medication is bitter-tasting and repugnant? Should the patient take the medication, or should he rebuff him, saying "My intellect has not ruled this medication to be appropriate for curing this disease, and I have not experienced it"? If he did the latter, you would doubtless consider him to be a fool, just as those who have vision consider you a fool to reject prophecy. If you say "How do I know[75] that the prophet is benevolent and is cognizant of this science of medicine?," I reply "How do you know that your father is benevolent, for it is not something you can perceive through the senses? Rather, you are cognizant of it by necessity and without a doubt, through indications of his circumstances and evidence of his actions in all his comings and goings."

Whoever looks into the sayings of the Prophet and the reports that have been related about him will acquire necessary knowledge that his benevolence towards his community is greater than the benevolence of the father towards his son. This can be seen in his keenness to guide people, his diligence to persuade people using affectionate, gentle, and kind means, to improve their morals, to resolve **[167]** their conflicts, and generally to do whatever will be of benefit to them in both religious and temporal matters. Moreover, if he considers the marvels apparent in his actions, the supernatural wonders that have been related of him in the Qur'ān, his utterances in the Ḥadīth,[76] and what he has said about

74 Alternatively, through observation (*mushāhadah*).

75 Literally, how am I cognizant of . . . (*fīma aʿrifu*); but here and in the next sentence, loosely, know.

76 Reading *wa ʿalā lisānihi fīl-akhbār* instead of *ʿalā lisānihi wa fīl-akhbār* (in his utterances and in the Ḥadīth).

the distant future – which has turned out as he predicted – he will come to know with necessity that the Prophet has attained a stage beyond the intellect, and that an eye has been opened that can reveal the supernatural that can only be apprehended by a select few, and those things that cannot be apprehended by the intellect. This is the method of acquiring the necessary knowledge by which to assent to the Prophet. If you experience the Qur'ān and contemplate it, and peruse the Ḥadīth, you will become cognizant of it firsthand. This much is sufficient to warn the so-called philosophers; we have mentioned it here because there is a dire need for it in these times.

(iv) As for the fourth reason for the weakening of faith, which has to do with the evil lifestyle of the religious scholars, it can be remedied in three ways.

First, we say: "You claim that the religious scholar eats forbidden things, though he is cognizant of the fact that they are forbidden. Meanwhile, you are cognizant of the prohibition on wine, pork, usury, slander, dishonesty, and defamation, yet you go ahead and do these things. You do so not because you do not have faith that they are transgressions but rather **[168]** because your appetites overwhelm you. His appetites are like yours and have overwhelmed him, just as your appetites have overwhelmed you. Moreover, what distinguishes him from you is his knowledge of things beyond these, which is irrelevant to the stringent restrictions against specific forbidden things." Similarly, many of those who have faith in medicine do not desist from fruits and cold water, even though the doctor has restricted them from having them. That does not prove that these things are not harmful or that faith in medicine is misplaced. The same applies to the transgressions of the religious scholars.[77]

Second, the common person can be told: "You ought to believe that the religious scholar considers that his knowledge will earn him credit in the afterlife and assumes that it will save him, on the grounds that the virtues of his knowledge will gain him leniency when it comes to his deeds. Though his knowledge may actually argue against him, it is indeed possible that it might elevate his rank. That is, even though he has neglected practice, he has his knowledge to vouch for him. However, if you

[77] In other words, religious scholars who commit transgressions are like doctors who follow an unhealthy diet. They do so not because they know something about the effects of food on the body that the rest of us do not, but simply because they are overwhelmed by appetite. Therefore, there is no reason to follow their lead.

model yourself after him, being a nonscholar,[78] you will have neglected practice while being devoid of all knowledge, so your practice will doom you and will be unable to intercede on your behalf."

Third – which is the true response – the real religious scholar does not commit a transgression except as an oversight, and he would definitely not persist in transgressions. For real knowledge is cognizance that transgressions are a lethal poison and that the afterlife is better than this life. Whoever is cognizant of that would never trade what is better for what is worse.

Such knowledge is not acquired from the types of sciences with which most people are preoccupied. That is why their knowledge only increases their willingness to defy God Almighty by transgressing against him **[169]**. Real knowledge, by contrast, makes one more reverent, fearful, and hopeful, and empowers one not to commit transgressions, apart from occasional oversights, which no one can escape from time to time and which do not indicate weakness of faith. The faithful person is subject to seduction and is repentant, but is far from persistence in and devotion to wrongdoing.

This is all I intended to mention by way of censuring philosophy and esoteric Instructionism, as well as their faults and the faults of those who deny them without method. We pray to God Almighty to number us among those he prefers and chooses, those he guides to truth and enlightens, those who are inspired to recollect Him to the point that they do not forget Him, those who are protected against their own evildoing to the point that they are not influenced by anyone but Him, and those he selects for Himself so that they do not worship anyone but Him.

[78] Literally, common person (*ʿāmmī*).

Ibn Ṭufayl, *Ḥayy bin Yaqẓān*

[26] Our worthy predecessors (may God be pleased with them) have related that one of the islands of India that lies below the equator is the island where humans are created without a father or mother and where trees bear women as fruit. This is the island that Masᶜūdī[1] calls the Island of Wāqwāq. For this island has the most temperate air of all the regions of the earth and is the most perfect because it is disposed to have the highest light[2] shine upon it. This is contrary to what the majority of philosophers and most eminent physicians believe. They hold that the most temperate part of the inhabited world is the fourth geographical zone.[3] If they say this because they have determined that there is no settlement along the equator due to terrestrial obstacles, then there is something to their statement that the fourth zone is the most temperate of all the remaining regions. However, if they simply mean that what lies along the equator is too hot, as the majority of them actually say, then they are wrong, and demonstration proves the opposite.

It has been demonstrated in the natural sciences that the generation of heat is caused only by motion, contact with hot bodies, and illumination. It has also been shown in these sciences that the sun is not hot in essence,

[1] Masᶜūdī (d. *c*. 956 AD) was an Islamic historian who was born in Baghdād, traveled widely in Asia, and died in Cairo.

[2] It is not clear what Ibn Ṭufayl means by 'the highest light' (*al-nūr al-aᶜlā*), perhaps more direct light.

[3] Following the Greek tradition, Islamic geographers divided the inhabited world into seven zones or climates (*aqālīm*, singular *iqlīm*), south of which are the regions to the south of the equator and north of which are the countries of the far north. The fourth zone, being the central zone, was often considered to be the most temperate and most fit for human habitation. (See *EI* entry on "iklīm")

nor does it have any of the qualities of mixtures.[4] In addition, it has been shown that the bodies that reflect[5] illumination most perfectly **[27]** are the polished nontransparent bodies, followed by dense unpolished bodies. As for transparent bodies that have no density, these do not reflect light in any manner. This is one of the things demonstratively proven specifically by Shaykh Abū ᶜAlī ibn Sīnā, and was not mentioned by any of his predecessors.[6] If this is in fact the case and these premises are true, then it follows that the sun does not heat the earth as hot bodies heat other bodies with which they are in contact, for the sun is not hot in essence. Nor is the earth heated by motion since it is at rest, and is in the same state at the time of sunrise and sunset, whereas its states of heating and cooling are clearly perceptibly different at these two times. Nor does the sun heat the air first, thereby heating the earth by the mediation of the heat of the air. How could that be, since we find that in hot weather the air nearest the earth is much hotter than the air that is distant from it at high altitudes? It remains that the sun's heating of the earth is solely by illumination. Heat always follows light, to the point that if light shines intensively on a concave mirror, it will ignite what is adjacent to it. It has been proven in the mathematical sciences by absolute demonstrations that the sun is spherically shaped, as is the earth, that the sun is much larger than the earth, and that what is illuminated of the earth by the sun is always [somewhat] greater than half. This illuminated half is at all times most intensely illuminated at its center, since that is furthest from the darkness at the circumference of the circle, and since more parts of it face the sun. What is nearer the circumference is progressively less illuminated, until one reaches darkness at the circumference of the circle, which part of the earth is not illuminated at all. A point is at the center of the circle of illumination only when the sun is at the zenith directly overhead. That is when the heat at that point will be greatest. If a point is far from where the sun is at its zenith, it will be intensely cold, whereas if it is located where the sun remains at its zenith it will be intensely hot. It has been proven in astronomy that the inhabitants of the regions of the earth that lie on the equator are directly under the sun at its zenith

[4] That is, because it is not composed of a mixture of the four elements.

[5] Literally, receive (*taqbal*); Ibn Ṭufayl seems to be operating with an optical theory according to which reflective objects first receive light, then transmit it again.

[6] In *Kitāb al-Najāt* (Part 2, Article 5), Ibn Sīnā states that celestial bodies are not hot and that they heat the earth by illumination rather than by conduction.

only twice a year: when the sun is in the house of Aries and when it is in the house of Libra. During the rest of the year, the sun spends six months to the south and six months to the north of them. They neither have excessive heat nor excessive cold. As a result, their conditions are similar [all year long]. This argument requires greater clarification than is appropriate for our purposes here, but we merely wanted to draw your attention to it because it is one of the things that vouch for the possibility of humans being created in that region without a mother or father, which was mentioned above.

Some have rendered judgment and considered the matter settled that Ḥayy bin Yaqẓān is among those who were created in that region without a mother or father [28]. Others have denied this, and have given another account, which we will relate to you. They say that facing that island was a great island, expansive, rich in resources, and populous, owned by a man who was intensely proud and jealous. He had a very beautiful sister, whom he prevented from marrying until he could find her an equal. But she married in secret a relative named Yaqẓān, in a manner that was acceptable according to the custom prevalent in their times. Then she became pregnant from him and bore a child. She was afraid that she would be found out and that her secret would be revealed, so she put the child in a chest and fastened it securely, having quenched his thirst by breastfeeding him. She then carried him to the seacoast at night in a company of servants and confidantes. Her heart was brimming with fervent love and concern for him, and she bade him goodbye, saying: "O God, you have created this child and he was nearly nothing;[7] you provided for him in the depths of the womb and cared for him until he was complete and fully formed. I now entrust him to your kindness, praying for your favor, in fear of this tyrannical, mighty, and obstinate king. I beg you to be at his side and not to forsake him, O most merciful of all." She then flung him into the sea, at a time when the tide happened to be running out powerfully. The current carried him that very night to the shore of the other island that was mentioned previously.

At that time the tide had reached a high point that it would not reach again for another year. The water surged and carried him to a thicket with fertile soil, sheltered from wind and rain, and protected from the sun by trees, which provided screening as it rose and set. When the water

[7] Literally, and he was nothing to be mentioned (*wa lam yakun shay'an madhkūran*); cf. Qur'ān 76:1.

receded and drained away, it left the chest that carried the child in place. The sands then blew up, accumulating and obstructing the entrance to the thicket so that the chest could not escape and the thicket was blocked **[29]** to water. The tides could not reach it. The nails of the chest had been loosened and its boards shaken when the water cast it into the thicket. Thus, when the child became hungry, squirming and crying in distress, his voice reached the ears of a doe that had earlier lost its young, when it had strayed out of its hiding place and was carried off by an eagle. When the doe heard the cry of the child, she thought it was her child. She followed the sound, imagining her offspring, until she reached the chest. As the child moaned and whined inside the chest, she prodded the chest with her hooves until a board broke off the top. The doe was moved [when she saw the child]. She bent over and caressed him, giving him her nipple to suck until the tasty milk quenched him. Then she began to care for him, nurture him, and protect him from harm. That is how those who deny spontaneous generation explain his origin. We will relate here how he progressed from one stage to the next until he achieved greatness.

As for those who claim that he was born of the earth, they say that a piece of clay was fermented underground on that island over a period of years, until heat and cold were mixed within it, as were moisture and dryness, in a balanced mixture at equilibrium. This piece of fermenting clay was very large, and parts of it were superior to other parts in terms of their temperate composition and their readiness for the formation of gametes. The center was the most temperate part and was most similar to the composition of a human being. The piece of clay generated steam as though it was boiling, due to its viscosity. In its center there appeared some viscous material and a very small swelling, divided in two with a thin film between them, and filled with a light vaporous body of a most temperate and appropriate disposition. At that point the spirit, which is "from the command of God," attached itself to it, adhering so tightly that it was difficult to separate either in perception or in intellect. It is clear that this spirit is constantly emanating from God Almighty, just as the light of the sun is constantly emanating to the world.

[30] Some bodies are not capable of reflecting light[8] at all, such as highly transparent air, and some are capable of partially reflecting, such as dense

[8] Literally, of illuminating (*yustaḍā'u bihā*).

unpolished bodies, which differ in the amount of light they reflect, and their colors differ accordingly. Some are very capable of reflecting light, such as polished bodies like mirrors and such things. If such a mirror is concave and shaped in a specific way, it can give rise to fire due to the intensity of reflected light. Similar things apply to the spirit that is "from the command" of God Almighty, which emanates eternally to all beings. The effect of this emanation is not found in some beings due to lack of disposition, namely the inanimate beings, which lack life altogether. They correspond to air in the analogy just mentioned. Others are affected by the emanation to some degree; these are the species of plants, which correspond to dense bodies in the analogy. Yet others are affected to a great degree; these are the species of animals, which correspond to polished bodies in the analogy. Some of these polished bodies are capable of reflecting[9] the light of the sun to a greater degree, due to the fact that they imitate the form[10] and image of the sun. Similarly, some animals are capable of reflecting the spirit to a greater degree, due to the fact that they resemble the spirit and have the same form, namely human beings. This is referred to in the words of the Prophet (may God bless him and grant him salvation): "God created Adam in his form." If this form is strengthened in him to the point that all other forms fade by comparison, until it is left on its own and the sublimity of its light burns everything in its path, then it will correspond to the reflecting mirror,[11] which is capable of burning other things. This is only possible for prophets (God's blessings upon them all). All this has been shown in the appropriate places. Let us return to conclude what they have related concerning that act of creation.

They said: When this spirit was attached to that lump, all faculties were subject to it, worshipped it, and were made perfectly subservient to it by the command of God Almighty. Another swelling formed opposite that lump, which was divided into [31] three cavities, separated by thin films and unobstructed passages, and they were filled with a similar type of vaporous body that filled the original lump, except that it was lighter. A host of subservient faculties dwelled in the three cavities that were

[9] Literally, receiving (*qubūl*); Ibn Ṭufayl reverts to speaking in terms of receiving light rather than illumination.

[10] Here and in what follows, there seems to be a deliberate ambiguity in the use of the word *ṣūrah*, which can mean form in a philosophical context and image in the analogy.

[11] Literally, the mirror that reflects itself (*al-mir'āt al-munʿakisah ʿalā nafsihā*).

divided from the first one, which were assigned to protect and oversee it, as well as to bring to completion all the processes that occurred there, from the trivial to the sublime, by the first spirit attached to the first lump. Also opposite this lump on the other side from the second lump, a third swelling formed, filled with a gaseous body, but heavier than the first two. In this lump was couched a group of subservient faculties, which were assigned to preserve it and oversee it. The first, second, and third lumps were the first things to be created from the larger piece of fermenting clay, in the order that we have mentioned.[12] They were in need of one another. The first needed to use and subjugate the other two; the other two needed the first as the ruled needs the ruler, or the governed the governor. Both needed the organs that were subsequently generated as the ruler needs the ruled. One of them, the second, was more complete in ruling than the third. When the spirit was attached to the first organ,[13] its temperature was raised and it came to be shaped like pineal fire. The heavy body surrounding it was shaped in the same fashion and formed into solid flesh, with a dermal[14] sheath preserving it. This entire organ is known as the heart. It needed something to supply and nourish it, since heat leads to decomposition and desiccation, and it needed something to constantly replace what was decomposed, otherwise it would not last long. It also needed to perceive what accorded with it so that it could attract it, and what conflicted with it so that it could repel it. The first organ [i.e. of the other two], along with the faculties that originated from it, met the first need, while the second organ met the second [32]. The organ that undertook perception was the brain and the one responsible for nourishment was the liver. Both of these organs needed the heart to supply them with heat and the faculties specific to them, which originate from them. For these purposes, passages and channels were fabricated between them, some wider than others as necessity dictated, which are the arteries and veins.

Then the proponents of spontaneous generation go on to describe the process of creation and all the organs just as the natural scientists describe the creation of the fetus in the womb, leaving nothing out, until its nature is perfected, its organs are completed, and it attains the point at which

[12] The three lumps are, respectively, the heart, brain, and liver. The second lump has three cavities, apparently corresponding to three lobes of the brain.

[13] That is, the first of the three organs (reading *minhum* instead of *minhumā*).

[14] The inferior or inner skin (*ṣifāq*), located beneath the skin and above the flesh.

the fetus emerges from the womb. In their description of the completion of this process, they refer to the large piece of fermenting clay, which had been equipped to produce all that is required for the creation of a human being, including protective layers to cover his entire body and other things. When he was complete, these layers were split open in a manner resembling labor, and the rest of the clay cracked, for it had become desiccated. The child then cried for help once its nourishment ran out and his hunger intensified. The doe that had lost her young responded to the cry. From this point onwards, what these people relate concerning the manner of his upbringing agrees with those of the first party.

All say: The doe that took care of him was fortunate to encounter abundance and fertile pastures, so her flesh increased and her milk was plentiful, and she was able to nourish the child in the best manner. She remained with him at all times, leaving him only to graze. The child was so attached to the doe that whenever she strayed from him, he would cry intensely and she rushed to him, though there were no aggressive predators on that island. The child was raised and nourished on the milk [33] of that doe until he reached the age of 2 and began to walk and teethe. He followed the doe around and she treated him kindly and was merciful towards him. She carried him to places where there were fruit trees and fed him the sweet ripe fruits that had dropped to the ground, breaking the ones with hard casings with her molars. When the child wanted milk she fed him, when he yearned for water she led him to water, when he was exposed to the sun she shaded him, and when he was cold she warmed him. When night fell she led the child to his first resting place, covering him with her body and with the feathers that had lined the chest when he was first placed there. In the course of their comings and goings they had been befriended by a herd of deer that wandered alongside them and spent the night wherever they did.

The child remained with the doe in that condition, imitating her sounds in his own voice, to the point that their voices became almost indistinguishable. He also managed to imitate closely whatever sounds he heard made by birds and other animals, for he was passionately motivated to do so. The sounds he repeated most often were those made by the doe in seeking help, expressing familiarity, summoning other animals, and in self-defense, for animals make different sounds in each of these different situations. The beasts felt affection for him and he reciprocated their affection, and they did not feel estranged from one another.

When images of things were impressed upon his soul after they had receded from view, he experienced attraction towards some and repulsion towards others. Thus it came to pass that he observed the animals and found that they were all covered with fur, hair, or feathers. He also noted their agility, ferocity, and the weapons they were equipped with to defend themselves against opponents, such as horns, incisors, hooves, spurs, and claws. Then he looked at himself and observed that he was naked, weaponless, sluggish in motion, and lacking **[34]** in aggression when beasts competed with him over fruit. They would seize the fruits from him and would always get to them first, for he was unable to defend himself or to elude any of the beasts. He saw that his peers among the offspring of deer had sprouted horns where they had none before and gained strength, having initially been slow-moving. He found that he lacked those things. On reflecting on this, he was unable to ascertain its cause. He would observe those animals with defects and deficient natures, but would not find among them any who resembled him. He also looked at the openings for excrement in all animals and found that they were always covered. The openings for solid excrement were covered by tails, while those for urine were covered by fur and similar things; their genitals were also more hidden than his.

All this distressed him and caused him grief. After worrying about it for some time, by the time he approached the age of 7, he despaired of becoming more perfect. Since his deficiency weighed upon him, he took some broad leaves and put them behind him and in front of him, and he made a belt around his waist from palm fronds and coarse grass, to which he attached the leaves. It was not long before the leaves wilted, dried out, and fell off. He then took other leaves and sewed them together with double knots and this time it lasted longer but that was not very long either. He also trimmed and straightened tree branches to use as sticks to fend off the animals that contended with him, attacking the weak and resisting the strong, thereby raising his own self-esteem and dignity. He found that his hands were far superior to their hands, for they enabled him to cover his genitals and to use sticks to protect his possessions, which allowed him to do without the tail and natural weapons that he desired. Meanwhile, he grew up and advanced beyond 7 years, and he persisted in taking great pains to restore the leaves with which he covered himself.

[35] At some point, he was of a mind to take a tail from one of the dead beasts to attach it to himself. But he saw that the living beasts protected their dead and fended off others, so he was unable to perform that action until one day he came across a dead eagle. He was guided to fulfill his wish, and when he found that there were no beasts protecting him at all, he seized the opportunity. He drew close to the eagle, cut off its wings and tail in separate pieces, then he smoothed and unruffled the feathers, and he removed the rest of its skin. He divided the rest into two pieces, one of which he strapped to his back and the other to his navel and what lies below it. He then attached the tail to his backside and the wings to his upper arms. This provided him with warmth and gained him some respect in the souls of all the beasts, which ceased to contend with him or oppose him.

None of the beasts approached him from that point onwards except the doe that had nursed and raised him. She never left him and he never left her. When she aged and weakened, he would take her to fertile pastures and gather sweet fruits to feed her. Frailty and weakness continued to take hold of her progressively until death, at which point all movement ceased and all her actions were disabled. When the boy saw her in that state, he was terrified, and his soul nearly welled over with sorrow. He called out to her using the sound to which she usually responded, crying out as loud as he could, but he still could not see any movement or change in her. He looked closely at her ears and eyes but could not detect an observable defect. He also inspected all her organs but could not find a defect in any of them. He longed to find the source of the defect so that he could remove it and restore her to her former state, but he was utterly incapable of doing so. He had been guided to this opinion[15] by a lesson that had been impressed upon his soul earlier. For he found that when he closed his eyes or covered them with something, he could not see anything until that impediment was removed. He also found that if he inserted his fingers into his ears and blocked them, he could not hear anything until that obstacle was taken away [36]. Moreover, if he grasped his nose with his hand, he ceased to smell anything until his nose was reopened. As a

[15] That is, the opinion that there must be a defect or impediment in one of her organs.

result, he came to believe that all sensations and actions have impediments that obstruct them, and that when these impediments are removed the actions resume.

When he inspected all the doe's visible organs, he could not find an apparent defect in them. Moreover, he noticed that she was generally incapacitated, not afflicted in any specific organ. So it occurred to him that the defect that had struck her was in an unseen organ, lying in the interior of the body, and that the action of that organ was indispensable for all the visible organs. When a defect struck this organ, general harm and overall incapacity ensued. He yearned to locate that organ and to remove whatever afflicted it, so that its condition could be rectified and it could transmit its benefit to the rest of the body. Thus, the actions of the doe would resume.

Before that, he had noticed that in the dead corpses of beasts and others, their various parts were solid throughout, except for the cavities in the skull, chest, and abdomen. It struck him that the organ that he sought would be found in one of those three places. Moreover, he had a strong presumption that it would be in the most central of those three locations, since he had become convinced that all other organs needed it, and it followed necessarily from that that it should be centrally placed. In addition, when he reflected upon himself, he felt such an organ in his chest. And when he considered[16] all his other organs – hand, foot, ear, nose, and eye – he found that he could endure being deprived of them and would be able to spare them. He was also able to do the same for his head and supposed therefore that he could do without it, but when he reflected upon the organ in his chest, he found that he was unable to spare it for an instant. Likewise, when he fought with beasts, the part he guarded most from their spikes was his chest, due to his awareness of what lay inside.

When his judgment settled on the fact that the organ that had become defective was located in the doe's chest, he resolved to [37] search for it and examine it, in the hope of finding it and eliminating the defect. But then he feared that this action itself would have a greater impact than what had happened to her already, and that his efforts might be in vain.[17] However, he reconsidered: Had he ever seen beasts and others who had

[16] Reading *yastaʿriḍ* instead of *yaʿtariḍ* (objected to).
[17] Alternatively, his efforts would be at her expense (*fa-yakūn saʿyuhu ʿalayhā*).

come into that condition and later recovered, returning to their original condition? He could find none. Thus, he despaired of her returning to her former condition if he left her alone, but he held out some hope of her being restored to that condition if he could find that organ and remove its defect. He determined to cut open her chest and to examine what lay inside. He made knife-like tools from the shards of hard stones and slivers of dry reeds, and he used them to make an incision between her ribs. Then he cut through the flesh between the ribs and reached the membrane[18] that lies under the ribs, which he found to be tough. This strengthened his assumption that such a membrane could only be for such an organ as the one he sought. He hankered to get past it to reach his desired goal. He tried to slit it open but found it difficult for lack of the proper tools, since his were made of stones and reeds. So he renewed his efforts and went about piercing the membrane carefully until it yielded and he reached the lung. At first, he assumed that it was what he was looking for, so he went about examining it and searching for the place that had a defect.

Initially, he only found one of the pair of lungs, which lies on one side. He noticed that it was displaced to [38] the side, whereas he believed that the organ he sought could only be at the center of the body by width, just as it was at the center of the body by length. So he continued to search in the middle of the chest until he found the heart enclosed in an extremely tough sheath,[19] which was strongly connected to it. The lung adjoined it on the side where he began to cut. He said to himself: "If the organ has on the other side what it has on this side, then it is truly central, and it must be what I am looking for. That is especially so given its fine location, superb shape, compactness, and the toughness of its flesh, as well as the fact that it is protected by this membrane, the likes of which I have yet to see around any other organ."

He then investigated the other side of the chest, where he found the membrane lining the ribs and he found the lung, as he had on the other side. At that point, he judged that that organ was indeed what he was looking for. He attempted to split it and to penetrate the pericardium, and after some exertion and duress, he managed to do so, but only after making great efforts. He unsheathed the heart and found it solid on all sides. He tried to detect some apparent defect in it, but could not find any. He then

[18] The pleura is a membrane that lines the thoracic cavity (parietal pleura) and covers the lungs (visceral pleura).

[19] The myocardium is a tough muscular wall surrounding the heart.

pressed his hand down on it and discovered that it contained a cavity. He said to himself: "Perhaps my ultimate goal is simply inside this organ, and I have yet to attain it." He cut it open and found two cavities inside, one on the right and another on the left. The one on the right was full of congealed blood, whereas the one on the left was completely empty. He said: "What I seek is surely located in one of these two chambers," and he added, "The right chamber[20] just contains congealed blood. Undoubtedly, it congealed only when the whole body came into this state." He had observed before that when blood flows out of the body it always congeals and coagulates, and this was blood like any other. "I see that this blood is present in all other organs, and is not specific to any particular organ. What I seek is not **[39]** something with this characteristic. Rather, it is what is specific to this location, something that I find I cannot do without for an instant, and for which this organ was originally created.[21] I have been wounded many times by beasts or rocks and much blood has flowed from me. But that did not harm me, nor did it make me lose any of my actions. What I seek is not in this right chamber. As for the left chamber, I find that it is quite empty and do not think that that is in vain. If each organ has an action specific to it, how could this chamber be in vain, especially given its splendor? Quite simply, I now see that what I seek was indeed in it, but it has abandoned it and rendered it empty. After that, the body became incapacitated, losing sensation and motion."

When he realized that what inhabited it had left that chamber before it broke down and passed into that state, he determined that it would be unlikely for it to return after the destruction and dissection that had occurred. He came to regard the body on the whole as base and valueless in comparison with that thing that, he believed, had inhabited it for some time and then had left it. After that, he focused his attention on that thing: What was it? How was it?[22] What connected it to this body? Where is it now? Which exit did it take when it left the body? What was the cause of its distress – in case it left unwillingly? And what caused it to have such an antipathy towards the body and to separate from it – in case it left willingly?

[20] That is, the right ventricle of the heart.

[21] Alternatively, which he had originally set out to find (*wa ilayhi kāna inbiʿāthuhu min awwal*). However, this change of pronoun ("he" instead of "I") would entail an interruption of the direct quotation.

[22] Alternatively, what qualities did it have (*kayf hūwa*)?

As his thoughts wandered in this manner, he forgot about the body and disregarded it. He came to know that the mother who had loved and nursed him was that very thing that had left the body. That was the source from which **[40]** all her actions issued, rather than the now defunct body. The entire body was merely an instrument for the other thing, on a par with the stick that he used to fight off the beasts. He transferred his relationship from the body to the owner of that body and its motive force, and all his longing was now directed towards it.

Meanwhile, the body decomposed and emitted unpleasant odors, which just increased his aversion towards it and caused him not to want to see it. Afterwards, he happened to witness a fight between two ravens that ended with one of them killing the other. The surviving raven began to scratch at the ground until it dug a hole, then interred the dead raven in the earth. He said to himself: "This raven has done well to bury the corpse of the other, even though it was wrong to kill the other raven in the first place. It is all the more fitting for me to perform such an action towards my mother." He dug a hole, laid his mother's body in it, and covered it with earth, continuing to reflect on that thing that had caused the body to function, which he still did not know.

However, from then onwards, he observed each individual deer and found that it had the same shape and form as his mother. He came to assume that each of them was moved and disposed by something similar to the thing that had moved and disposed his mother. As a result of that similarity, he felt affection towards all deer and was drawn to them. He remained in that state for a while, examining the species of animals and plants, wandering along the shore of that island, wondering whether he would find a creature similar to himself, since he saw that each individual animal and plant had many others resembling it. But he looked in vain. Since he had observed that the sea surrounded the island on all sides, he believed that his island was the only thing in existence.

[41] One day a fire happened to ignite in a thicket of reeds by the action of friction. When he stood to watch it, he was overwhelmed by the sight of an entity[23] that was so unfamiliar to him, and he stopped to marvel at it for a while. As he drew closer to it, he noticed that the fire had a piercing light and was capable of acting at a distance. As soon as it made contact with something, it consumed it and transformed it into itself. He was

[23] Literally, creature (*khalqan*).

transported with wonder at it, and[24] his God-given nature supplied him with the boldness and strength to stretch his hand out towards it to take something from it. When he touched it, it burned his hand and he was unable to take hold of it. Then he hit upon the idea of taking a smoldering stick that had not been completely consumed by fire. Grasping it by the intact end as it burned at the other end, he managed to hold on to it and to carry it to the place where he had made his dwelling, for he had earlier sought refuge in a den that he deemed fit for habitation.

Day and night, he continued to feed the fire with an ample supply of grass and wood and to watch over it with admiration and wonderment. He was especially drawn to it at night when its light and warmth took the place of the sun for him. As his fascination with the fire grew, he came to believe that it was the best thing he had. Observing that it always moved upwards and desired elevation, he assumed that it belonged to the celestial substances that he saw. By throwing things into it, he tested its power and found that it consumed things either quickly or slowly, depending on the disposition of that body to be burned. One of the things he threw into it in order to test its powers was a species of marine animal that had been washed up on the shore. As the animal cooked and gave off the smell of roast flesh, his appetite grew, so he ate a piece of it and enjoyed the taste. That is how he acquired the habit of eating meat, and how he came to master the skill of hunting and fishing.

[42] His fondness for fire increased, since it enabled him to secure good nourishment as never before. His enthusiasm for it grew as he witnessed its beneficial effects and its powerful capabilities. It occurred to him that the thing that had left the heart of the deer that had raised him was of the same substance as this being, or at least something related to it.[25] What confirmed this assumption for him was the fact that he observed the warmth of animals throughout their lifetime and their coldness after death – this was constant and unvarying. It was also confirmed by the warmth he felt in his own chest, at the point that corresponded to the place where he had cut open the deer. It occurred to him that he could take a live animal, cut open its heart, and inspect the cavity that he found empty when he cut open the deer, his mother. That way, he would be able to observe the cavity in the live animal while it was still full of the thing

[24] Omitting *bimā*.

[25] Alternatively, something of the same genus (*min shay'in yujānisuhu*).

that inhabits it, and determine whether it was of the same substance as fire and whether it possessed some illumination and heat.

He secured a beast, manacled it firmly, and cut it open in the manner in which he had the deer, reaching the heart. First, he inspected the left side of the heart, making an incision there, and found that cavity filled with a vaporous air resembling a white mist. He inserted his finger into it and found it so hot that he almost burned himself. At once, the beast died. He became convinced that the vapor was what moved that animal, and that every individual animal was the same: when the vapor parted, the animal died. He was then moved by the desire to investigate the rest of the organs of animals, their arrangements, conditions [43], quantities, and the qualities of their relations to each other. He also wanted to determine how they derived sustenance from this hot vapor so that they could go on living, how this vapor remained as long as it did, what it was derived from, and how it came about that it did not lose its warmth.

These questions he pursued by dissecting live and dead animals, continuing to inspect them closely, until he became an expert in this subject and attained the level of the most eminent natural scientists. He came to realize that each individual animal, no matter how numerous its organs and diverse its perceptions and motions, was a unity by virtue of that spirit, which constituted its single fixed principle, and from which proceeded its division into various organs. All bodily organs are mere servants or implements for that thing. The spirit disposes the body like someone who uses the perfect weapon to confront each opponent and stalk every prey, whether on land or on sea. Each genus is hunted with the proper hunting implement, and weapons are divided into those used in self-defense and those used as deterrents. Likewise, hunting implements[26] are divisible into those more suited to marine animals and those appropriate for land animals. Again, instruments for dissection can be divided into those appropriate for cutting, breaking, and piercing; though the dissected body is one, each instrument is disposed in a way that is suited to it, according to the desired goal. Similarly, if the animal spirit, which is one, uses the instrument of the eye then its action will be sight, whereas if it uses the instrument of the nose its action will be smell. If it uses the tongue the action will be taste, if skin and flesh the action will be touch, and if liver nourishing and being nourished [44]. Each of these actions has

[26] Arabic uses the same term (*ṣayd*) for hunting and fishing.

an organ that serves it and each organ is only able to complete an action when something reaches it from the spirit along the pathways known as nerves. If these paths are severed or blocked in some way, the action of that organ is disabled. These nerves receive the spirit from the interior of the brain, which derives it in turn from the heart. The brain contains many spirits, for it is a location that distributes it to many parts.[27] When any organ is deprived of this spirit for some reason or another, it will be put out of action. This corresponds to a discarded implement, which the agent can neither dispose of nor use beneficially. Moreover, if this spirit as a whole leaves the body or is dissipated in one way or another, the entire body will become incapacitated and will arrive at the condition of death.

This manner of reasoning allowed him to attain this level of rational speculation by the third seven-year period after his birth, which was his twenty-first year.

During the period mentioned he devised a number of useful inventions. He covered himself with the hides of animals that he dissected and wore them on his body. He made thread out of hair, the barks of stalks of mallow, hemp, and other plants with fibers. He first hit upon this idea when using alfa, from whose tough thorns and stalks, sharpened on stones, he made hooks. He discovered the art of construction when he observed the behavior of swallows. He built a depot and storehouse for his surplus food, which he secured with a door made of canes tied to one another, to prevent any animals from getting at it while he was absent on some errand or another [45]. He also domesticated birds of prey to use in hunting and raised chickens to benefit from their eggs and meat. From the hooves of wild cattle he fashioned spearheads and attached them to sturdy canes and the branches of beech trees, using fire and sharp stones to do so, thereby creating spear-like weapons. He made a shield from toughened hides. All this he did because of what he saw as his lack of natural weapons.

He observed that his hands were capable of supplying him with everything he lacked in that regard and that animals of all varieties no longer resisted him. Rather, they now fled from him and eluded him altogether by being swifter, so he fell back on his ingenuity. The most successful course, he thought, would be to domesticate some of the swiftest animals, treating them kindly by bringing them their proper food, until he was capable of

[27] Alternatively, consisting of many parts (*tatawazzaʿfīhi aqsām kathīrah*).

riding them and using them to chase other types of animal. The island contained wild horses and asses, so he took as many as he needed, tamed them until he was able to achieve his purpose, and attached laces and hides to them to create something like bits and saddles. He thereby achieved what he had hoped for and was able to pursue the animals that he had been unable to trap by using his ingenuity. He mastered all these things at the same time as he was occupied with dissection and desired to understand all the properties of the organs of animals and their peculiarities. All this took place within the period specified, namely 21 years.

After that, he pursued other interests, examining all bodies in the realm of generation and corruption: animals of all varieties, plants, minerals, rocks, soils, water, steam, snow, hail, smoke, ice, flame, and heat. He discovered that they had many characteristics and a variety of actions, as well as both similar and contrary motions [46]. He reasoned intently about these matters and verified them, finding that they were similar in some respects and differed in others. Insofar as they were the same, they were one, and insofar as they differed, they were various and multiple. Sometimes he would reason about the properties of things and what distinguished them from one another, and they would appear to be an immeasurably large multitude. Existence seemed to him to be an uncontainable, sprawling expanse. Indeed, even his own self[28] appeared multiple when he considered the variations among his organs, each of which was suited to an action and had a characteristic that was specific to itself. He would inspect each organ and find that each was capable of being divided into many parts. He would therefore judge that his essence was multiple, as he did for the essence of every other thing.

At other times, he would follow another line of reasoning, and would find that his organs, for all their multiplicity, were in fact connected to one another. They were not separate in any way, and were effectively one. Moreover, they were only different because of the differences among their actions, which were caused by what they received from the potentiality of the animal spirit, about which he had reasoned earlier. That spirit was one in its essence and was also the reality of the essence; all other organs were like instruments for it. By this method, his essence was unified for him.

[28] The Arabic *dhāt* can mean either self or essence, and there seems to be a deliberate ambiguity in this portion of the text, as Ḥayy is in the process of formulating the concept of essence. In what follows, I have translated it using both English terms, as seems appropriate.

He then moved on to other types of animal, and by the same type of reasoning, concluded that each particular one was a unity. Then he would look at a species, such as deer, horses, asses, and the various species of birds, and would find that the individuals of each species resembled one another in both external and internal organs, as well as in their senses, movements, and ends. He could find no differences among them – aside from slight things – by comparison to what they had in common. He judged that the spirit in each of these species was one thing, and that it differed [47] only in that it was divided among many hearts. If he could collect everything that was divided among these hearts and put them in one container, it would consist of one thing, as though it were water or some other liquid that had been divided among many bottles and then collected together again. Whether divided or collected it consists of one thing, it is only accidentally multiple in some respect. Based on this manner of reasoning, he came to regard an entire species as one thing, and took the multiplicity of the individuals of a species as corresponding to the multiplicity of organs in a single individual, which were not really multiple.

Conjuring up all the species of animals in his mind, he contemplated them, and found that they were all similar insofar as they all had perception, nutrition, and moved by volition wherever they wished. He had come to know that these actions were those specific to the animal spirit, and that all the respects in which they differed – aside from these commonalities – were not highly specific to the animal spirit. It became clear to him as a result of this contemplation that the animal spirit that was common to the entire genus of animals was one in reality. Wherever a slight difference arose that was specific to one species or another, this was comparable to a single quantity of water, divided among many bottles, some of which were colder than others, but which was actually one and the same. Those having the same degree of coldness were comparable to the specificity of the animal spirit in one species. Moreover, just as that water was a unity, the animal spirit was also a unity, even though it was accidentally multiple in some respect. According to this manner of reasoning, he discovered that the genus of animals was one.

Then he reexamined the different species of plants, finding that the individuals of each species resembled one another in their branches, leaves, flowers, fruits, and activity. He compared them to animals, and came to know that they had one thing in common, which corresponded to the spirit in animals, and that they were a unity in respect of that thing. He also looked at the entire genus of plants and judged that it was a unity insofar as plants all shared in the activity of nutrition and growth.

[48] Then he combined in his mind the animal genus and plant genus and found that all of their members shared in nutrition and growth, but that the animal genus added to the plant genus, perception, sensation, and motion. He also noted that plants sometimes exhibited something similar to these activities, such as the turning of flowers to face the sun, the motion of roots towards nutriment, and similar things. These contemplations led him to conclude that plants and animals are one, because of the one thing common to them both – though it was more complete and perfect in one of them, whereas in the other it was blocked by some impediment. It was comparable to one quantity of water that had been divided in two parts, one being solid and the other liquid. In this way, animals and plants were unified by him.

He then turned his attention to bodies that lacked perception, nutrition, and growth, such as rocks, soil, water, air, and flame, and found that they were all bodies with a certain height, width, and depth. He found that these bodies differed only in that some had color whereas others were colorless, some were hot while others were cold, and other such differences. He saw that hot bodies could become cold and cold bodies could become hot, and that water became steam and steam became water. He also found that burning objects were transformed into embers, ashes, flame, and smoke, and that when smoke encountered a stone arch it solidified there and became like any other terrestrial thing. As a result of these contemplations, he concluded that they were all one thing in reality, even though they were generally a multiplicity. This multiplicity was the same as that found amongst animals and plants.

When he went on to reason about the thing that unified plants and animals, he found that it was a body like these other bodies, with a length, width, and depth, which could be either hot or cold. Thus it was just like one of these other bodies that had neither[29] perception nor nutrition, but was different from them merely in the actions that issued from it by means of animal or plant instruments. Perhaps these actions were not essential but flowed to it from something else **[49]**; had they flowed

[29] Reading *lā taḥussu wa lā tataghadhdhā* for *taḥussu wa lā tataghadhdhā* (had perception and not nutrition).

to these other bodies they would have been similar. He reasoned about this thing in its essence, stripped of these activities – which according to preliminary opinion would appear to issue from it – and found that it was simply a body like any other. As a result of these contemplations, it became clear to him that bodies were one thing, whether animate or inanimate, in motion or at rest. But some of them had actions produced by instruments, and he did not know whether these actions were essential to them or whether they flowed to them from some other thing. From this perspective,[30] he saw nothing but bodies, and by this method, he discovered that existence as a whole was one. But by the first line of reasoning he regarded existence as an immeasurable and limitless multiplicity. He remained under the influence of this condition[31] for a period of time.

He then contemplated all bodies, whether animate or inanimate. At times they appeared to be one thing and at other times to be an endless multiplicity. Each of them, he observed, always had one of two features: it either moved upwards, like smoke, flame, and air when it was underwater, or else it moved in the opposite direction, downwards, like water, pieces of earth, animals, and plants. Each of these bodies always had one of these two motions, and would not rest unless an obstacle blocked its path. For instance, when a rock moving downwards encounters the solid surface of the earth it stops because it is unable to penetrate it; if it were able to do so, it would clearly not cease to move. That is why, when you lift it, you will find that it struggles to move downwards, seeking to descend. Similarly, when smoke rises, it will not veer from its course unless it encounters a solid dome to trap it, at which point it will twist right and left. If it manages to escape from the dome, it will penetrate the air in its ascent, since air cannot trap it. He also noted that when a leather skin is filled with air, fastened, and immersed in water, it seeks to ascend and will resist anyone who holds it underwater. It continues to do so until it attains the location of air, by emerging from under the water. At that point, it comes to rest and loses its former resistance and tendency to go upwards.

He reasoned: Were there any bodies lacking one of these two motions, or a tendency towards one of them **[50]** at any given time? He found no

[30] Literally, in this condition or state (*fī hādhihi al-ḥāl*).

[31] Presumably, the condition of alternately seeing existence as a unity and seeing it as a multiplicity.

such body among those around him, but he eagerly sought such a body, in order to determine the nature of bodies as such,[32] without being joined to any of the characteristics that give rise to multiplicity. When he failed to do so, he observed those bodies with the fewest characteristics predicated of them and found that they had, in some way, one of two attributes, which can be expressed as follows: heaviness and lightness. He reasoned about heaviness and lightness. Do they belong to body as such? Or do they belong to a concept[33] added to that of body? He ruled in favor of the latter, since he thought that if they belonged to body as such, then there would not exist a body without both of them. But we find that the heavy body does not have lightness, and the light body does not have heaviness. These are necessarily two different bodies, and each has a distinct concept added to its being a body. This concept is what differentiates each of these bodies from the other. If that were not the case, they would be the same thing in every respect.

He realized that the reality of each of the heavy and light bodies is composed of two concepts: one shared by both, namely the concept of body, and another specific to each, which is heaviness in one of them and lightness in the other. These concepts are joined to the concept of body, which is what moves one upwards and the other downwards. Similarly, he reasoned about all other inanimate and animate bodies and found that the reality of the existence of each [51] one of them is composed of the concept of body and of some other concept added to the concept of body, either one or more than one. The forms of the different bodies began to loom before him, and this is the first thing that appeared to him from the spiritual realm, since they are forms that cannot be perceived by the senses but are rather apprehended by a type of intellectual reasoning. Among the things that appeared to him from the spiritual realm was that the animal spirit whose location is the heart, as has been explained above, must also have a concept added to the concept of corporeality, equipping it by virtue of that concept to carry out these particular movements, which are specific to it, of the kinds of perceptions, varieties of sensations, and types of motions. That concept was its form and the differentia that

32 Alternatively, body *qua* body (*min ḥayth hūwa jism*).

33 The Arabic term *maʿnā* (concept, meaning) can have a range of connotations in medieval Islamic philosophy. But rather than translate it freely in this context, I have preferred to translate it literally, while drawing attention to the fact that in this sentence and in what follows, it is better understood as "property" or "attribute," or sometimes "form."

differentiated it from all other bodies. This is what theoreticians call the animal soul.

The same applies to the thing that takes the place for plants of natural heat for animals. It is something specific to them, their differentia, which theoreticians call the vegetative soul. Similarly for all inanimate bodies, which have, in addition to both animals and plants in the realm of generation and corruption, something specific to them, enabling each of them to perform their specific actions, such as the perceptible types of movements and the kinds of capacities.[34] That thing is the differentia of each of them, which is what theoreticians call its "nature."

When he understood by these speculations that the reality of the animal spirit, which he always yearned for, was composed of the concept of body as well as another concept added to that of body, and also that the concept of body was shared by all bodies and that the other associated concept was specific to a particular body, the concept *body* ceased to be of importance to him. So he set it aside and he fastened his thoughts on the second concept, which is what is expressed as the *soul*.[35] He yearned to explore it and committed himself to thinking about it, and in so doing he adopted the principle of reasoning that he would examine all bodies not insofar as they were bodies, but rather insofar as they possessed forms[36] that entailed specific properties that differentiated them from one another.

He pursued this inquiry and dedicated himself to it, and found that there was a set of bodies sharing a certain form that issued in a certain action or actions. He observed that a subset of this set, while sharing a form with this collection, added to it another form, from which certain other actions issued. He observed further that a subset of bodies within that subset, which had the first two forms, added a third form, from which certain actions issued that were specific **[52]** to them. An example of this would be all the terrestrial bodies, such as earth, rocks, minerals, plants, animals, and all other massive bodies, which constitute a single set sharing one form, which issues in a downward movement, provided they are not obstructed from moving downwards by some obstacle. A subset of this set, namely the plants and animals, while sharing this form with the previous set, adds to it another form, which issues in nutrition and growth. Nutrition occurs when the one receiving nutrition replaces

[34] Alternatively, qualities (*kayfiyyāt*). [35] The Arabic term *nafs* can also be translated as self.
[36] Alternatively, insofar as their essences were forms (*dhawāt ṣūwar*).

whatever has actually decomposed of it, with the help of the nutritive faculty, which transforms what it has come upon by means of the digestive faculty, with the help of the faculty of assimilation and the faculty of transport,[37] so that it is perfectly disposed to match the substance of the one receiving nutrition, in order to preserve the individual and perfect his capacity. Growth is augmentation by means of the faculty of growth, which increases the dimensions of the body, meaning height, width, and depth, according to natural proportions, with the nutriment that has entered its parts. Both of these actions are common to plants and animals, and issue necessarily from a form common to both, which is called the vegetative soul. Moreover, a subset of this subset, specifically animals, while sharing with the previous subset the first and second forms, adds a third form, which issues in perception and locomotion from one domain to another.

He also found that each species of animal has a specific property that sets it apart from other species and differentiates it from them, making it distinct from them. He knew that this issued from a form specific to it, which is additional **[53]** to the concept of the form that it has in common with other animals. Likewise, each species of plant is similar. It became clear to him that some of the perceptible bodies in the realm of generation and corruption acquire their reality from numerous concepts added to the concept of body, while others do so on the basis of fewer such concepts. He came to know that it was easier to be cognizant of those bodies with fewer concepts than those with more. He therefore first sought to understand the reality of the form of the thing that acquires its reality from the fewest things. He found that animals and plants acquire their reality from many concepts, due to the variety of their actions, so he postponed his reflections about their forms. He also found that some parts of earth are simpler than other parts, so he sought out the simplest of these he could find. Likewise, he found that water was a thing less composite than other things, given the paucity of actions issuing from its forms; similarly, for fire and air.

The first thing he assumed was that these four can be transformed into one another and that they had one thing in common, namely the concept of body, and that this thing [viz. the concept body] should lack any of the concepts that distinguish each of these four from the other. It cannot

37 It is not clear what precise function the faculty of transport (*al-wāṣilah*) is performing; it is not listed by Ibn Sīnā among the faculties of the soul.

move upwards or downwards, nor can it be hot, nor moist, nor dry, since none of these attributes is general to all bodies. Thus, these cannot be attributes of body insofar as it is body. If it were possible for a body to exist that had no form added to its being a body, it would have none of these attributes, and it could not have any attribute if that attribute did not generalize over all bodies that were informed with the various kinds of forms.

He reasoned: "Is there a single attribute that generalizes over all bodies, both animate and inanimate?" He found nothing that generalized over all bodies except the concept of extension, which exists in all of them in all three dimensions, expressed as height, width, and depth. He knew that this concept belongs to body insofar as it is body. However, he was unable to perceive the existence of a body possessing this attribute alone, which possessed no concept besides the extension just mentioned and wholly lacking all forms. He then reflected upon this extension in three dimensions. Was it the concept of body itself **[54]** and was there no other concept besides it? Or was that not the case? He observed that alongside this concept of extension there was indeed another concept, that in which extension alone existed and without which it could not subsist, just as that extended thing could not subsist on its own without extension.

He used an example drawn from perceptible bodies, which have forms,[38] to illustrate this idea. He observed that if one molded clay into a shape, such as a sphere, it would have height, width, and depth in certain quantities. Moreover, if that same sphere were then transformed into a cube or egg shape, its height, weight, and depth would change, and would take on other quantities, different from the previous ones. Meanwhile, the clay remained one and the same, unchanged, though it necessarily had a length, width, and depth, to some extent or another. It could not be stripped of them. In addition, because they succeeded it, it became clear to him that it was a concept on its own, and because it could not be stripped of them entirely, it became clear that they were of its reality.

By considering this example, it seemed to him that body, insofar as it was body, was in reality composed of two concepts: the first corresponded to the clay of the sphere in this analogy, and the other corresponded to

[38] Alternatively, whose essences are forms (*dhawāt al-ṣūwar*).

the height, width, and depth of the sphere, or cube, or any other shape that a body might have. It also seemed to him that he only understood the concept of body insofar as it was composed of these two concepts and that neither could do without the other. But what could change and take on many aspects was the concept of extension, which resembled form for many bodies, which have forms; whereas what remained in a fixed state was what corresponded to clay in the previous analogy, which resembled the concept of body for all bodies that had forms. This thing that corresponded to the clay in the analogy is what theoreticians call matter or prime matter, which is entirely bare of form.

When his reasoning reached this point, he withdrew somewhat from what is perceptible and became aware of the peripheries of the intellectual realm, but then he became nostalgic and longed for what he had become familiar with in the perceptible realm. So he retreated slightly and left body **[55]** as such, since that was something that was not perceived by the senses and was not tangible. Instead, he returned to the simplest perceptible bodies that he had observed, namely those four that his reasoning had previously hit upon.[39]

The first that he reasoned about was water. He observed that if it were left to what its form dictated, it evinced a perceptible coldness and sought to move downwards. If it were heated first, either by fire or by the heat of the sun, coldness would be eliminated first and it would continue to seek to move downwards. If it were heated further, it would no longer seek to move downwards and it would seek to move upwards instead. Thus, the two attributes that always issued from it and its form would be eliminated altogether. Since he was only cognizant of the two actions that issued from the form, when these actions ceased, the form was annulled.[40] The form of water was eliminated from that body when actions appeared from it that had a tendency to issue from another form. Another form originated in it, which had not been there before, and actions issued from the body by virtue of that form, which would not have had a tendency to issue from it before, while it retained the first form. Thus, he knew by necessity that each event[41] must inevitably have an originator. This example impressed

[39] That is, the four elements: earth, water, air, and fire.

[40] Literally, the judgment of the form was annulled (*baṭula ḥukm al-ṣūrah*). Ibn Ṭufayl uses a metaphor that suggests the reversal of a legal verdict.

[41] Alternatively, each existent (*kull ḥādith*).

upon his soul the agent[42] of the form, in a general way not in particular terms.[43]

He then went in pursuit of the forms that he had already come to know, one by one, and found that they were all originated and that they must necessarily have an agent. He then reasoned about the essences of the forms and found that they were none other than the dispositions[44] of bodies to issue forth those actions. For example, when water was heated to excess, it was disposed to move upwards and became suited to that. That disposition was its form, since there was nothing there but body and the things that could be perceived thereof, such as qualities and movements, which were not there before. There was also an agent that had originated in them, having not been there before. The suitability of the body for some movements rather than others, was none other than its disposition to its form. The same seemed to him to hold of all forms. It became clear to him that the actions issuing from them were not in reality due to them, but were rather due to an agent that carried out the actions attributed [56] to them. The concept that dawned upon him was the one expressed in the statement by the Prophet of God (peace be upon him): "I was the hearing by which he hears, and the sight by which he sees." And in the most masterful Revelation: "You did not kill them, but God killed them; and you did not throw when you threw, but God threw" [Qur'ān 8:17].

When something of the agent loomed before him in this general manner without particularity, he had an acute yearning to become cognizant of it in particular terms, for he had not yet left the perceptible realm. He began to seek this voluntary agent at the level of perceptibles, not knowing yet whether it was one or multiple. He perused all the bodies before him, which were always the objects of his reflection, and found that all of them were generated at times and corrupted at other times. Although he had not witnessed the corruption of the entire set of bodies, he had witnessed the corruption of its parts, such as water and earth. He saw that parts of them were corrupted by fire. Likewise, he saw that air was corrupted by extreme cold, producing ice, which then melted into water. Similarly, for all the bodies that he had observed: none of them were free of origination and none lacked the voluntary agent. He therefore cast them all aside and came to reflect upon celestial bodies.

42 The term for "agent" (*fāʿil*) is also used to refer to the Aristotelian efficient cause.
43 Reading *tafṣīl* (particular) for *tafḍīl* (preference).
44 Literally, disposition of a body (in the singular).

He reached this level of rational speculation at the end of four seven-year periods after his birth, which were twenty-eight years.

He knew that the sky and all the planets in it were bodies because they were extended in three dimensions [57]: height, width, and depth. None of them ever lacked this attribute, and whatever never lacks the attribute of extension is a body. Thus, they are all bodies. He then reflected: Are they infinitely[45] extended, having infinite height, width, and depth without end? Or are they instead finite, being bounded by limits at which they stop and after which there can be no extension? He was somewhat perplexed by this. But by the power of his reasoning and the cleverness of his mind, he observed that an infinite body was an absurdity, an impossible thing, and an unintelligible concept. This judgment was bolstered by many arguments that occurred to him, for he argued as follows. This celestial body is either finite on the side that faces me and that I can perceive, which I do not doubt because I can sense it with my eyes; or else it is finite on the opposite side, which is what I am doubtful of. However, I also know that it is impossible for it to extend infinitely on the opposite side, by the following argument. First, I imagine two lines [58] starting from this bounded side, traversing the thickness of the body infinitely in the direction of the extension of the body. Then, I imagine that a large segment is removed from one of these lines on its bounded side, and that the rest of the line is taken and laid at the bounded end of the line that remains whole.[46] If the mind then follows both lines in the direction that is said to be infinite, we will find one of two things. Either both lines will still extend infinitely and neither will be shorter than the other, which is impossible, since the line from which a segment has been taken would then be equal to the one that remained whole – just as it is impossible for the whole to be the same as the part. Or else the shorter line will not extend with the other line forever, but will rather fall short before it reaches its destination and will cease to extend along with it. This means that it will be finite, so if the segment that was taken from it at first, which is also finite, is restored to it, the whole will also be finite. But then it will be no shorter and no greater than the line that remained whole. Thus, this line will be the same as the other, and since it is finite, the other line will also

45 Literally, extended without end (*mumtaddah ilā ghayr nihāyah*). In Arabic, the terms for finite (with end) and infinite (without end) appear to be more intuitively graspable than the corresponding English terms, making this argument seem more accessible to an autodidact like Ḥayy.

46 Literally, from which nothing was taken (*lam yuqtaʿ minhu shay'*).

be finite. So the body in which these lines are supposed to be drawn will also be finite. But these lines could be drawn in any body, so every body is finite. Thus, when we suppose a body to be infinite, our supposition is false and impossible.[47]

When he had determined, thanks to his exceptional native intelligence that had discovered this argument, that the body of the sky was finite, he wanted to be cognizant of its shape and the manner in which it was intersected by the surfaces that bordered it. He looked first at the sun, moon, and other planets, and saw that they all rose in the east and set in the west. He saw that whichever one passed over the zenith traversed a great circle, whereas what diverged from the zenith to the north or south traversed a smaller circle. And what was further from the zenith on either side had a smaller circle than what was nearer. Moreover, the smallest circles in which the planets moved were two: one around the South Pole, which is the orbit of Suhayl,[48] and another around the North Pole, which is the orbit of al-Farqadayn.[49] Since his home, which we described earlier, was on the Equator, all these circles were perpendicular to the surface of his horizon and were similar to the south and north. Moreover, both polar axes were visible to him. He noticed that a planet traversing a large circle and a planet traversing a small circle, which rose together, would also set together **[59]**. The same applied to all planets at all times. So it became clear to him, as a result, that the celestial realm was shaped like a sphere. This belief was strengthened by the fact that he observed that the sun, moon, and other planets return to the east after setting in the west, as well as the fact that they appeared to him as large when they rose, when they reached the center of the sky, and when they set. If their orbits were not circular, they would necessarily have been closer to his sight at some times

47 In this passage, Ḥayy puts forward a proof that the universe is finite. Since it is not infinite on the side facing him, he starts out by supposing that it extends infinitely on the far side opposite him, and proves that this leads to an impossibility. He imagines two lines starting from the boundary of the celestial realm and extending infinitely outwards through it (call them AC and A'C'). Next, he imagines taking a line segment from the bounded end of the first line (AB), then adjusting it so that its bounded end (B) is aligned once again with the bounded end of the second line (A'). If both lines (BC and A'C') remain infinite, this leads to an impossibility since it effectively implies that the part (BC = B'C') is equal to the whole (A'C'). Alternatively, if the first line (BC) falls short of the second (A'C'), this implies that the first line (BC) is finite. But since the line segment (AB) that was taken from it is also finite, and adding two finite magnitudes results in a finite magnitude, the original line (AC) must have been finite to begin with, which is also impossible since it contradicts the initial supposition. He takes this as a *reductio ad absurdum* of the supposition that the celestial realm is infinite in extension.

48 The star Canopus.

49 Two bright stars (β and γ) of Ursa Minor.

than at others, and if that were so, then their magnitudes and sizes would have appeared differently in his sight, so that he would find them to be larger when they were near than when they were far, since their distances would have been different from his position – which is contrary to the first finding. Since that was not the case, he confirmed the sphericity of its shape.

He went on to examine the movement of the moon, observing that it went from west to east, as did the other wandering planets, until a large portion of the science of astronomy became evident to him. It became apparent to him that the motions of the planets occur in many spheres, all lying within one sphere, which was the highest and moved everything from east to west during the period of a day and a night. To explain how it moved and to become cognizant of it takes time and is proven in books. For our purposes, all that is needed is what has already been mentioned.

[60] When he achieved this level of cognizance, and he became acquainted with the fact that the entire celestial sphere and all that it contains is like one interconnected thing, and that the bodies that he reasoned about initially, such as earth, water, air, plants, animals, and the like, all lie within it and are not external to it, he likened it to an individual animal. The luminous planets correspond to the senses of the animal, while the various celestial spheres, which are connected to one another, correspond to the limbs of the animal. Meanwhile, what is within it of the realm of generation and corruption corresponds to what is inside the body of the animal including excretions and humors, within which an animal is frequently generated,[50] as in the larger world.

When it became clear to him that it was like a single individual in reality, a being in need of a voluntary agent, and when its many parts became unified for him, as a result of the same type of reasoning by which he unified the bodies that were in the realm of generation and corruption, he reflected on the entire world. Did it originate after having not existed, and did it come into existence after nonexistence? Or was it something that had always existed previously, having not been preceded by nonexistence in any way? He was puzzled by this, and neither of the two judgments carried greater weight with him. For when he leaned towards the belief in the preeternity of the world, he encountered many obstacles, such as the

[50] Presumably, spontaneous generation of parasites and other creatures living in the human body.

impossibility of the existence of what is infinite in time, by an argument similar to the one that he used to establish the impossibility of an infinite body. Likewise, he saw that this existence was not free of originated events, so that it was not possible for it to precede them, but what could not precede originated events, must also be originated. But when he leaned towards the belief in the origination of the world, he encountered other obstacles, such as the following one. He observed [61] that the concept of its origination after its nonexistence cannot be understood except as meaning that time preceded it, but time is part of the world and cannot be separated from it. Thus, the precedence of time over the world cannot be understood. Likewise, he said: "If it were indeed originated, it must have had an originator. Why did this originator, which originated it, originate it at this time and not before? Was it due to some new factor that occurred, which is impossible because there was nothing else in existence? Or was it due to a change that occurred in its essence? If so, what originated that change?"

He continued to reflect on this for several years, while arguments opposed one another, but neither of the two beliefs carried greater weight with him. When he was at a loss as to what to think, he began to reflect on what followed from each of the two beliefs, since what followed from each might be the same. He found that if he believed that the world was originated and emerged into existence out of nonexistence, it followed necessarily that it was not possible for it to come into existence on its own, and that it must have an agent that brings it into existence. This agent would not be perceivable by any of the senses, for if it were then it would be a body like any other, and if it were a body like any other, then it would be part of the world, would be originated, and would need an originator. If that second originator were also a body, then it would require a third originator, and the third a fourth, and so on in an infinite sequence, which is impossible. Therefore, it is necessary that the world has an agent that is not a body. If it is not a body, then there is no means of perceiving it by any of the senses, since the five senses only perceive bodies or what depends on bodies. If it cannot be perceived, then it cannot be imagined, for imagination is nothing but bringing forth the images of perceptibles in their absence. If it is not a body, then none of the attributes of bodies are applicable to it, beginning with the attributes of extension, height, width, and depth. It is exempt from all that and from all the attributes of bodies that follow from that. If it is the agent of the world, then it must have power over it and knowledge of it. "Does He not know what He created, for he is Kind and Discerning" [Qur'an, 67:14].

[62] He also observed that if he believed that the world was preeternal, and that nonexistence did not precede it, and that it had always been as it is, it would follow that its motion was preeternal and was infinite in the direction of its beginning, for it was not preceded by immobility at the point at which it started. Every motion necessarily requires a mover. The mover can either be a potentiality pervading a body – either that same body or a different body that is external to it – or else it can be a potentiality that does not pervade or is not present in a body. Every potentiality that pervades a body and is present in it is divided when that body is divided and multiplied when it is multiplied, such as, for example, the weight in a stone that moves it downwards. If the stone is divided in two halves its weight will also be divided in two halves, and if a similar stone is added to it then its weight will also be increased by the same amount. If it were possible to increase the stone forever infinitely, its weight would also increase infinitely. However, if the stone reaches a certain degree of magnitude and stops, the weight would also stop at that limit. But it has been demonstratively proven that every body is necessarily finite, hence every potentiality in a body is also necessarily finite. Thus, if we find a potentiality that produces an infinite action, then this potentiality must not be in a body. Moreover, we have found that the celestial sphere moves forever infinitely and without interruption, since we have supposed that it is preeternal and without a beginning. It follows necessarily from this that the potentiality that moves it is not in its body nor in another external body. It therefore belongs to something that is free of bodies, without any of the attributes of bodies.

It had already become apparent to him during his first reasoning concerning the realm of generation and corruption that the reality of the existence of each body is by virtue of its form, which is its disposition to undertake a variety of motions. By contrast, the existence it has by virtue of its matter is a weak existence that is almost inapprehensible. Thus, the existence of the entire world comes about by virtue of its disposition to be moved by this mover, which is free of matter and its attributes and is exempt from being perceived by the senses or conjured by the imagination, for God is above that. Moreover, if He[51] is the agent of the motions of the celestial realm, in their various types, which are actually unvarying and unflagging, then He must necessarily have power over it and knowledge of it.

Therefore, his reasoning led him to the same conclusion by this route as he had reached by the first route, and he was none the worse for his doubts concerning the preeternity or origination of the world. In either case, he determined that an agent existed that was not a body, not attached to a body, not detached from a body, and neither external nor internal to a body. For attachment, detachment, internality, and externality are all attributes of bodies, and He was exempt from these attributes.

[63] Since the matter of every body needs form, for it cannot subsist without it and does not have a fixed reality in its absence, and since form does not have true existence except by the action of this voluntary agent, it became clear to him that all existents need this agent for their existence, and that none of them could subsist without it. He was therefore the cause of existents and they were caused by Him, whether they were originated in existence and preceded by nonexistence, or whether they had no beginning in time and were never preceded by nonexistence. In either case, they are caused, need the agent, are dependent on Him for their existence, could not persist without His persistence, could not exist without His existence, and would not be preeternal were it not for His preeternity. Meanwhile, the cause, in essence, is capable of doing without them and is free of them. How could it be otherwise, since it has been demonstratively proven that His ability and power are infinite, and that all bodies and all that is connected to them or dependent on to them, even to some extent, including what lies above and below them, are His action and creation, and come after Him in essence if not in time.

Compare this to grasping a body with your fist, then moving your hand. The body would necessarily move along with the movement of your hand, a movement that comes after the movement of the hand in essence if not in time, since they began together. Similarly, the entire world is caused and created by that agent out of time. "His command, if He intends something, is only to say to it, 'Be,' and it is" [Qur'ān, 36:82].

[51] Even though Ḥayy does not seem to have formulated the concept of a personal God, I have used the masculine pronoun in conformity with the Arabic text.

When he found that all existents are the result of His action, he examined them thoroughly in order to appreciate the power of their agent and to wonder at the marvels of His handiwork, the acuity of His wisdom, and the subtlety of His knowledge. Signs of His wisdom and marvelous handiwork were clear to him in the most insignificant of existing things, let alone the most significant. This left him full of wonder, and he determined that this could only be produced by a voluntary agent at the height of perfection, indeed above perfection. "The weight of an atom escapes Him not in the heavens and on earth, nor anything smaller nor larger" [Qur'ān, 34:3].

[64] He proceeded to contemplate all types of animals, and how "He gave each thing its nature, then guided it" [Qur'ān 20:50][52] to use that nature. Had He not guided the animals to use those organs that were created for them in the ways that provide the benefits for which they were intended, animals would not have benefited from these organs and they would have been burdensome to them. He came to know that He was the Most Generous and Most Compassionate. Whenever something pertaining to existing beings seemed to him to be good, magnificent, perfect, strong, virtuous – whichever virtue it happened to be – he reflected and knew that it emanated from the excellence and action of that voluntary agent, may He be exalted. He knew that He was in essence greater and more perfect than all of them, as well as more complete, better, more magnificent, more beautiful, and more enduring. He also knew that there was no comparison between Him and the others. He continued to pursue all the attributes of perfection, and found that they pertained to Him and issued from Him, and that He was more deserving of these attributes than all other things beneath Him.

He also pursued all the attributes of imperfection and observed that He was innocent of them and exempt from them. How could it be otherwise, since imperfection simply means pure nonexistence, or what is related to nonexistence? And how could nonexistence be related to or come into contact[53] with the pure necessary existent in essence, the giver of existence to all existents? There is no existence but Him: He is existence, perfection, completion, goodness, magnificence, ability, and knowledge.

[52] Ibn Ṭufayl inserts the final pronoun into the Qur'ānic quotation.
[53] Reading *talāmasa* for *talammasa*.

He is Himself, and "Everything will perish but His countenance" [Qur'ān, 28:88].

He achieved this level of cognizance at the end of five seven-year periods after his birth, which was thirty-five years.

[65] His heart was so preoccupied with the agent that he became absorbed in thinking about Him to the exclusion of all other things. He was distracted from his previous examination and inspection of existents to the point that, from that time onwards, he could not set his sight on anything without seeing in it some trace of His handiwork. His thought would carry him immediately to the Maker, leaving the product behind. He yearned more keenly for Him and his heart turned away completely from the inferior perceptible realm and became attached to the superior intelligible realm.

When he acquired knowledge of that superior being, whose existence was fixed and uncaused, and who was the cause of the existence of all things, he wanted to know how he had acquired this knowledge and by what faculty he had apprehended this being. He examined all his senses, namely: hearing, sight, smell, taste, and touch, and found that they could not perceive anything that was not a body nor in a body. For hearing only perceives sounds, which occur when the air vibrates when bodies collide. Sight only perceives color, smell perceives odor, taste perceives flavor, and touch perceives texture, hardness, softness, roughness, and smoothness. The same goes for the imaginative faculty, which cannot apprehend anything that does not have a length, width, and depth. All things that can be perceived are attributes of bodies, and the senses cannot perceive anything else. That is because they are faculties that pervade bodies and are divisible[54] as bodies are divisible. Therefore, they cannot perceive anything but a divisible body. Since such a faculty pervades something that is divisible, if it perceives something, then that thing must necessarily be similarly divisible. Thus, every faculty that is in a body necessarily can only perceive a body, or what is in a body.

It became clear that this necessary existent was innocent of bodily attributes in every **[66]** way. Therefore, He could only be apprehended by way of something that was not a body, nor a bodily faculty, nor attached in any way to bodies. He could not be inside them, nor outside them,

[54] Ibn Ṭufayl seems to be saying that these faculties are physically embodied and have multiple functions. Compare what Ḥayy says about organs when he first dissects bodies (see [46]).

nor connected to them, nor detached from them. It had already become clear to him that he apprehended Him by his essence and that cognizance of Him became established within him. Thus, it became clear to him in this way that his essence, by which he apprehended Him, was something that was not bodily and that none of the bodily attributes applied to it. It also became clear that his apparent essence,[55] by means of which he apprehended bodily things,[56] was not his true essence, but that his true essence was that thing by which he apprehended the absolute necessary existent.

When he came to know that his essence was not this bodily frame that he perceived by his senses, which was contained within his skin, his body became completely unimportant to him. He began to reflect on that noble essence by which he apprehended the noble necessary existent. He reasoned as follows: Could that noble essence be annihilated, corrupted, or diminished, or would it persist permanently?

He observed that corruption and diminution were the attributes of bodies, which cast off one form and took on another, such as when water became air, or air became water, and when a plant became earth or ashes, and when earth became a plant. That is the meaning of corruption. As for those things that were not bodies and did not need bodies to subsist, which were completely exempt from bodily things, their corruption cannot even be conceived. When he had verified that his true essence could not be corrupted, he desired to know what condition it would be in if it cast the body aside and left it behind. It had become clear to him that it would only cast the body aside if it had ceased to be a suitable instrument for it. He examined all perceptual faculties and found that each of them sometimes perceives in potentiality and at other times perceives in actuality. For example, the eye when shut or averted from the object of sight **[67]**, perceives in potentiality. The meaning of "perceives in potentiality" is that it does not perceive now but that it will perceive in the future. In case the eye is opened and it receives the object of sight it perceives in actuality. The meaning of "perceives in actuality" is that it now perceives. Likewise, each one of these perceptual faculties can perceive in potentiality and in actuality. And if one of these faculties has not perceived in actuality at all, then it will not, while potential, yearn to perceive that which is specific

55 Alternatively, self (*dhāt*), again trading on the ambiguity in the Arabic term.
56 Alternatively, corporeal things (*jismīyyāt*).

to it, for it has not yet encountered it, as in those who are blind at birth. Meanwhile, if it had once perceived in actuality at some time then became perceiving in potentiality, it will continue, while potential, to yearn to perceive in actuality, because it has encountered that perceptible thing, has become attached to it, and has been drawn towards it. It is like someone who was sighted and became blind, and who continues to yearn for objects of sight.

The more complete, magnificent, and good the perceptible thing is, the greater will be the yearning for it, and the more intense will be the pain of losing it. That is why the pain that one experiences upon losing one's eyesight after being sighted is greater than the pain of losing one's sense of smell, for the things perceived by sight are more complete and better than those perceived by smell. Now suppose that something exists that is infinitely perfect, and endless in goodness, beauty, and magnificence, and He is above perfection, magnificence, and goodness – for there is nothing in existence that is perfect, good, magnificent, and beautiful that is not produced by Him and does not emanate from Him. Whoever loses the ability to apprehend that thing after having encountered Him, will necessarily be in infinite pain for as long as he is deprived of Him, just as he will be in a state of uninterrupted joy, endless bliss, and infinite delight and happiness, when he constantly apprehends Him.

It had already become clear to him that the necessary existent has all the attributes of perfection and is exempt from and free of the attributes of deficiency. It also became clear to him that the thing through which he arrives at His apprehension does not resemble bodies and is not corrupted as they are. As a result, it became apparent to him that if someone has an essence that is prepared to have such an apprehension and he casts off his body at death, then there are three possibilities. The first possibility is that, he had not encountered the necessary existent at all before death, during the time that he was in control of the body, not having had contact with Him or heard of Him. Such a being will not yearn for that existent and will not be pained by losing Him when he separates from his body **[68]**. All bodily faculties are extinguished with the expiration of the body, so they do not yearn for the needs of these faculties, do not long for them, and do not feel pain at being deprived of them. This is the condition of all nonrational beasts, whether they have the form of humans or not. The second possibility is that he may have encountered this existent before the time of death, while he was in control of the body, and have become acquainted with that existent and come to know His perfection, grandeur, power, ability, and goodness. But he may have turned away from Him, following his passion, and have met his end in this condition. Such a person would be deprived of the vision,[57] while still yearning for it. He will remain in a state of prolonged torment and infinite pain. He will either extricate himself from this pain after protracted efforts and will have a vision of what he yearned for earlier, or else will remain eternally in pain, depending on his disposition towards one or another of these two courses during his bodily life. The third possibility is that one encounters the necessary existent before parting from the body and devotes himself completely to Him, committing himself to reflect on His exaltation, goodness, and magnificence, never turning away until he meets his end, will be in a state[58] of approaching and having a vision of Him in actuality. If he parts from the body, he will remain in infinite joy and permanent bliss, happiness, and gladness, due to the constancy of his vision of the necessary existent, as well as the clarity of that vision and its freedom from confusion or blemishes. He will shed the bodily faculties with their sensual needs, which are pains, evils, and obstacles, by comparison with that state.

When it became clear to him that the perfection of his essence and its joy can come about only with the constant help of that necessary existent, **[69]** he resolved to have a vision of Him always in actuality, so that he would not avert his eyes even for a instant, until he met his end in this state of vision in actuality, and his joy would be continuous and uninterrupted by pain. This is what the shaykh and imām of Ṣūfism al-Junayd referred to when he told his companions just before his death: "This time is being taken from God Almighty,"[59] and proceeded to the sanctity of prayer.

He then began to reflect on how he would be able to achieve this permanent vision in actuality, and would not be distracted from it. So he reflected attentively on that existent at every hour. However, his reflection would be disrupted as soon as he caught sight of a perceptible thing, heard a sound made by some animal, imagined some likeness or another, felt a pain in one of his limbs, experienced hunger, thirst, cold, or heat, or needed to get up to satisfy his curiosity. The state of vision would then come to an

57 Ibn Ṭufayl uses a term (*mushāhadah*) deployed by the Ṣūfīs to denote a state of mystical insight.
58 The Arabic term *ḥāl* is that used to denote the mystical state by the Ṣūfīs.
59 Alternatively, "This is a time taken from God Almighty." The sense seems to be that any period of time is better spent worshipping God, even when one is on the verge of death.

end and he would be unable to return to it without exerting some effort. He feared that he would meet his end while he was distracted[60] and that he would be consigned to permanent agony and the pain of being veiled in obscurity.[61] That condition saddened him and the remedy defied him.

He undertook an examination of all species of animals, observing their actions and the purposes behind them, in order to determine whether any of them were aware of this existent and had Him as their aim. That way, he reasoned, he might learn from them how to bring about his own salvation. But he found that all of them aimed merely at providing nourishment for themselves, and at satisfying their appetites by supplying themselves with food, drink, sex, shade, and warmth. That is how they occupied themselves day and night until their time was up and they died. He could not find a single one that deviated from this course[62] or aimed at anything else at any point. Clearly, therefore, they were not aware of that existent nor did they yearn for Him, and they had not even encountered Him in any way. Thus, they were all headed towards nonexistence or to a condition resembling nonexistence. When he had rendered this judgment regarding animals, he knew that it applied all the more to plants, since plants were capable of only some of the sensations that animals had. If the more perfect in sensation had not arrived at this cognizance, it was unlikely that the less perfect would – not to mention that he also observed that the actions of plants never went beyond nutrition and reproduction.

[70] After that, he reasoned about the planets and the celestial sphere, finding that their motions were all regular and proceeded in an orderly fashion, and that they were transparent and luminous, far from accepting change and corruption. He had a strong intuition that they had essences that were different from their bodies, which were cognizant of the necessary existent. He also intuited that these cognizant essences were not bodies nor imprinted in bodies, like his own cognizant essence. How could they not have such essences that were free of bodily[63] attributes, while he did have such an essence, even though he was weak, sorely in need of sensory things, and was one of the corruptible bodies? Despite his inadequacy, this did not prevent him from having an incorruptible essence that

[60] Literally, in a condition of distraction.

[61] Literally, the pain of the veil (*alam al-ḥijāb*). Ibn Ṭufayl may have in mind the veil that separates believers from nonbelievers, as mentioned at several points in the Qur'ān (see e.g. Qur'ān 7:46, 17:45), or perhaps the pain of being separated from the necessary existent.

[62] Literally, opinion (*ra'y*).

[63] Alternatively, free of corporeality (*al-barī'ah ʿan al-jismānīyyah*).

was free of bodies. In this way, it became clear to him that the celestial bodies were all the more worthy of this. He knew that they were cognizant of the necessary existent and had a permanent vision of Him in actuality, for the obstacles that barred him from constantly having that vision were sensory impediments, the likes of which the celestial bodies did not have.

Then he reflected as to why this essence, by virtue of which he resembled the celestial bodies, was exclusive to him alone among the many different species of animal. It had earlier become clear to him from considering the four elements and their transformation into one another, that nothing on the face of the earth maintains its form. Rather, generation and corruption always succeed one another in these bodies, and most of them are mixed and composed of contrary things, which is why they are headed for corruption. None of these things is pure, though what is nearly completely pure and without defect is very far from corruption, such as bodies of gold and ruby. Similarly, celestial bodies are simple and pure, and that is why they are far from corruption and why forms do not succeed themselves in them.

It also became clear to him at that point that the reality of some bodies in the realm of generation and corruption consists in a single form added to the concept of body, which are the four elements,[64] while the reality of other bodies, such as plants and animals, consists of something more than that. A thing whose reality consists in fewer forms will also have fewer actions and will be further from life. The complete absence of form prevents it from having an entry into life and puts it in a condition resembling nonexistence. Whatever has a reality that consists in more forms will have more actions, and its entry into the condition of life will be more lasting. If these forms are such that there is no way for them to part from the matter that is specific to them, life will be more apparent, lasting, and potent. The thing that lacks form entirely is prime matter[65] or matter; no trace of life [71] is to be found in it and it resembles nonexistence. The four elements, each of which consists of one form, are in the first ranks of being in the realm of generation and corruption, and they compose the things that have many forms. These elements are very weak in life, in that they only have one motion. They are weak in life simply because

64 The Arabic term (*isṭaqis,* plural *isṭaqisāt*) corresponds to the Greek *stoikheion* (element).

65 The Arabic term (*hayūlā*) corresponds to the Greek *hulē* (prime matter).

to each of them there is a clearly opposite contrary, which opposes it by reason of its nature and requires it to change its form. Thus, its existence is ephemeral and its life is weak. Meanwhile, plants are more potent in life and animals are yet more apparent in life. This is because those compounds that are dominated by the nature of a single element can be overpowered by the natures of the other elements, which can extinguish their potentialities. That compound then becomes effectively of the same nature as the dominant element and is therefore only slightly worthy[66] of life, just as that element itself is only very slightly worthy of life. As for those compounds that are not dominated by a single element, the elements in them are well balanced and at equilibrium. In such a compound, none of the elements will extinguish the potentiality of any other, but they will instead act upon each other in an equal fashion. None of the elements will have actions that are more apparent in the compound and none of them will prevail over it. It will thus be far from resembling each one of the four elements and its form will seem not to have a contrary, thereby becoming worthy of life. When this balance increases, being more complete and further from imbalance, it will be yet further from having a contrary, and its life will be more perfect.

Since the animal spirit that is located in the heart is highly balanced, being lighter than earth and water, and heavier than fire and air, it lies practically at the center and is not opposed by any of the elements in a clear manner. That is why it is disposed to take on an animal form. He saw that it followed necessarily from this that the most balanced of the animal spirits must be disposed to the most perfect life in the realm of generation and corruption. That spirit must be close to being considered without a contrary form, which is why it resembles the celestial bodies whose forms do not have contraries. The spirit of that animal will be as though it were in the center in reality, in between the elements that do not move upwards at all and those that do not move downwards. Moreover, if it were possible to set it at the midpoint between the center of the world and the highest point reached by fire, and if it were not corrupted, then it would be fixed there, seeking to move neither upwards nor downwards. If it were displaced from that location it would move around the center, just as **[72]** the celestial bodies move. And if it were to move in place, it would revolve around itself and would be spherical in

66 Alternatively, only slightly hospitable to life (*lā yasta'hil . . . min al-ḥayāt illā shay'an yasīran*).

shape, for it could not be otherwise. Thus, it was very similar to the celestial bodies.[67]

Since he had considered the conditions of animals and had not found any that could be assumed to be aware of the necessary existent, and he knew from his essence that it was aware of Him, he concluded therefore that he was the animal with a balanced spirit, who resembled all the celestial bodies. It became clear to him that he was different from all other species of animal. Indeed, he had been created for a different purpose and had been prepared for something great, for which no other species of animal had been prepared. It was honor enough for him that the baser of his two parts, namely the bodily part, was the one that most resembled the celestial substances, which are external to the realm of generation and corruption and exempt from the incidence of imperfection, transformation, and change. Meanwhile, his more noble part is the thing by which he was cognizant of the necessary existent. This[68] cognizant thing is godly and divine, cannot be transformed, is incorruptible, and none of the attributes of bodies applies to it. It cannot be perceived by any of the senses, cannot be imagined, and one cannot arrive at cognizance of the necessary existent by any other instrument, but can only arrive at Him through it. For He is the Cognizant, the Cognized, and Cognizance itself; the Knower, the Known, and Knowledge itself. He does not fluctuate in any respect, for fluctuation and detachment are attributes of bodies and the dependents of bodies, and there is no body there, nor bodily attributes, nor bodily dependents.

When he became clear as to the manner in which he differed from other types of animal, namely his resemblance to the celestial bodies, he saw that it was his duty to be receptive to them and to imitate their actions, and to make efforts to emulate them. He also found that his more noble part, by which he was cognizant of the necessary existent, resembled the necessary existent in some respect, since it was exempt from bodily attributes, just as the necessary existent was. Moreover, he determined that he must strive to acquire His attributes for himself, in any way possible, to adopt His character,[69] to take His actions as a model, to endeavor to implement His

[67] These are properties of the animal spirit that are specific to human beings.

[68] The subject here switches in midstream. At first, Ibn Ṭufayl is speaking about the soul, but then he shifts to speaking about what is cognized by the soul. (Note the epistemological doctrine of the unity of the cognizer with the cognized.)

[69] Alternatively, adopt His ethics (*yatakhallaq bi-akhlāqih*).

will, to submit matters to Him, to comply wholeheartedly with all His judgments both outwardly and inwardly, so that He would be pleased with him. He would do all this even if it brought pain and harm to his body, indeed even if it ruined his body entirely.

[73] In addition, he observed that he resembled all the other animals when it came to the base part of him that belongs to the realm of generation and corruption, which is the opaque, dense body that demands of him various types of perceptible things, including food, drink, and sex. He also observed that that body was not created for him in vain, nor was it joined to him for no reason, so it was his duty to attend to it and improve it. This attention should be given by way of actions that resemble the actions of the other animals. Thus, he had a duty to perform actions with different aims, of the following three kinds: (1) activities emulating the nonrational animals; (2) activities emulating the celestial bodies; (3) activities emulating the necessary existent. The first emulation was his duty insofar as he had an opaque body with divisible organs, different faculties, and a variety of ends. The second emulation was his duty insofar as he had an animal spirit, which is located in the heart and is a starting point for the rest of the body and its faculties. The third emulation was his duty insofar as he was himself, that is, insofar as he was the essence by which he was cognizant of the necessary existent. He had already understood that his happiness and triumph over adversity could come about only as a result of the constancy of his vision of this necessary existent, to the point that he could not turn away for an instant. He then reasoned concerning the manner in which he could achieve this constancy, and his reasoning led him to the conclusion that he must adopt these three kinds of emulation.

The first emulation would not help him to attain this vision at all, but would rather distract and impede him from achieving it. That is because it involves conduct concerning perceptible things, and perceptible things are barriers [74] that obstruct that vision. However, this emulation was simply required to preserve the animal spirit, by which he could achieve the second emulation, that of the celestial bodies. Necessity dictated that he take this course, even though it is not free of harm.

The second emulation would enable him to attain a great portion of the constant vision, but it would be a vision tainted by impurity. For whoever constantly experiences that type of vision will thereby intellect his own essence, as will become evident in due course.

The third emulation would enable him to attain a clear vision and pure absorption, which gives no consideration to anything but the necessary existent. Anyone who has this vision in this manner will have lost his own[70] essence, which will be obliterated and fade away. The same applies to all other essences – whether they are numerous or few – apart from the essence of the One, the True, the Necessary Existent, may He be exalted and elevated.

It became clear to him that his ultimate goal was the third emulation, that he could not achieve it unless he practiced and adopted the second emulation for a long period of time, and that this period could only endure by means of the first emulation. He also came to know that the first emulation, though necessary, was essentially a hindrance but accidentally a help. Since it was necessary, he compelled himself not to give this emulation any more than its necessary share, which is the least amount that suffices for the persistence of the animal spirit.

He found that there were two things that made the persistence of the animal spirit necessary **[75]**. The first was nutrition, which provided incoming sustenance and excreted what had decomposed. The second was external protection and fending off various types of harm, including cold, heat, rain, exposure to the sun, and ferocious animals. He observed that if he were to partake necessarily of this emulation in a random and haphazard fashion, then he would become too self-absorbed without noticing. So he found that it would be prudent of him to impose restrictions and fix limits that he could not exceed. It became clear to him that the restrictions should concern the things that he could nourish himself with, their kinds, their amounts, and the time that could elapse before he went back to this emulation.

He first examined the kinds of things that he could nourish himself with, and found that they were divided into three varieties: (1) Plants that were not yet fully grown and had not completely reached their goal, which are the various types of moist leafy plants that he could be nourished by; (2) The fruits of plants that had ripened completely and had issued seeds to produce others to perpetuate their species, which are the various types of moist and dry fruits; (3) Animals that he could be nourished by, whether land or sea animals. He had already determined that all these kinds were created by the action of the necessary existent, by whose proximity and

70 Alternatively, the essence of his soul (*dhāt nafsih*).

emulation he could attain happiness. Inevitably, nourishing oneself by means of these kinds would bar them from reaching perfection and would interrupt the ultimate goal intended for them. That would be a disruption of the action of the agent, which would be contrary to his goal of achieving proximity and emulation. Thus, he saw that the correct course would be to desist from nourishing himself altogether. However, that was impossible for him to do, for withholding nourishment would lead to the corruption of his body. Moreover, that would, in turn, be a greater disruption of the agent than the first course of action, for he was more noble than those things whose corruption would be the cause of his continued existence. He found it easier to accept the lesser of the two harms and indulged in the lighter disruption. If some of these kinds of plants and animals were not to be found, he decided that he would take whatever he could, in amounts to be clarified in due course **[76]**. However, if all of them were in existence, he would have to select among them whatever would not lead to a great disruption of the action of the agent, such as the flesh of fruits that had completely ripened and had successfully produced seeds to reproduce their kind. He would do so on condition that he would preserve those seeds, not eating them, allowing them to rot, or casting them in a spot that was not suitable for planting, such as rocks, swamps, and the like. If he was unable to find such fruits with nourishing flesh, such as apples and pears, he would have to take either those fruits whose seeds were the only source of nourishment, such as walnuts and chestnuts, or the leafy plants that had not yet reached perfection. In both cases, he did so on condition that he sought out those that were most abundant and prolific, and that he did not pull up their roots or destroy their seeds. In the absence of these, he would have to partake of animals or of their eggs, on condition that he took the most abundant and that he did not destroy an entire species. That is what he decided concerning the kinds of things that he could be nourished by.

When it came to the amounts of nourishment that he could partake, he found that they should be sufficient to fend off hunger and should not exceed that. As for the times that should elapse between each return to the first emulation, he found that if he had taken as much nourishment as he needed, he would be satisfied with that and would not partake of any more, until he was overcome with a weakness that interrupted some of the activities that he was obliged to perform in the second emulation, which will be described in what follows. When it came to the necessity of preserving the animal spirit so that it could provide him with external protection, his task was made easier by the fact that he covered himself with skins and had a home that sheltered him from external contingencies. So he was satisfied with that and no longer concerned himself with it, all the while committing himself to the rules of nutrition that he had drawn up for himself, as described above.

[77] He then turned to the second activity, which was the emulation and imitation of the celestial bodies, including the acceptance of and subordination to its traits and attributes. These attributes were arranged into three categories. The first category consisted of those attributes that they have in relation to what lies beneath them in the realm of generation and corruption, namely what they provide it with in terms of essential warming, accidental cooling, lighting, evaporation, and condensation, in addition to all the other things by means of which they are disposed to receive the emanation of spiritual forms from the necessarily existing agent. The second category consisted of their essential attributes, such as transparency, luminosity, purity, exemption from opacity and all types of contamination, and circular motion, some around themselves and others around other points. The third category consisted of the attributes they have in relation to the necessary existent, such as their having a vision of Him constantly without being distracted from Him, yearning for Him, acting according to His judgment,[71] commitment to carrying out His will, and never moving except by His volition and within His control.[72] He therefore made an effort to emulate them in each of these three categories.

He emulated the first category of attributes by making a commitment never to come across any need, defect, harm, or obstacle affecting any animal or plant, which he was able to remove, without removing it. When he saw a plant screened from the sun, entwined with some other plant that was harming it, or parched to the point that it was dying, he would remove that screen [78] if it were removable, separate the harmful plant from the other without damaging the harmful one, or undertake to water it if possible. When he came upon an animal pursued by a hyena,[73] pricked by a thorn or spike, with something harmful in its eyes or ears, or overwhelmed

[71] Alternatively, His wise maxims (reading *ḥikamihi* instead of *ḥukmihi*).

[72] Literally, within its grasp or fist (*qabḍatihi*).

[73] Earlier, Ibn Ṭufayl had said that there were no predators on the island [see 32], but according to one source hyenas were not classified by Arab writers with the hostile predators (*sibāʿ*).

by thirst or hunger, he would take it upon himself to relieve it or to bring it food and water. When he noticed that some obstacle like a rock or landslide had impeded a stream flowing to water a plant or animal, he removed it. He persisted in pursuing this emulation diligently until he achieved his goal.

He emulated the second category of attributes by committing himself to purifying himself constantly, removing blemishes and impurities from his body, cleaning himself with water often, and scrubbing his nails, teeth, and underarms. He also anointed himself with whatever types of plant fragrances and aromatic oils he could find, and made sure his clothes were clean and sweet-smelling, to the point that he radiated goodness, beauty, cleanliness, and fragrance. He also undertook a variety of circular motions, sometimes circumnavigating the island by walking along its coast and wandering around its coves. At other times, he would move around his house or the surrounding land, walking or running around it a number of times. At yet other times, he would spin around himself to the point that he passed out.

He emulated the third category of attributes by reflecting attentively on the necessary existent, then severing all perceptual attachments, shutting his eyes and blocking his ears. He made every effort not to pursue his imagination and exerted all his strength not to think of anything but Him, without associating anything else with Him. To help himself achieve this, he spun about himself, gradually speeding up the pace of rotation. When he [79] rotated quickly all perceptible things were lost to him, imagination was weakened, along with all other faculties that needed the bodily instruments. Meanwhile, the action of his essence, which was free of all body, was strengthened. At times, his faculty of reflection was cleared of all defects and he was able to have a vision of the necessary existent, but then the bodily faculties would come rushing back in, ruining his state and casting him among the lowest of the low. Then he would recommence, and if he ever found himself overcome with a weakness that diverted him from his purpose, he took some nourishment in accordance with the conditions mentioned.

After that, he would resume the emulation of the celestial bodies in the three categories mentioned, persisting in it for some time, while he struggled and contended with his bodily faculties. At times when he was able to overcome these bodily faculties, his reflection would be cleared of defects and something of the state of the third emulation would loom before him. Then he began to seek the third emulation and aspire to achieve it. He examined the attributes of the necessary existent, for it had already become clear to him during his theoretical reasoning and before embarking on his practice that these attributes were of two kinds: positive attributes such as Knowledge, Power, and Wisdom, or negative attributes such as exemption from corporeality and its dependents and anything remotely related to body. The positive attributes must be exempt in this way so that they do not contain bodily attributes, including multiplicity. His essence is not multiplied by these positive attributes, but resolve themselves into one concept, which is the reality of His essence. So he began to seek means of emulating Him in each one of these two respects.

He came to know that the positive attributes all pertain to the reality of His essence and that they were not multiple in any way, since multiplicity is an attribute of bodies. He also knew that His knowledge of His own essence was not a concept added to His essence, but rather that His essence was the knowledge of His essence, and knowledge of His essence was His essence. Therefore, it became clear to him that if it were possible for him to know his own essence, the knowledge by which he knew his essence would not be a concept added **[80]** to his essence, but would be himself. Thus, he saw that emulation of His positive attributes was merely to know Him without associating Him with any attributes of bodies. So he occupied himself with that.

As for the negative attributes, they all come down to exemption from corporeality. Therefore, he began to shed bodily attributes from his essence, many of which he had already cast off in his previous exercise, in which he aspired to emulate the celestial bodies. However, he had kept many remnants, such as circular motion – motion being one of the attributes most specific to bodies – and attention to animals and plants, including caring for them and removing obstacles for them. These are also bodily attributes, since they are first perceived[74] by bodily faculties, in the first place, and are also taken[75] up by bodily faculties. So he began to shed all these matters, since none of them were worthy of the state that he now sought. He now restricted himself to being still in the confines of his cave, with his head bowed and his eyes lowered and averted from all perceptibles and bodily faculties. His entire concern and all his reflections were concentrated on the necessary existent by Himself and without partner.

[74] Literally, seen (*yarāhā*). [75] Literally, toiled or labored at (*yakdaḥ fī amrihā*).

Whenever his imagination chanced upon anything else, he made an effort to expel and repulse it. He trained himself to do so, and persisted in this for a long time, spending several days without nourishment or motion.

At the height of his struggle, all essences would sometimes disappear from his recollection and reflection, with the exception of his own essence, which would not recede from him even when he was absorbed in having a vision of the first existent, the true necessary existent. That caused him distress, for he knew that it was a defect in the pure vision and a dilution of the observation. He continued to seek his own obliteration and to seek fidelity in the vision of the Truth, until he attained it, and the heavens, earth, and everything in between them receded from his recollection and reflection, including all spiritual forms and corporeal potentialities, and all immaterial potentialities, which were the essences that were cognizant of existence. His essence receded along with the rest of the essences; all vanished and faded away, becoming like so much scattered dust. Only the one true permanent existent remained, making the statement, which was not a concept added to His essence: "To whom does dominion now belong? To God, the One, the Victor" [Qur'ān 40:16]. He understood His speech and heard His call, and he was not prevented from understanding by the fact that he could not speak. He became absorbed in this state [81] and had a vision of what no eye had seen nor ear had heard, and what had not occurred to the heart of any human being. Do not engage your heart in the description of something that has not occurred to any human heart. Many of the things that can occur to human hearts are incapable of being described; what of something that cannot occur to a human heart by any means, something that does not pertain to its world or state? I do not mean by "heart" the body of the heart or the spirit that lies inside its cavity, but rather the form of that spirit, whose potentiality emanates to the human body. Each of these three could be called the "heart," but there is no means for this state to occur to any of these three, and the only things that can be articulated are those that can occur to one of them.

Whoever wishes to articulate that state wishes the impossible. It would be comparable to someone who wanted to taste dyed colors insofar as they were colors, say, insisting that blackness be sweet or sour. Nevertheless, we will not withhold from you certain signs to indicate the vision he had of the wonders of that station, by way merely of putting forth similes rather than of approaching the threshold of truth, for there is no means to determine what is in that station except by attaining it. Now listen with your heart's ear to what I will point out to you and look at it with your intellect's eye, that you might perhaps find within it some guidance to the main road. My only condition is that you not seek more of me in plain speech at this time than what I am entrusting to these pages, for space is tight and it is dangerous to aim at precision[76] in one's expressions concerning something about which one must not speak.

I say: He was obliterated to his own essence and to all other essences, seeing nothing in existence but the One, the Living, the Everlasting, and he had the vision he had, then he returned to observe other things. When he awoke from that state, which is similar to a state of inebriation, it occurred to him that his essence could not be distinguished from that of the Almighty Truth, and that the reality of his essence was the essence of the Truth. The thing that he had originally assumed was his essence, which he distinguished from the essence of the Truth, was nothing in reality. Indeed, there was nothing but the essence of the Truth, which is comparable to the light of the sun that falls upon dense bodies and is reflected[77] in them. If he is compared to the body in which the light is reflected, then he is nothing in reality but the light of the sun.[78] If that body were to cease to exist, then its [reflected] light would be extinguished but the light of the sun would remain as it is, neither diminished by its presence nor augmented by its absence.

If a body capable of reflecting[79] the light of the sun is created, it will reflect it; and if that body ceases to exist, then the reflection will cease to exist[80] **[82]** and will have no meaning. His supposition was bolstered by the fact that it had become clear to him that the essence of the Almighty Truth is not multiple in any way, and that His knowledge of His essence is His essence itself. It followed from this that whoever acquired the knowledge of His essence had also acquired His essence. Since he had acquired this knowledge, he had acquired the essence. But this essence can only be acquired by His own essence, and its acquisition is itself His essence, so he was the essence itself. The same holds for all immaterial essences that

[76] Literally, to control (*al-taḥakkum*). [77] Literally, appears (*yaẓhar*).

[78] Presumably, Ḥayy's body is compared to the dense body and his soul, which is his essence, is compared to the light reflected by that body.

[79] Literally, receiving (*qubūl*), here and in what follows.

[80] Reading *fa-idhā ʿadima al-jism ʿadima dhālika al-qubūl* instead of *fa-idhā ʿadima al-jism dhālika al-qubūl*, which does not make sense.

can be cognizant by means of that true essence, which he had originally regarded as being multiple. By this supposition, they became one thing.

This specious argument would have been established in his soul had God in His mercy not corrected him and set him right with His guidance. He came to know that this specious argument was stirred up within him merely because of the vestiges of the darkness of bodies and the impurity of perceptibles. For multiplicity and scarcity, unity and union, combination, conjunction, and separation, are all bodily attributes. Those immaterial[81] essences that were cognizant of the essence of the Almighty Truth cannot be said to be either a multiplicity or a unity, because they are free of matter. Multiplicity is merely the distinctness of essences from each other, and unity can only occur by contact. None of this can be understood except by means of the composite concepts entangled with matter. However, it can be very awkward to articulate these things, for if you denote these immaterial essences in the plural according to our usual expression that will produce the illusion of the concept of multiplicity, even though they are free of multiplicity. Meanwhile, if you denote them in the singular that will produce the illusion of unity, which is impossible for them.

At this point, I feel as though I am confronted by bats that are blinded by the sun and move in a frenzied fashion. I will be told:[82] "You have gone so far in your excessive scrutiny that you have been stripped of the nature of rational creatures and cast off rational judgment. One of the judgments of reason is that something is either [83] one or many." Let this interlocutor dampen his enthusiasm, curb the ardor of his tongue, question himself, and consider the example of the base perceptible realm that he is in the midst of, as did Ḥayy bin Yaqẓān. He would pursue one line of reasoning and find that it was an immeasurable and unlimited multiplicity. Then he would pursue another and find it to be one. He remained hesitant, unable to affirm one of the characterizations or the other. That is because the basis of the perceptible realm is plurality and singularity, by means of which one understands its reality, wherein there is detachment and contact, isolation and distinctness, and similarity and difference. What is one to suppose of the divine realm, about which one cannot say "all" or "some," and about which one cannot utter any audible expression without producing an illusion that differs from reality? No

[81] Here and elsewhere, considering *mufāriqah* as shorthand for *mufāriqah lil-māddah*.
[82] Literally, he (presumably, an imagined interlocutor) will say (*wa yaqūl*).

one can be cognizant of it but those who have a vision of it, and its reality can be proven only for one who has acquired it.

With regards to his [i.e. the interlocutor] saying that "you have been stripped of the nature of rational creatures and cast off rational judgment," we concede that to him and leave him to his reason and his rational beings. What he and his like mean by "reason" is simply the rational faculty that examines the particular perceptible existents and derives the universal concept. The rational beings that he refers to are those who reason in this manner. Since our speech is of a kind that transcends that, let those who are only cognizant of perceptibles and their universals stop up their ears. Let them return to their own group who "know but the outward appearances of the temporal life and turn away[83] from the afterlife" [Qur'ān 30:7].

If you are one of those who is convinced by the use of allusions to and signs of the divine realm, and you do not load utterances with the meanings that they are usually made to bear, we will provide you with more of the vision of Ḥayy bin Yaqẓān in the station of truth, which was mentioned before. We say: After pure absorption, complete obliteration, and real attainment, he had a vision of the outermost sphere of the heavens, which has no body. He observed an essence free of matter, which was not the essence of the True One **[84]**, nor the essence of the sphere itself, nor something else. It was like the image[84] of the sun that appears in a polished mirror, which is not the sun, nor the mirror, nor something else. He observed that the immaterial essence of that sphere had a degree of perfection, magnificence, and goodness that were indescribable by any tongue and too subtle to be dressed up with any letter or sound. He saw that it was in a state of utmost joy, happiness, bliss, and gladness, as it had a vision of the essence of the Almighty Truth. In addition, he had a vision of the immaterial essence of the next heavenly sphere, the sphere of the fixed stars. This was neither the essence of the True One, nor the essence of the immaterial outermost sphere, nor itself, nor something else. It was like the image of the sun that appears in a mirror that has reflected the image from another mirror, which faces the sun. He also saw that this essence had magnificence, goodness, and joy, as did the essence of the highest sphere. He also had a vision of the next sphere, which is the sphere of the planet Saturn, and beheld its immaterial essence. It was

83 The Qur'ān has "are ignorant of" (*ghāfilūn*), instead of "turn away from" (*muʿraḍūn*), but cf. also Qur'ān 21:1.

84 The Arabic *ṣūrah* is also the term for the philosophical concept of form.

not identical with any of the essences of which he had previously had a vision, nor was it something different. It was as though it were the image of the sun that appears in a mirror that has in turn reflected an image from a mirror facing the sun. He also found this essence endowed with magnificence and joy, as he had the others. He continued to have a vision of the immaterial essence pertaining to each sphere, which was not one of the essences that preceded it nor something else, as though it were the image of the sun being reflected from one mirror to another, ranked in the fixed order of the heavenly spheres. For each of these essences, he had a vision of goodness, magnificence, joy, and gladness, the likes of which no eye had seen, nor ear had heard, nor had occurred to the heart of any human being.

This continued until he came to the realm of generation and corruption, which is entirely contained within the sphere of the moon. He found that this sphere had an essence that was free of matter and was not identical to any one of the essences that he had had a vision of before, nor was it another thing **[85]**. This essence has seventy thousand faces, each face has seventy thousand mouths, and each mouth has seventy thousand tongues glorifying the essence of the True One, venerating it, honoring it, and never flagging. He found that this essence, which produced in him the illusion of multiplicity though it was not in fact multiple, possessed the same perfection and joy as the ones he had seen before. It was as though this essence was the image of the sun in shimmering water, which reflected the image from the last of the reflecting mirrors in the order given, beginning with the first mirror, which faced the sun itself. He then had a vision of his own immaterial essence, which we would have said was a part of the seventy thousand faces, had they been divisible. Had this essence not originated after having not been in existence, we would have said that it was identical with the seventy thousand faces; and had it not been specific to his body when his body originated, we would have said that it had not been originated. At this level, he had a vision of essences such as his own, for bodies that had once been but had vanished and for bodies that were still in existence. If it were permissible to say of them that they were many, then they would be infinite; and if it were permissible to say that they were one, then they would be united.

He observed that his own essence and the other essences at his level had an infinite share of goodness, magnificence, and joy, of a sort that no eye had seen, nor ear heard, nor had occurred to any human heart. No one is capable of describing it or intellecting it save the cognizant attainers. He had a vision of many immaterial essences that were like tarnished mirrors, overcome with malice **[86]**, encircling the polished mirrors that reflected the image of the sun, but with their surfaces averted. He found disgrace and deficiency in these essences, of a kind that had never even occurred to him. These essences experienced unending pains and indelible sorrows, were enclosed in torment[85] and veiled with fire, oscillating between repulsion and attraction. He also had a vision of other essences, different from the tormented ones, which loomed then vanished, alternately coming together then breaking up. He concentrated his attention on them and observed them intently, seeing a great horror, a grave calamity, an urgent throng, and momentous judgments, as well as fashioning, life-breathing, creation, and destruction.[86] But as soon as he had confirmed their existence, his senses returned to him and he became aware of his state, which resembled a fainting spell. He lost his footing in that station, and the perceptible realm loomed once again, banishing the divine realm. For their concurrence in one state was not[87] unlike that of two cowives – satisfying one offends the other.

You might say: "It appears from what you have said about this vision that if the immaterial essences belong to an eternally existent incorruptible body like the heavenly spheres, then they are also eternal. But if they pertain to a corruptible body like rational animals, then they will be corrupted, fade, and vanish, as suggested by the simile of the reflecting mirrors. The image only remains as long as the mirror remains, and if the mirror is corrupted then the image will also be corrupted and annihilated." I say to you: "How quickly have you forgotten your vow and withdrawn your pledge! Did we not preface these remarks by saying that the articulation of these things is strained, and that expressions invariably give rise to an illusion different from reality? The illusion that you conjured up has tripped you up, for you have taken the simile to be the same as what it represents in every respect." This must not even be done in ordinary types of discourse. It is still less permissible here, given that the sun, its light, image, and shape, as well as the mirrors and the images

[85] Cf. Qur'ān 18:29.

[86] Ibn Ṭufayl is clearly expressing an apocalyptic vision, and the terms used are mainly Qur'ānic terms to describe creation and the Day of Judgment.

[87] Reading *illā ka-ḍurratayn*, instead of *ka-ḍurratayn*, which makes more sense given traditional Islamic beliefs about the difficulty of satisfying cowives.

reflected in them, are all things that are inseparable from bodies, and cannot subsist without them. Thus, their existence is dependent on them and they are extinguished with their expiration.

As for the divine essences and the godly spirits, they are all free of bodies and their dependents, being completely exempt from them. They are neither connected nor attached to them, and the extinction and persistence of bodies, as well as their existence and nonexistence, are all equivalent to them. However, their connection and attachment to the essence of the One True Necessary Existent is such that He is their beginning, origin, cause and creator, giving them [87] persistence and supplying them with everlasting and continued existence. They have no need of anything, but rather bodies are in need of them. If their nonexistence were possible, all bodies would cease to exist with them, for they are the origins of matter; just as, if it were possible for the essence of the True One to cease to exist (may He be praised and glorified above that, for there is no God but He), all these essences would also cease to exist, as would all bodies. The entire perceptible realm would also cease and no existent would remain, for everything is interconnected. The perceptible realm is dependent on the divine realm, as though it were its shadow, whereas the divine realm can do without it and is free of it. Nevertheless, it is impossible to posit the nonexistence of the perceptible realm since it is necessarily dependent upon the divine realm.[88] It is corrupted by being transformed, not by ceasing to exist entirely. That is what the cherished Book spoke of when it mentioned this concept in describing the alteration of mountains into wool,[89] of people into moths,[90] the contraction[91] of the sun and moon, and the bursting of the seas, "on the day that the earth and heavens are transformed into something else" [Qur'ān 14:48]. This much is all that I can show you at this time of the vision of Ḥayy bin Yaqẓān in that lofty station. Do not seek more than this in utterance, for that is not feasible.

But I can divulge the completion of his tale, God willing. When he returned to the perceptible realm, after having wandered on his journeys, he grew weary of the burdens of the temporal life and he longed fervently for the afterlife. He sought to return to that station in the same way that he had done so originally and managed to attain it more easily than his

[88] This is impossible presumably because the divine realm exists necessarily.
[89] Cf. Qur'ān 101:5, 70:9. [90] Cf. Qur'ān 101:4. [91] Cf. Qur'ān 81:1.

first attempt, remaining in it longer than he had before. But once more, he returned to the perceptible realm. After that, he endeavored to attain the station again. This time it was even easier for him than the first and second times, and he remained there longer. Over time, the attainment of that lofty station continued to come more readily to him and his stays lengthened, to the point that he was able to attain it whenever he wished and did not leave until he wanted to. He would remain there at that station, quitting it only for the sake of his bodily needs, which he had reduced to an absolute minimum [88]. At this point, he wished that God would relieve him of his body, which required him to relinquish that station, so that he could dedicate himself permanently to his joy and be free of the pain that he encountered when he abandoned his station for the sake of bodily needs.

He remained in this state until after the seventh seven-year period following his birth, which was fifty years.

Ibn Rushd, *The Incoherence of the Incoherence*

[512] *Abū Ḥāmid al-Ghazālī said:* The first issue concerning the natural sciences is the judgment of the philosophers that the connection that is observed to exist between causes and effects is a necessary relation, and that there is no capability or possibility of bringing the cause into existence without the effect, nor the effect without the cause.[1]

The first issue must be disputed, since denying it is the basis of affirming miracles that interrupt the habitual [course of events], such as converting a stick into a serpent, reviving the dead, and cleaving the moon. Those who regard the habitual course [of events] as being necessitated consider all these things to be impossible. They attach a figurative interpretation to the Qur'ānic passages concerning the revival of the dead. They say that God intends in these passages to refer to eliminating the death that is ignorance by means of the life that is knowledge. They have interpreted the conversion of the stick into the deceiving [serpent] in terms of Moses' refutation of the doubts of the unbelievers by means of the clear divine argument. As for the cleavage of the moon, they have often denied its occurrence, claiming that it has not been recurrently corroborated by a sound tradition.

The philosophers have only affirmed the existence of miracles that interrupt the habitual [course of events] in the following three cases.

One of them concerns the imaginative faculty. They have claimed that when it becomes dominant, powerful, and is no longer preoccupied with the senses or other concerns, it discerns the Preserved

[1] Ghazālī goes on to mention three other issues in the natural sciences about which he also disagrees with the philosophers.

Tablet.[2] Thus, the forms of future particulars are imprinted on it. This occurs during wakefulness for prophets and during sleep for other people. This is the prophetic property of the imaginative faculty.

The second is a property of the theoretical rational faculty attributable to the faculty of intuition, which is the speed of moving from one piece of knowledge to another. Many clever people discover the proof as soon as what is to be proven is mentioned to them, or discover **[513]** what is to be proven by themselves once the proof is mentioned to them. Generally speaking, if the middle term occurs to them, they will discover the conclusion, and if the terms of the conclusion are present to their minds, the middle term that links the two terms[3] of the conclusion will also occur to them.[4] People differ in this respect: some discover these matters by themselves, others do so with the least amount of prompting, and yet others only apprehend them with prompting after considerable effort. If, at one extreme, the deficiency could be so severe that a person may have no intuition at all and may not be disposed to understand intelligibles even after being prompted, then at the other extreme, the power[5] of intuition could be so great as to enable someone to discover all or most of the intelligibles in a very short period of time and with the greatest ease. There is quantitative variation when it comes to all or some inquiries and there is qualitative variation also, so that this can be achieved most quickly and easily. Many a pure sacred soul can intuit all the intelligibles without pause in the shortest period of time; this is the case with the prophet who has a miraculous theoretical faculty and does not need instruction in the intelligibles, but rather seems to be self-taught. This is the one described in the verse: "its oil is almost luminous without being touched by fire, light upon light" [Qurān 24:35].

The third concerns the practical faculty of the soul, which can reach a point whereby natural things are affected by it and subjugated to it. For example, when one of our souls conjures up an image of something, the bodily organs and the soul's faculties come to its service, moving towards the imagined objective. If one imagines something tasty one begins to

[2] The Preserved Tablet (*al-lawḥ al-maḥfūẓ*), which is mentioned at Qur'ān 85:22, is the tablet kept in heaven containing the original copy of the Qur'ān as well as the record of "all things, past, present, and future" (*EI* entry on "lawh").

[3] Literally, the two extremes (*ṭarafay*).

[4] Consider the syllogism: "All As are B. All Bs are C. Therefore, all As are C." B is the middle term, and A and C are the two terms of the conclusion.

[5] Alternatively, faculty (*qūwwah*).

salivate at the mouth and the salivating faculty responds by flowing with saliva from the source. Also, if a person imagines sexual intercourse the faculty responds by making his penis erect. Again, if a person walks along a plank suspended in the air between two walls, he has a heightened illusion of falling, which makes the body react to this image and fall; whereas if the plank had been lying on the ground he would have walked along it without falling. This occurs because bodies and bodily faculties were created to serve souls and be subjugated to them, and this varies in accordance with the purity of souls and their power. It is not unlikely for the power of the soul to reach such an extent that the natural power outside the prophet's own body would become subservient to it. That is because his soul does not inhere in his body; instead, it has a kind of attachment and yearning towards governing his body, which was created in its very nature. Thus, if it is possible for his body parts to obey his soul, it is not impossible for other bodies to obey it as well. His soul may aspire to stir up wind, bring down rain, provoke a thunderstorm, or produce an earthquake afflicting some group of people. The occurrence of these things depends on the incidence of cooling, heating, or movement of the air **[514]**. This cooling or heating can originate from his soul, and these things can be generated by him without the presence of an observable natural cause. This would be a miracle pertaining to the prophet, though it only happens in air that is disposed to receive it, and it cannot go so far as to convert wood into an animal or cleave the moon, which is not receptive to fracture.

That is the philosophers' creed concerning miracles. We do not deny any of the things they have mentioned, nor do we deny that these are among the things that occur to prophets. However, we reject the fact that they confine themselves to these and that they disallow the conversion of a stick into a serpent, the revival of the dead, and other matters. Thus, it is necessary to delve into this issue in order to affirm miracles, as well as for another reason: to vindicate what Muslims have agreed to, namely that God Almighty is capable of everything. Let us address the matter at issue.

I say: The ancient philosophers have not contributed any statement to the discourse concerning miracles, since, according to them, these are things that must not be subject to scrutiny and regarded as open questions, for they are the principles of religious laws. Those who examine and doubt them deserve punishment according to them, as do those who examine the other general principles of religious law, for example: Does

God exist? Does happiness exist? Do the virtues exist? The philosophers hold that the existence of these things must not be doubted and that their manner of existence is a divine matter that human intellects are incapable of apprehending. The reason for that is that these are the principles of the actions that render a human being virtuous, and there is no route to acquiring knowledge except by way of acquiring virtue. Therefore, one must not subject to scrutiny the very principles that lead necessarily to virtue before the acquisition of virtue itself. If **[515]** the theoretical[6] arts cannot be completed without principles and starting points that are taken for granted by the practitioner from the outset, that is all the more the case with practical matters. As for what Ghazālī has ascribed to the philosophers concerning the causes of miracles, I do not know of any who have said this apart from Ibn Sīnā. If the existence of these things is verified and it is possible for a body to change by means of something that is not a body or a bodily power without transformation,[7] then what he has said concerning that cause is possible. But not everything that is possible by nature is within the ability of a human being to perform. What is possible for a human being is well known, and most things that are possible in themselves are impossible for humans. Thus, one can assent to the prophet's bringing about something extraordinary[8] that is impossible for a human being and possible in itself,[9] without being required to state that things that are impossible according to reason are possible for prophets. If you contemplate the miracles whose existence has been verified, you will find that they are all of this kind, the clearest of which is God's Holy Book, whose extraordinariness is not based on testimony[10] like the conversion of a stick into a snake. Rather, its miraculousness has been established through the senses and through reflection for every human being who has existed or will exist until the Day of Judgment **[516]**. This miracle

[6] Alternatively, the scientific arts, or the sciences (*al-ṣanā'iᶜ al-ᶜilmīyyah*).

[7] A transformation (*istiḥālah*) is a change in which the same matter takes on a different form, e.g. when water turns to steam. Here, Ibn Rushd is discussing the possibility of changes that take place without transformation.

[8] Though Ghazālī uses the verb *kharaqa* and the adjective *khāriqah* to indicate an interruption in the course of nature, Ibn Rushd seems to be using the noun form *khāriq* here to indicate an extraordinary event, and one which is humanly impossible but not metaphysically or logically impossible.

[9] It is not clear why Ibn Rushd thinks that a prophet can bring about something impossible for a human being, since they are human beings themselves; perhaps he means, impossible for an ordinary human being.

[10] Alternatively, hearsay (*samāᶜ*).

has thereby surpassed all other miracles. Let someone who is not content to pass over this issue in silence be satisfied with that. In addition, let such a person recognize that the select assent to prophets in another way, which is mentioned by Abū Ḥāmid elsewhere. That is the action issuing from the attribute by which the prophet is termed a prophet, namely acquaintance with what is hidden,[11] and setting down laws that accord with the truth and produce deeds that bring happiness to all of humanity. As for what Ghazālī has ascribed to the philosophers concerning visions, I know of none of the ancients besides Ibn Sīnā[12] who has said this. What the ancient philosophers say about inspiration and visions is only that they are from God the Blessed and Almighty, by the mediation of a spiritual and immaterial existent, which is the bestower of the human intellect, according to them. The most proficient philosophers call this the "Active Intellect" and in the religious law it is called an "angel."

Let us now return to what he has said concerning the four issues.

[517] *Abū Ḥāmid al-Ghazālī said:* The connection between what is habitually believed to be the cause and what is believed to be the effect is not necessary, according to us. Rather, whenever there are two things, if neither is the same as the other, the affirmation of one does not include the affirmation of the other, and the negation of one does not include the negation of the other, then the existence of one does not necessitate the existence of the other, nor does the nonexistence of one necessitate the nonexistence of the other. That includes, for example, quenching thirst and drinking, satiety and eating, burning and contact with fire, light and sunrise, dying and slitting the throat, restoring health and taking medicine, diarrhea and taking a laxative, and so on for all the observed connections in medicine, astronomy,[13] and the arts and crafts. The connection between these things and what precedes them is decreed by God Almighty, who created them in succession. It is not necessary in itself nor inescapable, but rather proceeds by His decree. It is within His ability to create satiety without eating, death without the slitting of the throat, continuation of life with the slitting of the throat, and so on for all the other connections.

[11] Alternatively, the future, occult, or supernatural (*al-ghayb*).

[12] Ibn Rushd seems to have misspoken here; Ibn Sīnā cannot be considered one of the ancients.

[13] Though Ghazālī later usually uses *ʿilm al-nujūm* for astrology, astronomy seems more appropriate in this context. Note that *aḥkām al-nujūm* is the term most often used for astrology, while, *ʿilm al-hay'ah* is usually reserved for astronomy; however, astronomy was often considered the part of astrology that had a purely descriptive role (cf. *EI* entry on "nudjūm").

The philosophers have denied this possibility and have claimed its impossibility. Since it would take too long to investigate all of these innumerable cases, we will consider just one example, which is burning and the contact of cotton with fire. We allow that it is possible that there can be contact between cotton and fire without **[518]** burning and that it is possible that cotton could be converted into smoldering ashes without having had contact with fire. However, the philosophers deny this possibility. This issue can be discussed by considering three positions.[14]

The first position is the opponent's claim that the cause[15] of burning is fire alone, and that it is a cause by nature[16] not by choice, for it is not possible for it to refrain from what is in its nature after contact with the substratum that is ready to receive it.

This is what we deny, for we say instead that the cause of burning, by creating blackness in the cotton, separating its parts, and rendering it burnt and charred, is God Almighty, either through the mediation of the angels or without mediation. Fire itself is inert and has no action. What proof is there that it is the cause? Their only proof is the observation of the occurrence of the burning upon contact with the fire. But observation proves that the occurrence took place upon contact with fire, not that the occurrence took place by virtue of contact with fire, nor that there was no cause but fire.

There is no disagreement with the philosophers over the fact that the union of the spirit with the faculties of cognition[17] and that locomotion in the sperm of animals is not generated by the natures contained in heat, coldness, moisture, and dryness. We also agree that the father is not the cause[18] of the embryo by virtue of depositing the sperm in the uterus, nor is he the cause of its life, vision, hearing, and the other features[19] that it has. It is well known that these things come into existence at that point, but no one would say that they come into existence by virtue of the father. Rather, they exist due to the First, either without mediation or by the mediation of the angels who are charged with these originated things. This is one of the things affirmed by the philosophers who avow

[14] For the second position, see [525], but it is unclear which is the third position attributed to the philosophers.

[15] Alternatively, efficient cause or agent (*fāʿil*).

[16] Alternatively, it is a natural not a voluntary cause (*fāʿil bil-ṭabʿ lā bil-ikhtiyār*).

[17] Alternatively, faculties of perception (*mudrikah*); however, Ghazālī seems to have in mind more than just the five senses.

[18] Alternatively, efficient cause or agent (*fāʿil*).

[19] Literally, concepts (*maʿānī*).

the existence of the Creator, and they are the ones with whom we are in dialogue. Thus, it is clear that the existence of something upon the occurrence of something else does not prove that that thing exists by virtue of the other.

We can further clarify this by means of an example. Suppose that there is a congenitally blind man whose eyes are blocked by some membrane and who has not heard from others about the difference between night and day. Now suppose that the membrane is removed from his eyes during the day and he opens his eyelids. When he sees colors, he will assume that the cause[20] of the perception of the forms of colors in his eyes is the opening of his eyes, and that so long as his eyesight is good, his eyes are open **[519]**, the membrane is lifted, and the particular thing in front of him is colored, it necessarily follows that he will see, and that it would be rationally impossible for him not to see. But when the sun sets and the air is darkened, he will know that the light of the sun is the cause of the imprinting of colors in his vision.

Why is our opponent sure that the principles of existence do not contain causes from which these originated things emanate upon contact between them? Surely, because they are stable, do not cease to exist, and are not moving bodies that may disappear. If they were to cease to exist or disappear, we would apprehend the difference and would understand that there was another cause behind what we observe.[21] Indeed, this is inescapable in accordance with their own starting point. That is why the discerning philosophers have agreed that the originated things and accidents that occur upon contact between bodies, or generally, whenever their relative positions change, are simply emanations from the bestower of forms,[22] which is an angel or a group of angels. Thus, they have said, the imprinting of the forms of colors in the eye is due to the bestower of forms, whereas the presence of the sun, good eyesight, and colored bodies are mere instruments and dispositions that enable the substratum to receive these forms. They have applied this to all originated things.

[20] Alternatively, efficient cause or agent (*fāʿil*).

[21] The analogy seems to have the following sense. The philosophers are like the blind man from whose eyes the membrane has been lifted. The blind man assumes that the sun is not the cause of his seeing, just as the philosophers assume that the principles of existence are not the causes of existing things, since they are stable and unvarying. However, after sunset the blind man realizes that the sun is the real cause; similarly, if these principles of existence were to be suspended, philosophers would come to understand that they were the real causes.

[22] That is, the Active Intellect.

This refutes the claim that fire is the cause of burning, food is the cause of satisfying hunger, medicine is the cause of health, and so on for other causes.

I say: It is sophistry to deny the existence of the efficient causes that are observed in sensory things. A person who makes this statement is either renouncing with his tongue what lies in his heart, or has been taken in by a sophistical doubt that he has been exposed to in this regard. For someone who denies that cannot maintain that every action must have a cause.[23] As to whether these causes are sufficient in themselves to produce their effects, or whether the effects come about also **[520]** by means of an external cause, which may be separate or not – that is something that is not self-evident, but requires extensive investigation and examination.

If they have embraced this objection concerning efficient causes that are perceived to act upon one another due to what has been stated here by Ghazālī concerning the effects whose causes are not perceived,[24] they are wrong to do so. Those things whose causes are not perceived and unknown are sought precisely because their causes are not perceived. Since those things whose causes are not perceived are unknown by nature and are sought, it follows necessarily that those things that are not unknown do have perceptible causes. This objection is the work of someone who does not distinguish between those things that are self-evident and those things that are unknown. Thus, what has been advanced under this heading is mere sophistry.

Furthermore, what do they say about essential causes, which are such that an existent cannot be understood without understanding them? It is self-evident that things have essences and attributes, which dictate the specific acts of each existent, and with respect to which the essences, names, and definitions of things differ. If each existent did not have a specific action, it would not have a specific nature, and if it did not have a specific nature, it would not have a specific name or definition. Thus, all things would be one thing, or rather not even one thing, since we could ask of that one thing: does it have an action or reaction specific to it or not? If it does have one specific action, then **[521]** since specific actions issue from specific natures [it will have a specific nature]. And if it does not have

[23] Alternatively, agent or efficient cause (*fāʿil*).

[24] Presumably, these unperceived causes are some of the things that Ghazālī has already mentioned, e.g. the cause of life in the embryo, which is God or the Active Intellect (i.e. the bestower of forms). Later, these are referred to as the "separate principles."

one specific action, then the one would not be one. Moreover, if the nature of the one is revoked, then the nature of the existent is also revoked, and if the nature of the existent is revoked, that entails nonexistence.

As for the question of whether the actions issuing from each existent lead necessarily to those acts, or whether they lead to them for the most part, or whether both are possible, that is an inquiry that should be pursued and investigated. Any action and reaction between two existents takes place only by adding to it one of an infinite number of things. This additional thing may in turn be dependent on another. That is why it cannot be affirmed that whenever fire comes close to a susceptible body, it will necessarily act upon it. For it is not unlikely that there could be another existent additional to the susceptible body that impedes the action of the fire, as is said to be the case with talc and other things. But that does not necessitate divesting fire of the attribute of burning, so long as it alone retains the name and definition of fire.

All originated existents have four causes: efficient, material, formal, and final. This is something self-evident, as is the fact that they are all necessary for the existence of their effects, particularly those that are a part of the effect itself, namely what some have called the "material cause" (and others call the "condition" or "substratum") and what some have called the formal cause (and others call an "attribute of the soul"). The theologians admit that these are necessary conditions with respect to **[522]** what is conditioned. For example, they say that life is a condition of knowledge. Similarly, they admit that things have real natures and definitions, and that these are necessary to the existence of existing things. They apply this judgment in the same fashion to both observables and unobservables. In addition, they do the same for what ensues from the substance of a thing, which is what they call an "indication."[25] For example, they say that perfection in an existent is an indication that its cause[26] is rational, or that the fact that an existent is intended for a purpose is an indication that its cause has knowledge of it.[27]

Intellect is nothing over and above the apprehension[28] of existents along with their causes, and this is what distinguishes it from other cognitive faculties. Thus, if you abolish causes, you abolish the intellect. The art

25 Alternatively, proof, or sign (*dalīl*). 26 Alternatively, efficient cause, or agent (*fāʿil*).

27 Ibn Rushd seems to be thinking of the claims that are sometimes made by theologians in putting forward something like an argument from design to prove the existence of God.

28 Reading *idrāk* for *idrākih*.

of logic states that there are causes and effects, and that the effects are apprehended perfectly only when their causes are apprehended. Thus, abolishing these things abolishes knowledge and annuls it. It entails that nothing can be known at all in the sense of real knowledge, but rather only assumed, and that there can be no demonstrative proof or definition either. It also abolishes the various types of essential predicates from which demonstrative proofs are constructed.

If one argues that there is no necessary knowledge in any case, then it follows that that statement is not necessary either. Alternatively, one might acknowledge that some things are necessary while others **[523]** are not, adding that the mind sometimes makes assumptions when judging them and is under the illusion that they are necessary when in fact they are not. The philosophers do not deny that, and allow that it is possible to call such things "habit." But if that is not what they mean by the term "habit," then what else can they mean? Do they mean that it is (1) a habit of the agent, (2) a habit of existents, or (3) our own habit when we make judgments concerning these things? (1) It is impossible for God Almighty to have a habit, for a habit is a trait[29] acquired by an agent that necessitates the repetition of an action in most cases. But God Almighty states: "You will find no alteration in God's course, nor will you find any change in God's course" [Qur'ān 35:43]. (2) If they mean a habit in existents, habits can be possessed only by those who have souls. If a habit exists in something that does not have a soul, it is in reality the nature of that thing. But it is not possible for existents to have a nature that dictates a certain effect either necessarily or for the most part.[30] (3) If it is our own habit in making judgments concerning existents, that is nothing but an act of the intellect that is dictated by its nature, by virtue of which it is what it is. The philosophers do not deny this kind of habit, for "habit" is a vague term. But if one investigates the term one finds that its one underlying meaning is that of a conventional[31] action. For example, when we say that it is the habit of *A* to do *p*, what we mean is that he does it for the most part. If that is what they mean by "habit," all existents would be

[29] The term *malakah* is often translated as "habit" and contrasted with *ʿādah* (custom); however the latter is here translated as "habit."

[30] Presumably, because a thing's nature dictates only that it happen necessarily; when something happens for the most part, it is no longer its nature. Something happens for the most part not when it is dictated by a thing's nature, but when external causes intervene to prevent it from happening in some instances.

[31] Alternatively, hypothetical (*waḍʿī*).

conventional, and there would be no wisdom **[524]** [in the universe] from which to ascribe wisdom to the Agent.

As we have already stated, there is no doubt that these existents can act upon one another, though they are not sufficient in themselves to produce such actions, but rather need an external agent whose action is a condition of their action, indeed of their very existence. However, concerning the essence of this agent or agents there is disagreement among the philosophers in some respects and agreement in others. They all agree that the First Agent is free of matter, and that the action of this Agent is a condition for the existence of existing things and their actions. Moreover, they also agree that these things receive the action of the Agent by the mediation of something that He intellects, which is different from these existing things. Some of them consider this medium to be the celestial sphere alone, while others think that it is the celestial sphere along with another existent that is free of prime matter, which is what they call the "bestower of forms." This is not the place to investigate these differing opinions. This concept is the most noble thing investigated by the philosophers. If you are interested in these matters, you must pursue them in their proper place.

There is disagreement among the philosophers mainly concerning the origination of substantial forms, in particular those pertaining to the soul, for some of them are not able to ascribe these **[525]** to the action of the hot, cold, moist, and dry elements, which are the causes of the generation and corruption of natural things, according to them. Others, the materialists, relate every observable thing that does not have an observable cause to the hot, cold, moist, and dry elements. They say that when these elements are mixed in certain ways, these things are generated and that they are dependent on those mixtures, just as colors and all other accidental properties are generated. The other philosophers have occupied themselves in refuting them.

Abū Ḥāmid al-Ghazālī said: The second position[32] concerns those who admit that effects emanate from the principles of originated things, but maintain that the dispositions to receive forms are due to present observable causes. Moreover, they claim that these principles issue in certain effects necessarily and naturally, as light issues from the sun, and not by way of deliberation and choice, though substrata differ in their

[32] For the first position, see [518].

dispositions to receive that light. Thus, a polished body receives the sun's rays and then reflects them to illuminate another location, while clay does not receive them. Air does not impede the penetration of rays of sunlight, whereas rocks do. Some things soften in the sun while others harden; some whiten like the fuller's cloak while others darken like his face. The principle is the same but the effects are different because of the difference in the dispositions of the substratum. Similarly, whatever emanates from the principles of existence issues from them without restraint or deficit, but rather the shortcoming is in the substrata. If that is the case, then whenever we suppose that fire exists with its attributes and two similar pieces of cotton come into contact with fire in the same manner, it is inconceivable that one would burn and not the other, since there is no choice in the matter. Based on this concept, they have denied that Abraham (peace be upon him) fell in the fire without burning, while the fire remained fire. Rather, they claim that this is only possible by divesting **[526]** the fire of its heat, which makes it no longer fire, or by changing the essence of Abraham (peace be upon him), and converting him into a rock or some other thing that is unaffected by fire. But neither of these is possible.

I say: Those philosophers who claim that sensory existents do not act[33] upon one another, but rather that the cause is an external principle, cannot say that their apparent effects on one another are wholly deceptive. Rather, such a philosopher would say that they act upon one another with respect to their dispositions to receive the forms from the external principle. However, I do not know of any philosopher who says so in all cases. The philosophers only say so about the essential forms, not the accidents.[34] All the philosophers agree that heat causes similar heat, and so on for all four elemental qualities, in such a way as to conserve the heat of the element of fire and the heat produced by the celestial bodies. None of the reliable philosophers have said what Ghazālī has ascribed to them, namely that the various separate[35] principles act by nature not by choice. Rather, according to them, anyone with knowledge is an agent by choice, though he always chooses the side of virtue, issuing in the more virtuous of two opposites.

[33] Alternatively, do not cause one another, or do not act causally upon one another (*fāʿilah*).

[34] That is, some philosophers say that existing things receive their essential forms from an external principle.

[35] Alternatively, the immaterial principles (*al-mabādi' al-mufāriqah*). Ibn Rushd is referring to the celestial intelligences.

This choice is not made in order to perfect the agents' essences, for there is no deficiency in their essence **[527]**, but rather to perfect thereby some other existents that have deficiencies in their natures.

As for the objection that Ghazālī ascribed to the philosophers regarding the miracle of Abraham (peace be upon him), that is something that only the heretics among the Muslims have held. The wise among the philosophers do not permit discourse or dialogue concerning the principles of religious law. According to them, anyone who does so requires a stern reprimand. Since every art has basic principles that must be accepted by anyone who investigates it, who must not challenge them by negating or refuting them, so also the practical religious art is most worthy of such treatment. According to the philosophers, adherence to the religious virtues is necessary for the very existence of human beings insofar as they are human beings, or rather insofar as they are knowing human beings. That is why all humans are obliged to accept the principles of religious law and why they must emulate the religious lawgiver. Renouncing or disputing them amounts to nullifying the existence of the human being. That is why heretics must be killed. What must be said in this regard is that these principles are divine matters that surpass human intellects. Thus, they should be acknowledged despite ignorance of their causes. That is why we do not find any of the ancient philosophers discussing miracles, despite their appearance all over the world, for they are the principles upon which religious laws are established, and the religious laws are the principles of the virtues. Nor have they discussed what is said about what happens after **[528]** death. If a person is raised according to the religious virtues, he will grow up to be completely virtuous. Moreover, if after some time, he is fortunate enough to be one of the religious scholars who are secure in their knowledge and he comes upon an interpretation of one of the religious principles, he is duty-bound not to divulge that interpretation, but rather to say with the Almighty: "Those secure in knowledge say, 'We believe in it; it is all from our Lord'" [Qur'ān 3:7]. These are the definitions of the religious laws and of the scholars.

Abū Ḥāmid al-Ghazālī said: There are two ways of responding to this. The first is to say that we do not accept that the principles do not act with choice and that God Almighty does not act by means of His will. We have already refuted this claim of theirs in discussing the issue of the origin of the world. Since it has been established that the Agent gives rise to burning by will when the cotton makes contact with fire, it is rationally[36] possible for Him not to give rise to the burning when contact takes place.

I say: What he states here to his opponent, concerning what he has the illusion of establishing, is precisely what his opponent resists and states that there is no proof of, namely that the First Cause causes burning without an intermediary created by Him in such a way that the burning arises from the fire. Such a claim would repudiate what the senses tell us **[529]** about the existence of causes and effects. None of the philosophers doubts, for example, that the burning produced in the cotton by the fire is [in fact] caused by the fire. However, they do not think that that is so absolutely, but rather due to an external principle, which is a condition for the existence of the fire, not to mention its ability to burn. They merely disagree as to what[37] the principle is, whether it is separate, or an intermediary between the originated thing and the separate principle, which is different from fire.

Abū Ḥāmid al-Ghazālī replied on behalf of the philosophers: It will be said that this will lead us into flagrant absurdities. If one denies the necessity between effects and their causes, and [the connection between them] is related to the will of the Creator,[38] and if His will does not have a definite method that pertains to it, but may rather be variable and diverse, then we must allow the possibility that there are wild animals, raging fires, towering mountains, and armed enemies in front of us, which we do not see because God Almighty has not created in us the ability to see them. It would be possible for someone to leave a book in his house only to find it, on his return, converted into a rational and obedient young boy, or into an animal. Alternatively, if the man leaves a boy in his house it is possible that he might return to find him converted into a dog, or ashes into musk, or a rock into gold, or gold into a rock. Moreover, if he were asked about any of this, he would be obliged to say: "I do not know what is in my house at this very moment, but rather all I know is that I left a book at home, which may now be a horse whose urine and dung have soiled the study," and "I left a piece of bread in the house that may have been converted into an apple tree, for God Almighty is capable of all things." It is not necessary for a horse to be created from semen, nor for a tree to be created

36 Literally, it is possible according to reason or the intellect (*amkana fil-ʿaql*), but it would seem as if Ghazālī wants something stronger than logical possibility, perhaps metaphysical possibility.

37 Alternatively, as to the quiddity (*mā hūwa*) of the principle.

38 Literally, of its Inventor (*mukhtariʿihā*).

from seed. Indeed, it is not necessary that they be created from anything at all, for God might create things that were not in existence before. Moreover, when a man sees a human being he has never seen before and is asked to say whether he has been born into the world **[530]**, he should demur, saying: "It is possible that some of the fruits in the market were converted into that human being. God is capable of every possible thing, and this thing is possible, so one must hesitate before answering." Many variations can be conceived on this theme, but this much will suffice for our purposes.

When Ghazālī said this on behalf of the philosophers, he also put forward a reply, saying: The response to this is as follows. If it were established that humans cannot be given knowledge of the nonexistence of what possibly exists, then all these absurdities would necessarily follow. But we harbor no doubts concerning these images that you have conjured up, for God Almighty has created the knowledge in us that these possibilities were not caused by him. We never claimed that these things were necessary, but rather that they were possibilities that may or may not occur. The habitual repetition of certain events, time after time, firmly entrenches their occurrence in our minds according to past habit. It is possible for a prophet to know by the methods mentioned by the philosophers that so-and-so will not return from his travels tomorrow, but his return remains possible even though the prophet knows that this possibility will not occur. Likewise, one can look at an ordinary person and know that he does not know what is hidden[39] about something or other, and cannot apprehend intelligibles without being taught, yet also not deny that his soul and intuition may be strengthened to the point that he may apprehend what the prophets apprehend. The philosophers have admitted this possibility, even though they know that it will not occur. If God were to interrupt this habit by making it happen during a time when habits are interrupted, these items of knowledge would be expunged from people's hearts and God would not create them. Therefore, there is nothing to prevent something from being possible within the capabilities of God Almighty, while he has the foreknowledge that he will not act in such a way at that time – though it is possible for him to do so at certain other times. Moreover, He creates in us the knowledge that he will not act in that way at that time. Therefore, the statements attributed to us are complete distortions.

[39] Alternatively, the future, or the occult (*al-ghayb*).

I say: If the theologians acknowledge that contraries are equally possible in existents, that contraries are equally possible for the Agent, and that one of the contraries is selected by the will of an agent whose will does not adhere to a rule, whether always or for **[531]** the most part, then all these flagrant absurdities do indeed follow necessarily from the theologians' position. That is because certain knowledge is cognizance of a thing as it really is. Thus, if all that exists is the possibility of two contraries relative to the receptacle and the Agent, then there will be no stable knowledge of anything at all, even for an instant. If we suppose the agent to have this attribute, then he would lord over existents like a despotic king who acts as the highest ideal in his kingdom. No one in the kingdom could represent him and no one would be able to ascertain any laws to which he referred, or even a habit.[40] It follows necessarily that we would be ignorant by nature of the actions of such a king, and we would be ignorant by nature that any action of his that came about would continue to exist at any given point.

Abū Ḥāmid al-Ghazālī attempts to avoid these absurdities by saying that God Almighty creates in us the knowledge that these possibilities only occur at specific times, namely at the time that a miracle occurs. But this is an unsuccessful attempt to avoid the absurdities, for the knowledge that is created within us is always dependent on the nature of the existent. True belief[41] is belief that something is in its existing condition. Thus, if we have knowledge of these possibilities, then the possible existents must be in a condition that is related to our knowledge of them, either through themselves, or the Agent, or both. This condition is what they term "habit." If this condition, which they call "habit," cannot possibly **[532]** be in the First Agent, it must be in existents. But that is what the philosophers term "nature," as we have already said. Likewise, God's knowledge of existents must be necessarily related to existents, though it is the cause of those existents. That is why it follows necessarily that existing things occur in accordance with His knowledge. For example, if God informs the prophet of Zayd's arrival, its occurrence in accordance with the knowledge is simply caused by the fact that the nature of the existent is dependent on God's eternal knowledge. Knowledge, insofar as it is knowledge, is not related to something that does not have a settled nature.

[40] It is not clear why Ibn Rushd denies that it can be a habit. This much at least seems as though it may be granted to Ghazālī.

[41] Alternatively, true judgment (*al-ṣādiq*).

The knowledge of the Creator is the cause of the existent having the nature attached to it. Our ignorance of possibilities is simply a matter of our ignorance of that nature, which dictates its existence or nonexistence. If contraries in existents were truly equal in relation to themselves and their efficient causes, then it would follow necessarily that those things would be neither existent nor nonexistent, or both existent and nonexistent at once. That is why one of the two contraries must prevail in existence. The knowledge of the existence of that nature is what necessitates[42] that one of the two contraries must occur, and the knowledge that is related to it either precedes it **[533]**, which is the knowledge that causes it, namely eternal knowledge, or is dependent upon it, namely noneternal knowledge.

Being apprized of what is hidden[43] is nothing more than acquaintance with this nature. Having knowledge when we do not have a prior proof of this knowledge is what is called in ordinary people "vision" and in prophets "inspiration." The eternal will and eternal knowledge are what necessitate this nature in existents. That is the meaning of the words of the Almighty: "Say: no one in the heavens or on earth knows what is hidden but God" [Qur'ān 27:65]. This nature may be necessary or it may occur for the most part. As we have said before, dreams and inspiration are just means of being informed of the nature of possible existents. The arts that claim to provide cognizance of what exists in the future simply glean trivial effects of this nature, character, or whatever you want to call it, namely the very same settled thing to which knowledge relates.

Abū Ḥāmid al-Ghazālī said: The second response[44] that will save us from these flagrant absurdities proceeds by admitting that fire was created in such a way that if it makes contact with two similar pieces of cotton, it will burn them both and will not distinguish between them so long as they are really similar in every respect. However, we can still allow for the possibility that the prophet may be cast in the fire without burning, either by altering the attributes of the fire or the prophet. God Almighty

42 The necessitation need not be causal, since as he explains in the next sentence, it is only in the case of divine knowledge that the knowledge causes the prevalence of one of the two contraries; in the case of human knowledge, the causal relation is reversed (the prevalence of one of the two contraries causes our knowledge of a thing's existence). Still, if we have knowledge of its existence, then that necessarily implies that one of the two contraries must have prevailed.

43 Alternatively, the future, or what is absent (*al-ghayb*).

44 This response seems to be advanced for the sake of argument. It represents another way out and consists in acknowledging that existing beings have a nature but maintaining that this nature is not unalterable by God. Thus, it does not reflect Ghazālī's occasionalist position, but an attempt to show that the philosophers can have their natures without denying the possibility of miracles.

or the angels may create an attribute in the fire that limits its heat to its own body, preventing it from extending beyond it. This would preserve the fire's heat and enable it to have the form and reality of fire, while ensuring that its heating effects do not go beyond it. Alternatively, an attribute can be created in the body of a human that repels the effects of fire, while not divesting the body of being flesh and bones [534]. We find that someone who covers his body in talc and then sits in a lighted oven is not affected by the fire. Someone who has never observed that would deny it. Our opponent's denial that God is able to establish an attribute in the fire or the human body that prevents burning is similar to a denial by someone who has never observed talc and its effects. Many wonders and marvels are within God's capabilities and we have not observed them all, so why should we deny their possibility and judge that they are impossible? Similarly, resurrecting the dead and converting a stick into a serpent is possible by the following means. Since matter is receptive to anything, earth and the other elements can be transformed into a plant, a plant when eaten by an animal can be transformed into blood, blood can be transformed into semen, and semen flows into the uterus and generates an animal. This occurs habitually during a lengthy period of time, so why does our opponent consider it impossible for it to be in God's capability to conduct matter through these stages in a shorter time than has previously been the case? Moreover, if it is possible for it to occur in a shorter time period, then there is no limit to it being shortened further, and the actions of these powers may be speeded up to the point that they result in a miracle for the prophet.

If it is asked: Does this arise from the soul of the prophet or from another principle at the suggestion of the prophet? We respond: Does what you have admitted, in terms of the possibility of rain, lightning, and earthquakes being produced by the power of the prophet's soul, arise from his soul or from another principle? Our position on this issue is like yours on that. In both cases, it would be preferable for us to ascribe[45] it to God Almighty, either without an intermediary or through the mediation of the angels. But the timing of its propitious occurrence is due to the prophet's turning his attention to it; he specifies its appearance according to the order of goodness for the continuation of

[45] Literally, to relate (*iḍāfah*).

the order of religion. That is what makes its existence prevail [at that time]. The thing in itself is possible and the principle behind it is magnanimous and generous. But the miracle does not emanate from Him unless the need for it makes its existence prevail when goodness pertains to it. And goodness only pertains to it if the prophet needs to establish his prophecy in order to spread goodness.

All this is in harmony with their line of argument and they must accept it necessarily, since they have admitted that the prophet is endowed with a special property that is different from the habit of other people. The possible scope of this property cannot be determined by the intellect, so why should one falsify what has been passed down and recurrently corroborated, or what religious law has said is to be believed? In general, the only thing that receives the animal form is sperm, and the animal faculties emanate to it from the angels, which are the principles of existents according to the philosophers. The only thing that has been generated from the sperm of a human is a human being and from the sperm of a horse is a horse, for the fact that the sperm issues from a horse necessitates that the form of a horse will prevail over other forms, and accordingly, it will receive nothing but the prevailing form **[535]**. That is why wheat does not grow from barley or apples from pear seeds. We also find that some kinds of animals are generated from earth and do not procreate, such as worms, while others are both generated from earth and procreate, such as mice, snakes, and scorpions, which are generated from earth. Their dispositions to receive forms differ for reasons that are hidden from us and are not within the power of human beings to ascertain. According to the philosophers, forms do not emanate from the angels haphazardly or according to whim; rather, what emanates to each substratum is only what can be specifically received according to its own disposition. These dispositions are different and their principles, according to the philosophers, are due to the combinations[46] of the stars and the various relative positions of the heavenly bodies in the course of their motions. This makes it clear[47] that the principles of dispositions comprise wonders and marvels, to the point that they enable those proficient in talismans to mix these celestial powers with mineral properties[48] by means of the science of the

46 Alternatively, admixtures, or configurations (*imtizājāt*).
47 Reading with Marmura *ittaḍaḥa* instead of *infataḥa* (opens).
48 See note 68 in Ghazālī, "Rescuer from Error."

properties of mineral substances[49] and the science of astrology, giving shape to these terrestrial things and seeking a favorable ascendant star for them. Thus, they have effected wondrous things in the world with these talismans, such as for example driving out snakes and scorpions from one country, bedbugs from another country, as well as other things that are apprehended by the science of talismans. Since the principles of dispositions are incapable of being enumerated, we are not apprized of their inner secrets, and we have no way of listing them, how do we know that it is impossible for certain dispositions to occur in some bodies, and that it is impossible for these bodies to pass through a number of stages in a short period of time in such a way as to be disposed to receive a form that they were not disposed to receive before, thereby eventuating in a miracle? Those who deny it do so simply because of a lack of appreciation of and familiarity with higher beings, as well as inattentiveness to God's secrets in creation and in nature. Whoever has examined[50] the wonders of the sciences would on no account rule out God's ability to effect what has been related concerning the miracles of prophets.

Our opponents may say: We agree with you that every possible thing can be decreed by God Almighty and you agree with us that every impossible thing cannot be decreed. Now some things are recognized as impossible, others as possible, and yet others are such that the intellect is not able to determine whether they are impossible or possible. What is the limit[51] of the impossible according to you? Does it come down to the conjunction of affirming and negating the same thing? If so, you should say that for any two things, so long as they are not identical to one another, then the existence of one does not require the existence of the other. You should also say that God Almighty is able to create a will without knowledge of what is willed, and knowledge without life. In addition, say that God can move the hand of a dead man, seat him upright, and make him write volumes and practice arts while he has his eyes wide open and is gazing at his work – though he cannot see, has no life in him, and no ability, since these orderly actions are created by God Almighty by moving the man's hand and the motion is from God Almighty. However, if you allow that possibility, you invalidate the difference between voluntary motion

[49] Alternatively, mineral gems (*jawāhir*), if Ghazālī is using the term in its original, nonphilosophical sense.

[50] Alternatively, inductively examined (*istaqra'a*).

[51] Alternatively, definition (*ḥadd*).

and a shiver. An intentional action would no longer indicate knowledge or the ability of the agent. It would also follow that God ought to be able to transmute genera, converting substance into accident, knowledge into ability, black into white, and sound into smell, just as he can turn the inanimate into animate and **[536]** rock into gold, among the countless other impossibilities of which it would necessarily follow that He is capable.

The response to this is that the impossible cannot be decreed [by God], where the impossible is simply the affirmation of something along with its negation, or the affirmation of the more specific along with the negation of the more general,[52] or the affirmation of two things along with the negation of one of them. What cannot be reduced to these things is not impossible, and anything that is not impossible is capable of being decreed. The conjunction of blackness and whiteness is impossible because what we understand from the affirmation of the form of blackness in the substratum is the negation of the form of whiteness, as well as the existence of blackness. Thus, since the negation of whiteness is understood from the affirmation of blackness, then the affirmation of whiteness along with its negation is impossible. Again, it is impossible for a person to be in two places [at once] because we understand from his being at home that he is not outside his home, so it is not possible to decree that he be outside his home while he is at home, which we understand to negate his being outside his home. Likewise, we understand by "will" the pursuit of something known, so if pursuit were to be ordained without knowledge that would not be will, since it would negate what we have understood. In addition, knowledge cannot be created in the inanimate because by "inanimate" we understand something that has no apprehension. Thus, if apprehension has been created in it, it is impossible to designate it "inanimate" in the sense that we have understood. Meanwhile, if there is no apprehension, calling it "knowledge" when the substratum does not apprehend anything is [also] impossible. That is why this is impossible.

Concerning the transmutation of genera, some theologians have said that that is within God's capability. We say that it is irrational for one thing to become another. For example, if blackness were to be changed into ability, then either the blackness remains or not. If it is nonexistent, then it has not really been changed but has rather been annihilated and

[52] Ghazālī means, for example, the affirmation of redness with the negation of color.

something else has been brought into existence instead.[53] If it exists along with ability, it has not really been changed but rather something else has been added to it. Moreover, if blackness remains and ability is nonexistent, then it has not been changed but has rather remained as it was. By contrast, when we say that blood has been converted into sperm, we mean that the very same matter has shed one form and taken on another. The end result is that one form has been annihilated and another form has originated, while the same matter has persisted and taken on two different forms successively. And if we say that water has been changed into air by heating we mean that the matter that is capable of receiving the form of water has shed that form and received another form. The matter is common among them while the form[54] changes, as when we say that the stick has changed into a serpent or that earth has been changed into an animal. However, no matter is shared among an accident and a substance, nor among blackness and ability, nor among the other genera, which is why it is impossible to transform them into one another. But when it comes to God Almighty's moving the hand of the dead man and setting him up in the form of a living person who can sit and write in an orderly manner with his hand, that is not impossible in itself so long as we attribute the effects to the will of a voluntary agent. Rather, it is merely unusual because it goes against the habitual [course of events]. Our opponents are wrong to say that this invalidates the assertion that **[537]** intentional action is an indication of the knowledge of the agent. For the agent here is God Almighty, who intends it and has knowledge[55] of it. As to the statement that this leaves no difference between a shiver and voluntary motion, we reply as follows. We simply apprehend this difference from our own case, since we have observed a difference between the two states in ourselves, and we articulate this difference by referring to it as ability. Moreover, we recognize two possible divisions corresponding to the two different states: the first state is the bringing into existence of motion with ability, and the second state is the bringing into existence of motion without ability. Then, when we look at another person and observe many orderly motions, we come to know that they are endowed with ability [and therefore that these motions

53 Ghazālī seems to be saying that for A to be converted into B there must be something that persists throughout the change; otherwise, one should say that A is annihilated and B is created in its place.

54 Reading *ṣūrah* for *ṣifah* (attribute).

55 Reading *ʿālim bihi* (has knowledge of it) instead of *fāʿil lahu* (is the agent of it).

are voluntary].[56] These items of knowledge are created by God Almighty in the habitual course of things, according to which we apprehend one of the two possible divisions and do not ascertain the impossibility of the second division, as claimed above.

I say: When Ghazālī saw the utter absurdity and unacceptability to human reason of the statement that things do not have specific attributes and that each existent does not have a form from which its actions follow, he granted this statement and went on to deny two other positions. The first denial leads him to say that it is possible for these attributes to be present in an existent without having the effects that they habitually have. For example, it is possible for fire to possess heat without burning the thing it comes close to, even if that thing has a tendency to burn when fire comes close to it. The second denial amounts to the position that the forms specific to each existent do not have matter that is specific to them.

The first statement may[57] be granted to him by the philosophers, for the actions of the causes are necessary, but not the issuance of those actions by the causes, because of the **[538]** external things [i.e. additional contributing causes]. It is not impossible for fire to come into contact with cotton at a certain time without burning it, so long as there is something present that when joined with cotton renders it unreceptive to burning, as talc is said to do with animals.

As for the second statement, that matter is a condition for the existence of material existents, the theologians are unable to deny that. That is because, as Abū Ḥāmid al-Ghazālī points out, there is no difference between both affirming and negating something, and affirming it and negating part of it at the same time. Since all things consist[58] of two attributes, a general one and a specific one – which the philosophers express by saying that the "composite definition" consists of genus and differentia – there is no difference between revoking the existent and revoking one of these two attributes [i.e. genus and differentia]. For example, the definition of a human being consists of two attributes, one of which

56 The objection that Ghazālī seems to be responding to is this: if all human action is ultimately caused by God, then what is to distinguish a voluntary action from a mere reflex (e.g. a shiver)? He responds that when we perform voluntary actions we notice that we have ability (or power) over them. Thus, we divide all bodily motions into voluntary and nonvoluntary motions, and go on to apply this distinction to the motions of others (presumably by analogy). Of course, the fact remains that on his view the ability that we observe in our own case is a mere illusion.

57 Alternatively, it is not unlikely (*lā yubʿid*) that the philosophers would grant the first statement.

58 In other words, they possess two attributes (an instance of mixing the formal and material modes).

is general, namely animal, and the other is specific, namely rational. Just as revoking rationality is a revocation of humanness, so also revoking animalhood is a revocation of humanness. That is because animalhood is a condition of rationality, and once the condition is revoked so is the conditioned. The only disagreement between the theologians and the philosophers on this score concerns certain particular matters, regarding which the philosophers' view is that general and specific attributes are both conditional, while the theologians disagree [holding that only the specific attributes are]. For example **[539]**, according to the philosophers, heat and moisture are conditions of life in corruptible living creatures, since these attributes are more general than life, just as life is more general than rationality. The theologians do not see things this way, which is why you hear them say that[59] moisture is not a condition of life. Similarly, for the philosophers, having a specific shape is a condition of life, which is specific to an existent having that shape. If it were not a condition, one of two things would be possible: that specific shape would exist in an animal without its action existing at all, or else that specific shape would not exist.[60] For example, the hand for them is an instrument of the intellect, which issues in intellectual acts, such as writing and the other arts. If it were possible for the intellect to exist in inanimate things, it would be possible for the intellect to exist without the acts produced by it. This would be like the possibility of heat existing without heating what has a tendency to be heated by it.

According to the philosophers, each existent has a definite quantity, even though this quantity may be accidental in particular existents, and a definite quality, even though this quality may also be accidental. Similarly, it has a this-ness,[61] since existing things are definite for them, and their times of persistence are also definite **[540]**, even though they may also

[59] Omitting *al-hay'ah* (form), which does not make sense here. What would make more sense is a word meaning warmth or heat (e.g. *ḥarārah* or *sukhūnah*) but there seems to be no textual support for this.

[60] The sense here is unclear, but perhaps what Ibn Rushd has in mind is that having a specific shape is an essential attribute of a living thing, and that it cannot exist without having that shape (and this also applies to the shapes of particular living organs). As he goes on to suggest, it is essential to a human hand that it have the particular shape that it does; otherwise it could not issue in its specific actions. For example, human life cannot exist in something that has the shape of a table. Compare Aristotle's denial of the Pythagorean view that any soul can be embodied in a body, no matter what its shape, and his insistence that each body has its own particular form and shape (*De Anima* 407b24).

[61] Alternatively, haecceity (*innīyyah*).

have accidental properties, which are however also definite. There is no disagreement among the philosophers and theologians over the fact that when existing things have matter in common, matter with this attribute sometimes receives one of the two forms and sometimes receives its contrary. That is the case with the forms of the four simple bodies [i.e. elements], namely fire, air, water, and earth. However, the disagreement concerns those things that do not have any matter in common or whose matter is different. Can these things receive one another's forms? An example would be something that is observed to be receptive of some form or another only by way of numerous intermediaries. Can such a thing be receptive to the last form without intermediaries?[62] For example, the four elements are combined in such a way that a plant is created out of them, then that plant nourishes an animal, out of which is created sperm and blood, and out of the sperm and blood an animal is created. As God Almighty has said: "We have created the human being from an extract of clay, then we have rendered him a clot of blood in a secure location," until the end of the verse, "Blessed be God, the most excellent of creators" [Qur'ān 23: 12–14]. The theologians say that the form of a human can inhere in soil without any of the observed intermediaries. The philosophers reject this, saying that if this were possible, it would have been wise to create human beings without these intermediaries, and the creator who created them with this attribute would be the best and most able creator **[541]**. Each of the two groups claims that what they say is self-evident, but neither has a proof of their creed. Therefore, you must consult your heart; what it tells you is what you are obliged to believe and what you are entrusted with. May God make you and us the party of truth and certainty.

Some Muslims have maintained that God Almighty can be said to be able to conjoin contraries. Their specious argument is that the determination of our intellect that rules this out is simply something imprinted on the intellect, and that had it been imprinted with the possibility of that, it would not have denied it but would have allowed it to be possible. It follows necessarily from their view that the intellect does not have a settled nature, nor do existing things, and that the true beliefs that the intellect has are not dependent on the existence of these things. The

[62] It is not clear why, if they are eventually transformed as a result of a long chain, they do not have any matter in common – unless the receptivity of the matter changes in the process.

theologians have shied away from this view, but had they adopted it, that would have been a more defensible position than the impossibilities that their opponents confront them with on this topic. For their opponents are faced with accounting for the disparity between what the theologians have affirmed and what they have negated in this regard, and they find it difficult to do so, finding only vague statements. That is why we find that those who are proficient in the art of theology have resorted to denying the necessity between the condition and the conditioned, a thing and its definition, a thing and its cause, and a thing and its proof **[542]**. All this takes us deep into the opinions of the sophists and is meaningless. Among the theologians, this position has been taken by Abū al-Maᶜālī.[63] The universal argument that dispels these objections is as follows. All existing things can be divided into contraries and correlates. If it were possible for correlates to be separated, then it would be possible for contraries to be conjoined. But contraries cannot be conjoined, so correlates cannot be separated. This is God Almighty's wisdom in existing things and his course in creation, and "you will find no alteration in God's course" [Qur'ān 33:62, 35:43, 48:23]. The human intellect is intellect to the extent that it apprehends this wisdom. Moreover, the existence of this wisdom in this manner in the eternal intellect is the cause of its existence in existing things. Therefore, the human intellect is not contingent and could not have been created with different attributes, as Ibn Ḥazm[64] has been deluded into thinking.

[63] Abū al-Maᶜālī ᶜAbd al-Malik al-Juwaynī (1028–85 AD) was a jurist and theologian who was the teacher of Ghazālī and "probably the first to wish to establish a juridical method on an Ashᶜarī basis" (*EI* entry on "al-Djuwaynī").

[64] Abū Muḥammad ᶜAlī bin Aḥmad bin Saᶜīd Ibn Ḥazm (994–1064 AD) was an Andalusian poet, historian, jurist, philosopher, and theologian, whose "tendency is to reduce the importance and the range of application of logical procedures conceived as the instruments of an independent reason" (*EI* entry on "Ibn Ḥazm").

Index

CAMBRIDGE TEXTS IN THE HISTORY OF PHILOSOPHY

Titles published in the series thus far

Aristotle *Nicomachean Ethics* (edited by Roger Crisp)
Arnauld and Nicole *Logic or the Art of Thinking* (edited by Jill Vance Buroker)
Augustine *On the Trinity* (edited by Gareth Matthews)
Bacon *The New Organon* (edited by Lisa Jardine and Michael Silverthorne)
Boyle *A Free Enquiry into the Vulgarly Received Notion of Nature* (edited by Edward B. Davis and Michael Hunter)
Bruno *Cause, Principle and Unity* and *Essays on Magic* (edited by Richard Blackwell and Robert de Lucca with an introduction by Alfonso Ingegno)
Cavendish *Observations upon Experimental Philosophy* (edited by Eileen O'Neill)
Cicero *On Moral Ends* (edited by Julia Annas, translated by Raphael Woolf)
Clarke *A Demonstration of the Being and Attributes of God and Other Writings* (edited by Ezio Vailati)
Classic and Romantic German Aesthetics (edited by J. M. Bernstein)
Condillac *Essay on the Origin of Human Knowledge* (edited by Hans Aarsleff)
Conway *The Principles of the Most Ancient and Modern Philosophy* (edited by Allison P. Coudert and Taylor Corse)
Cudworth *A Treatise Concerning Eternal and Immutable Morality* with *A Treatise of Freewill* (edited by Sarah Hutton)
Descartes *Meditations on First Philosophy* with selections from the *Objections and Replies* (edited by John Cottingham)
Descartes *The World and Other Writings* (edited by Stephen Gaukroger)
Fichte *Foundations of Natural Right* (edited by Frederick Neuhouser, translated by Michael Baur)
Herder *Philosophical Writings* (edited by Michael Forster)
Hobbes and Bramhall on Liberty and Necessity (edited by Vere Chappell)
Humboldt *On Language* (edited by Michael Losonsky, translated by Peter Heath)
Kant *Critique of Practical Reason* (edited by Mary Gregor with an introduction by Andrews Reath)
Kant *Groundwork of the Metaphysics of Morals* (edited by Mary Gregor with an introduction by Christine M. Korsgaard)
Kant *The Metaphysics of Morals* (edited by Mary Gregor with an introduction by Roger Sullivan)
Kant *Prolegomena to any Future Metaphysics* (edited by Gary Hatfield)
Kant *Religion within the Boundaries of Mere Reason and Other Writings* (edited by Allen Wood and George di Giovanni with an introduction by Robert Merrihew Adams)
La Mettrie *Machine Man and Other Writings* (edited by Ann Thomson)
Leibniz *New Essays on Human Understanding* (edited by Peter Remnant and Jonathan Bennett)
Malebranche *Dialogues on Metaphysics and on Religion* (edited by Nicholas Jolley and David Scott)

Malebranche *The Search after Truth* (edited by Thomas M. Lennon and Paul J. Olscamp)
Medieval Islamic Philosophical Writings (edited by Muhammad Ali Khalidi)
Melanchthon *Orations on Philosophy and Education* (edited by Sachiko Kusukawa, translated by Christine Salazar)
Mendelssohn *Philosophical Writings* (edited by Daniel O. Dahlstrom)
Newton *Philosophical Writings* (edited by Andrew Janiak)
Nietzsche *Beyond Good and Evil* (edited by Rolf-Peter Horstmann and Judith Norman)
Nietzsche *The Birth of Tragedy and Other Writings* (edited by Raymond Geuss and Ronald Speirs)
Nietzsche *Daybreak* (edited by Maudemarie Clark and Brian Leiter, translated by R. J. Hollingdale)
Nietzsche *The Gay Science* (edited by Bernard Williams, translated by Josefine Nauckhoff)
Nietzsche *Human, All Too Human* (translated by R. J. Hollingdale with an introduction by Richard Schacht)
Nietzsche *Untimely Meditations* (edited by Daniel Breazeale, translated by R. J. Hollingdale)
Nietzsche *Writings from the Late Notebooks* (edited by Rüdiger Bittner, translated by Kate Sturge)
Novalis *Fichte Studies* (edited by Jane Kneller)
Schleiermacher *Hermeneutics and Criticism* (edited by Andrew Bowie)
Schleiermacher *Lectures on Philosophical Ethics* (edited by Robert Louden, translated by Louise Adey Huish)
Schleiermacher *On Religion: Speeches to its Cultured Despisers* (edited by Richard Crouter)
Schopenhauer *Prize Essay on the Freedom of the Will* (edited by Günter Zöller)
Sextus Empiricus *Outlines of Scepticism* (edited by Julia Annas and Jonathan Barnes)
Shaftesbury, *Characteristics of Men, Manners, Opinions, Times* (edited by Lawrence Klein)
Adam Smith, *The Theory of Moral Sentiments* (edited by Knud Haakonssen)
Voltaire *Treatise on Tolerance and Other Writings* (edited by Simon Harvey)